ADVANCE |
Soul of a Professor

"Authentic memoirs require the courage to reveal vulnerability, weakness, and inner struggle. As I read this piercing narrative, I was getting to know someone at once blessed with gifts and burdened with daunting personal challenges—someone with the determination to construct a meaningful and productive life. *Soul of a Professor* reminds us that being a human isn't easy, while offering guidance and inspiration to navigate the journey."

—**Jonathan Balcombe**, Author of *Super Fly* and *What a Fish Knows*

"Lisa Pruitt's memoir, *Soul of a Professor,* shines a light on living behind a façade. She shares her inner world as she bravely tells her personal story. We see not just a successful professor but a woman who strives to find her place in this world. In this deeply personal story, Lisa shows us her soft underbelly and the strength she draws from nature and horses."

—**Kami Guildner**, Business Coach for Women of Influence, Host of Extraordinary Women Radio and Extraordinary Women Ignite Conference

"You will be engaged. You will reflect. You will gain a deeper understanding of your own winding road of self-loathing and self-love. This memoir, which is unequivocally a profound journey, is a raw and unbridled storm of uneasy truths usually untold. The reader is allowed to walk a tightrope into the author's vulnerability and her hard-earned wisdoms. Lisa shows us how an unexpected and unyielding love can lift the shroud of despair and darkness and bring redemption and light."

—**Dr. Kedrick Perry**, Vice President for Equity and Inclusion, Loyola University, New Orleans

"The prose is careful and immediate, working to convey Pruitt's work toward healing with conviction. Split into five parts, the book traces her progressive transformation. References to Pruitt's age, the duration of her marriage, and her engineering life mark the passage of time with grace. The early chapters, which cover her frantic bulimic and anxious episodes, are short but coherent in revealing childhood pains. Later, the passages lengthen to encapsulate a wider range of experiences. Their pacing matches Pruitt's growing maturity, becoming less frantic and more meditative. And Pruitt's recovery is captured in open, patient terms, with longer, more detailed anecdotes that include scenery and rich emotional descriptions. These later passages sit with Pruitt's emotions rather than running from them. Throughout, succinct conversations are used to break up Pruitt's ruminating inner monologues. And the book balances its rough moments with its peaceful ones well, so that no one period dominates its work, which is expansive in its scope and appeal.

"*Soul of a Professor* is an inspiring memoir about a lengthy search for a higher calling."

—*Foreword* **Clarion Reviews**

"By sharing her raw and emotional story, Lisa tears down the image of a successful young engineer rising rapidly through the ranks of academia. She describes her own path out of an extremely dark personal and professional timespan, which includes the beautiful relationships she built with her horses. Her humanity, and ultimately her courage, shine through this memoir."

—**Dr. Ayyana M. Chakravartula**, Failure Analysis and Strategy Lead, Google

"As a professor in the Department of Mechanical Engineering at UC Berkeley, Lisa Pruitt is well known for her research in biomaterials, excellence in teaching, and mentorship. Her many accomplishments provide a rosy image of a highly successful career. In *Soul of a Professor*, Lisa shares an authentic journey through personal struggles to pursue a healthier lifestyle balanced with a high-stress career."

—**Grace O'Connell**, Professor of Mechanical Engineering and Associate Dean for Inclusive Excellence, College of Engineering, UC Berkeley

"Lisa's memoir as a successful engineering professor and her healing journey with horses is vivid, sensitive, and alluring. It is a dramatically courageous tale of a woman who has bridged two very different worlds: a life of structure and form juxtaposed with a life that is sensate and intuitive. In *Soul of a Professor*, Lisa shares her most vulnerable moments to overcome addiction, let go of shame that is not even hers to bear, and find her eagle wings to soar untethered by the expectations of others. As 'Fire Horse,' Lisa sets the example for how to live like a horse and allow emotions to be a part of our life's adventure, thus adding a richness to our life experience.

"This book is a must-read for anyone who wants to change the world by being authentic and sharing their truth. Lisa shows us the path as she un-engineers her life to take a stand for her true self and embrace her own worthiness. Thank you, Lisa, for showing the way to authentic power, grace, and dignity."

—**Ariana Strozzi Mazzucchi**, Founder of Equine Guided Education, Author of *Horse Sense for the Leader Within* and *The Water Calls: One Woman's Journey to Reclaim Her Dignity and Freedom*

"Pruitt's prose is solid and her metaphors convincing, as when she describes her armor making her as 'unyielding as structural steel.' She's humble about her professional successes, stressing instead the irony that, as an engineer, she didn't anticipate she was driving herself to fracture.

"In her work with her horses ... the prose and Pruitt as a character come alive, as she describes the many instances in which JJ serves as a 'beacon of light' in her recovery. Pruitt finds real healing when she begins to integrate her passion for horses with her academic work, and ... the concluding chapters soar with narrative detail and meaning.

"While readers who don't share Pruitt's past addictions or passion for horses may find less to identify with, the story of her struggles is uplifting and a solid addition to the genre of addiction and recovery memoir."

—**BlueInk Review**

Soul

OF A PROFESSOR

Memoir of an Un-Engineered Life

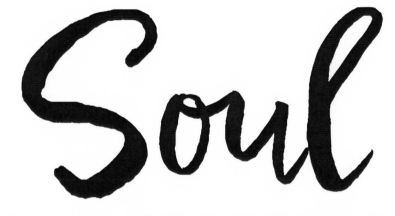

Soul
OF A PROFESSOR
Memoir of an Un-Engineered Life

LISA A. PRUITT, PhD

MERRY DISSONANCE PRESS   CASTLE ROCK, COLORADO

Soul of a Professor: Memoir of an Un-Engineered Life
Published by Merry Dissonance Press, LLC
Castle Rock, CO

FIRST EDITION 2022

Publisher's Cataloging-in-Publication data

Names: Pruitt, Lisa A., author.

Title: Soul of a professor : memoir of an un-engineered life / Lisa A. Pruitt, PhD.
Description: Castle Rock, CO: Merry Dissonance Press, 2022.

Identifiers: ISBN: 978-1-939919-67-0

Subjects: LCSH Pruitt, Lisa A. | Horsemanship--Therapeutic use. | Human-animal
relationships. | Horses. | Animals--Therapeutic use. | Self-actualization (Psychology). |
College teachers--Biography. | Women college teachers--Biography. | BISAC BIOGRAPHY
& AUTOBIOGRAPHY / Personal Memoirs | BIOGRAPHY & AUTOBIOGRAPHY /
Women
Classification: LCC RM931.H6 .P78 2022 | DDC 615.8/515/092--dc23

ISBN 978-1-939919-67-0

Book Interior and Cover Design © 2022
Cover Design by Victoria Wolf, wolfdesignandmarketing.com
Cover Art by Nima Nia, PhD
Book Design by Victoria Wolf, wolfdesignandmarketing.com
Editing by Donna Mazzitelli, writingwithdonna.com

All Rights Reserved by Lisa A. Pruitt and Merry Dissonance Press, LLC

This book reflects the author's present recollections of experiences
over time. Some names have been changed, some events have been
compressed, and some dialogue has been recreated.

For JJ
The love of my life and my spirit horse

PROLOGUE

The Darkest Hour Is Before the Dawn

S orrow pours down my cheeks. I can barely make out the silhouette of my long-legged thoroughbred across the field. Standing outside the gate to his pasture, I reflect on the failures of my life—a bittersweet irony, as one of my specialties as a professor is failure analysis. When I teach my engineering classes, we analyze failures as learning opportunities. At this juncture, I can't fathom how my personal failures could possibly be educational life lessons. Outwardly, I have achieved impressive academic success as a full professor with a highly respected portfolio of research, mentoring, and teaching. Inwardly, I feel unworthy and under-accomplished—an impostor in the world of academia.

My façade of success is crumbling. Throughout my life, I have struggled with anxiety, depression, and addiction. I failed to show up for my first marriage, for which I feel a visceral sense of shame and guilt. My sense of self is lost. My body is broken and exhausted. I have spent much of my life strengthening my academic armor—but like many engineering materials, strength comes at the expense of flexibility. In engineering parlance, my internal flaws have finally coalesced into a critical length, and I am on the verge of catastrophic failure. This is my darkest hour, and I do not know if I have the will to keep going.

I step through the pasture gate and watch my beautiful horse eating his dinner hay. *Who will care for him if I am gone?* With this thought, the energy shifts. JJ looks at me from across the pasture. Drawn to me as if by an electric current, he crosses the field to greet me as my body stays still. JJ stops at my side, and his knowing eyes look into mine—the immensity of this magnificent being engulfs me. Something stirs deep within. He wraps his head over my shoulder and lays his muzzle on my chest, enveloping me in a proverbial horse hug. Whether we stand together for minutes or hours, I do not know. As this splendid creature fills the empty vessel of my body with unconditional love, a flame of hope ignites. I receive a clear directive: I must not give up.

Months later, through the unyielding guidance of my bright chestnut horse, I find myself at a ranch that specializes in equine-guided education. This serene oasis is nestled within the rolling hills of the Sonoma Coast. I am here to work with a modern-day medicine woman who serves as my life coach. She reinforces what I have long known: horses heal people.

Standing in the round pen with JJ at my side, I gaze beyond the metal bars serving as our enclosure toward the vast sky and surrounding meadows. The serenity of the vista is lost on me at this moment because I am facing the most probing question of my life: *How is it that I have simultaneously reached the pinnacle of my academic career and hit rock bottom in my personal life?*

Standing outside the pen, my life coach questions the source of my deep-rooted beliefs and perceived failures. Her questions tangle my mind like the web of an angry spider. *What is the source of my unworthiness?*

Why do I hide behind an academic façade? How have I worked myself into utter exhaustion? I know the answers, but I have never openly shared the depths of my personal story. My fear is palpable. Deep within me resides a little girl still struggling with her perceived imperfections and embodied emotions, what Eckhart Tolle refers to as one's "pain body." I am assured that by working through my life story, I will find my healing medicine. With my spirit horse at my side, I bring myself back to the beginning.

PART
ONE

The Wrong
Daughter

1
Seeds of Darkness

The wintry February air penetrates the ice-clad windows of our small New England home. I am nearly two years old, and the chill settles in my little bones. I awaken to the sound of distant sobs, like the howling of a mother wolf at a burgeoning moon. My mother's sadness permeates the air.

Baby sister's crib is empty this morning. Just yesterday, I had quietly climbed into her crib, her bright moon eyes beckoning me. I held her as my mother had shown me, always supporting her head. Her bright red lips cooed at me, the creases of her little pinkies grasping my own tiny hands. I had rocked her like she was my own baby doll.

A visceral darkness is in our home. I hear the click of the bedroom door. Daddy steps in, and I see tears well up in his eyes. He picks me up, and his arms envelop me in a hug. Something is wrong. I hold him tighter.

"Daddy, where is baby?" I ask.

"God has taken Karen back to heaven," his voice cracks.

"Why?" I ask.

"I don't know," he answers, tears spilling down his cheeks. "Mommy's crying."

"Mommy is very sad. Let's not speak of Karen in front of Mommy. I hear that the priest has arrived. I need to speak with him. Can you be a good girl and play quietly with Mrs. Beasley?"

I grab my doll and rock her gently. She can never substitute for baby Karen. Today I feel my sister's absence in my heart. Torrents of tears stream down my face. The fabric of my soul has been ripped open.

Did I cause this? I wasn't supposed to climb into her crib. I was never supposed to hold her unless my parents were present. Is God angry with me? Did he take my baby sister away as my punishment?

Our massive German shepherd comes into the room as my father leaves. I find solace in King, nestling my head into his thick, soft fur. His chocolate-brown eyes stare into mine as he licks the sorrow from my face.

I overhear the priest outside the door, "Babies must be baptized to get into heaven." My parents' sobs reverberate through our home.

My heart breaks open. *Why did God take her and not me?* The seeds of darkness take root in this crucible of loss. A sense of unworthiness settles into the void once occupied by my baby sister and will serve as an internal flaw waiting to expand. A thought etches its way into my mind: *God took the wrong daughter.*

2

Early Years

The Christmas tree sings as her lights twinkle and dance across the room. I listen to its gentle melody as I watch the glow of reds, blues, yellows, and greens share their light. This is my third Christmas, and three stockings hang by the chimney. There should be four. My heart still aches for the loss of baby Karen.

Each night, I pray to God to bring my baby sister back. Each morning, I check her crib, but it has remained vacant since this past February. Our home has not felt the same since she left us. *Maybe I am not worthy of a baby sister?*

I learn from Daddy that the crib will soon have another baby. Mommy's expanding tummy has restored a smile to her face, but it has rekindled my fear. *I don't want God to take another sister.*

Today, we visit Santa at the department store. He sits on a big velvet chair in front of a massive tree, with snow on his shiny black boots. Mommy places me on his lap, and as I grasp the candy cane in my fist, it snaps.

"What would you like for Christmas?" Santa asks.

I think of all the toys that I want, but then I remember what I want more than anything. "Santa, can you bring Karen back home?"

"Only if you are a good girl. Ho, Ho, Ho!" he says.

Tears well up in my eyes. *I am not a good girl. I should not have been in her crib.* I will never see Karen again.

Decorated with pine boughs and lights, our home is ready for Christmas, but darkness looms just beneath the festive surface. I can't seem to let go of my sadness.

"Let's make pine cone wreaths today," Mommy says.

Our kitchen smells like a forest as we sit at the table and glue pine cones onto the circular frames. Mommy's wreath looks beautiful. She completes hers with a plaid taffeta bow and hangs it on the door. My wreath looks like a motley porcupine. My fingers stick together with sap, my lower lip quivers with escalating frustration. Pussy Cat rekindles my smile when she steals the ribbon and chases it around the kitchen floor. Mommy and I laugh.

My father works long days. Each night, I sit on his lap after dinner and listen to his stories. As King settles at my father's feet, I beg my father to tell me another story about Brer Rabbit.

"Please, Brer Fox, oh please, don't throw me in the briar patch," Daddy pleads in his high-pitched Brer Rabbit voice. I laugh, and my lower lip retreats.

Sometimes, Daddy lets me color on his graph paper, and I get to pretend that I'm an engineer too.

On the weekends, we visit my mommy's parents. On the long, quiet car ride, I stare out the window and look for the telltale river, indicating we're close to Nana and Grandpa's apartment.

"Mommy, look at the angels in the sky!" I say with excitement.

"Those are seagulls," she tells me. I am convinced they are angels taking someone to heaven. I wish they would bring Karen back. Our home seemed happier before she was taken nearly a year ago.

Nana greets us at the door when we arrive, her silver curls caked with flour and her apron showing evidence of Christmas cookies.

"Hi, Nana," I say. "Is Auntie Jackie here?"

"She was supposed to be here an hour ago," Nana says, rolling her eyes.

My mother laughs. "Auntie Jackie is always late."

Nana invites me into her kitchen, the sweet scent of her sugar cookies filling the air. She has already rolled her dough and cut them into Christmas trees. My job is to sprinkle the sugar. My pudgy little fingers splatter the cookie sheet with red and green sugar crystals.

"Twelve minutes," says Nana.

It feels like an eternity until I hear the magical buzzer. My stomach growls as the sweet essence of her cookies teases my nose. Nana peeks into the oven. "Just another minute," she says.

I anxiously await my treat. Nana gives me a crisp cookie and a cold glass of milk. Both disappear quickly, and I ask for another cookie.

"That's enough. You don't want to get fat," says Nana.

Grandpa is reading his newspaper, but once Nana leaves the kitchen, he peeks over his paper and gives me a smile. Then he fetches me another cookie.

"Thank you, Grandpa," I say.

"It's our secret," he says with a wink.

I eagerly wait for Auntie Jackie. When she arrives, I greet her at the front door, grab hold of her long trench coat, and hug her tightly, basking in her perfumed scent. Auntie is drinking a coffee milkshake. "Here you go, kiddo," she offers. I slurp down its creamy sweetness, and my inner sadness melts away.

"I have a gift for you, Lisa Anne Prune-Pit," she announces as she pokes my round tummy.

I quickly tear open the wrapping. "I love paints. Thank you!"

Auntie Jackie sets me up in the kitchen to make a painting. Nana tells her to spread Grandpa's newspaper on the table so I don't make a mess. My auntie curses under her breath. She smiles at me as if to say, "Don't use those words!" It's her "auntie language."

I dip my fingers liberally into the paint pots, filling the canvas with red and black. It captures my love for Auntie Jackie and the sadness I feel for losing Karen.

Nana frowns. "Why don't you choose pinks or pastels?" she asks.

"I like these colors," I say. I feel my lower lip protrude.

"I think your art is beautiful. I am going to frame it," says Auntie Jackie.

In January of 1969, my new baby sister arrives. Santa must have misunderstood. I asked for baby Karen. I want to be a good sister, but envy wells up in my body. Beth has the full attention of my parents and every other person who comes over to see her.

"What a beautiful baby!" they gush. I feel invisible.

A visceral sense of jealousy settles in. Beth and I look nothing alike—she has big blue eyes and tight little curls in her hair. She looks like my mother. Auntie Jackie also has eyes like the sky. She jokes that my eyes are brown because I'm "full of crap." Outwardly, I laugh at this, but inwardly, I weep.

My mother tells me I look just like my father did when he was a boy. *Does a little girl really want to look like her father?* I have a short pixie cut, and if I have to look like a little boy, then I am going to act like one. Instead of donning dresses, I find myself in the dirt alongside my father in the garden. King follows me everywhere. He is my best friend.

I try to avoid being around Beth because I feel unworthy when I am near her. I believe that I somehow caused Karen's death. *What if I cause something to happen to this baby sister? Will God send me straight to hell? Why am I here? It should be Karen who is the big sister to baby Beth.*

I am convinced my mother loves her more than she loves me. I can never seem to find my smile around my sister or mother. Mommy jokes that I should be called "Lisa the lip," which only makes me pout more. I find my smile when I spend time with King and Daddy in the garden.

In April, my mother invites some family members and children to our home for my third birthday party. My envy temporarily melts away as I intoxicate myself with chocolate cake. Jackie and I each eat a second piece of cake when Nana isn't looking. Auntie Jackie says with a chuckle, "I guess I have to start my new diet tomorrow." I don't know what a diet is, but my mommy and auntie are always talking about them.

One of the little boys at the party takes my balloon and then hits me when his mother isn't looking. Auntie Jackie catches him and stares him down cold. Darryl is mean. He pushes me down in the dirt when we are outside and away from the adults. King threatens him with a low growl. I retreat behind my protector.

When I am four years old, I go to the Pied Piper nursery school. Wooden tables covered with art supplies dot the large schoolroom. There are lots of children my age, but I can't seem to find my voice or make friends at school. The children make fun of me because I eat the creamy paste used for art. "You're gross," snickers one of the boys. I abandon the paste but begin to eat the erasers off the end of my pencils. I dread school.

"Can I stay home?" I ask.

"You need to go to school so that you can get smart," Daddy replies.

"I want to be smart like you someday," I say.

"You will be," he says and gently ruffles my hair.

One afternoon, when I get home from school, I find Beth watching cartoons on TV. King is lazing beside her. I feel a stab of jealousy and quickly fetch a milk bone to lure my dog away. Another day, I catch her playing with the little bird that Daddy and I rescued from the yard. She has Charlie bird in our Little People dollhouse. I blame her when he dies the next day. Meanness wells within me—I must wait for my revenge.

Months later, I make my masterpiece: a mud pie with a delicate balance of sand, dirt, and water. I offer it to my sister as we play in the sandbox.

"Mommy made you this pie. She will be sad if you don't eat it," I say.

Little Beth takes a bite of my dirt delicacy. I laugh. She cries, getting our mother's attention. I'm in trouble, again. "Lisa Anne Pruitt! You are older. You should know better," Mommy scolds.

I can't seem to find it in myself to be kind to my little sister. Last week, I pinched her fingers with my Tonka truck. The week prior, I plucked the head off her Skipper doll and tossed it out the car window after she put chewing gum in my hair. I am always to blame, even when Beth starts the battles. "You're older, and you should know better," little Beth says in her toddler's voice, mimicking our mother. My anger festers.

I am still convinced my mother loves Beth more than she loves me. I am the naughty sister. We are yin and yang—she is the good daughter, and I am the bad one. *Karen would have been a nice girl. She would have loved her little sister and not disappointed her parents. God, why did you take Karen and not me?*

8

One weekend, my father takes King for a ride. King's tail wags as he follows my father out of the house. He loves car rides.

"Where is King?" I ask as I notice my father has returned alone.

"Come sit on the sofa with me," Daddy' says, his eyes filling with tears.

"King has been put to sleep," he tells me.

"When will he wake up?" I ask. My palms begin to sweat.

"He won't wake up. He has gone to heaven."

"What do you mean?" I ask as my tears build alongside my fear and anger.

"King was too protective of you. He threatened to bite children."

"What children?" I ask through misted eyes. *Only mean children who push me when parents aren't looking?*

I'm off the sofa in an instant. I run to the bathroom and slam the door. I am angry at God. I am angry at Daddy and the children who taunted King. I scream into my bath towel, and hot tears flood my face.

I have lost my baby sister and now my protector. They are both in heaven, and I will never see them. I am not worthy of heaven. *Maybe I was never worthy of them?* Darkness consumes me. My inner flaw of unworthiness expands.

3

Learning Is Elementary

On my first day of elementary school, my mother walks me to the bus stop at the end of our street. The big yellow monster pulls up, bursting with children. Its mouth opens and swallows me whole. The noise of the children is deafening, yet my heart booms in my ears. My six-year-old body is filled with fear.

At school, we get our desks and learn where to put things. I sit quietly in my seat, watching the other children play. I am dreadfully shy and afraid to speak to anyone. At recess, we get to go out to the playground. I recognize Darryl because our mothers are friends. When he plays at our home, he calls me a "stupid, useless girl." Is he the reason I no longer have King? I hide on the playground so he doesn't see me.

I sit on a curb where I can watch the children play. I want to be home where I can climb my trees and disappear. A little girl with long red hair comes up to me and sits beside me. I am mesmerized by her blue eyes. They remind me of my periwinkle crayons.

"Hi, my name is Sharon. What's your name?"

"Lisa," I whisper.

"Would you like to be my friend?" she asks.

I nod, and she takes my sweaty hand in hers. I feel the warmth of her fingers wrap around mine. I am so grateful to have a friend. Sharon remains my only true friend throughout elementary school.

Ms. Miller, my first-grade teacher, has a pixie haircut and a fiery demeanor like Tinkerbell. Her discriminating eyes peer at me through her Coke-bottle glasses. She assigns me to a small wooden desk in the back of the room. I fidget with my sharpened pencils, and one finds its way to my mouth, where I nibble away its eraser bottom. I try to pay attention when she speaks, but I don't understand the math on the blackboard. I doodle on my paper.

"Lisa, pay attention!" she snaps.

Her sharp tone startles me, and I withdraw into myself. Nothing she teaches penetrates my brain. Basic concepts elude me. When graded papers are returned to us in math class, I learn that "F" is for failure. I immediately rip the letter off the paper, stuff the grade into my mouth, and swallow it when no one is looking. On the bus ride home, I rip the remainder of the incriminating paper into small pieces. I stuff down my stupidity.

I only bring home my A papers. I need good grades to make up for being a naughty girl at home.

My scheme catches up with me at the parent-teacher conference.

"Lisa, have you forgotten to bring some of your math papers home?" my father asks.

"No," I lie.

"I've only seen your A grades, but it seems you have received some other papers that I haven't seen. Where did they go?" he presses.

"I ate them," I say, ashamed.

"Your teacher and I decided it would be best if we moved you to another math class where the pace is a bit slower," he says. "I know how smart you are. I will help you with your schoolwork at night," he adds with a smile.

"Don't you have your own homework to do?" I ask.

"No. I gave up my school to focus on family," he says.

I feel sadness well up inside. I don't want my daddy to give up his school because I am not smart. I will work hard and make my daddy proud of me.

After the dinner dishes are cleared, Daddy takes an orange from our fruit bowl. "We're going to use this to learn fractions," he says with a smile.

He peels the thick skin away from its citrus meat. Its pungency wakens my senses. He sections the orange into quarters to show me that the four parts make the whole orange. We then section these pieces, and I learn equivalent fractions. When the math lesson is over, we eat the fruit.

Daddy makes learning fun. He answers my questions about nearly anything I can imagine. Sometimes I don't ask him questions because his answers get too complicated. I still don't understand why the sky is blue but it is not really blue. I want to be smart like my father. I want him to be proud of me—I don't want to disappoint him. I must get better grades at school.

I will spend much of my life trying to chase down a sense of worthiness through academic success.

On the weekends, Daddy takes me and Beth to the Boston Museum of Science. Mommy joins us after she takes Nana grocery shopping.

Overlooking the Charles River, the multistory center houses a multitude of scientific exhibits. The museum is captivating and daunting all at once.

"It's like an amusement park for our brains," Daddy says with a laugh.

"Daddy, can we go see Spooky the owl?" He is my favorite. His magnificent brown feathers cling to his expansive wings; his amber eyes enchant me as he turns his head nearly all the way around. I sit on the floor and watch him perched on the trainer's gloved hand. I so desperately want to pet him. The handler brings him back to his cage, and another trainer comes out with a large snake. She invites us to touch him. I work up my bravery; his skin feels like cold leather. I would rather pet the owl. I expect that his feathers are soft like rabbit fur.

"Daddy, can we go to the planetarium next?" Beth asks.

In the planetarium, I stare up at the stars on the curved roof above my head. I pray to God to see if somehow Karen found her way to him. Every day, Karen invades my thoughts. When I think about her, I feel sad, and when I feel sad, I think about her. Every mistake I make seems to call in some rhetorical banter: *Would Karen have done this? It is Karen who is worthy of this life. Not me.*

Daddy brings me back down to earth, telling us about his work as an engineer and why it is important for space exploration. I have no idea what he is talking about, but I nod my head as if I understand his language of mathematics and engineering. Someday, my sister and I will speak his scientific language fluently. Today, I just ask if we can see the owl again.

4

Red Sox and Green Monsters

Dandelions sprout up over the grassy field, and butterflies flicker across my baseball cap. Boredom consumes me. None of the softballs ever get to the outfield. I throw off my softball glove and pick flowers for my mother, then practice my cartwheels.

"Lisa, pay attention! It's time for our team to hit," yells my softball coach.

It's my turn at bat. The ball rises way up in the air before crossing home plate. My eyes try to follow the softball, but I lose track as it gets to the plate. I swing and miss. I then miss the next ball and the one after that.

"Strike three! You're out," grumbles the umpire.

Tears well up in my eyes. Our team loses. The coach tells my parents that he is going to put me in the position of catcher so I will pay attention. I am sad on the drive home—I am seven years old, and I want to be good at something. *Karen would be good at softball.*

"Mommy and Daddy, can you help me get better at softball?" I ask.

"We'll practice hitting the ball this weekend," Daddy promises.

We start practicing in the local field on the weekends. My father teaches me to bat and field. He also plays catch with me every night when he gets home from work. I quickly learn all the rules of baseball and listen to the Red Sox games on the radio with him. Carlton "Pudge" Fisk is my favorite player because he is the Red Sox catcher. He wears number twenty-seven. I have his baseball card. I want to play as well as Pudge does.

"Can we go to Fenway sometime and see the Green Monster?" I ask.

"Someday," Daddy replies.

"When I grow up, I'm going to play for the Red Sox. I'm going to hit baseballs over the Green Monster and help them win a World Series," I say. My father laughs, in part because he knows I have a great passion for baseball but also because he knows firsthand the limitations that society will impose on me because of my gender.

"You can do anything as long as you work hard," he encourages. This little seed will blossom within and ultimately bolster me in my chosen field of engineering and academia.

The following April arrives, and I see my birthday card on the table. My father jokes that I was really born on April Fool's Day, but we celebrate on April second so I don't get upset. When I see the contents of my card, I no longer care if I am a fool. I see the tickets emboldened with Red Sox on the front. "Mommy and Daddy, thank you so much!" I say breathlessly.

When we arrive at Fenway, I breathe in the scent of fresh grass and hot dogs. I gaze at the massive backdrop known as the "Green Monster" and hear the snap of baseballs assaulting leather. I watch in awe.

"Daddy, I see number eight," I say.

"Wave your ball to him," Daddy suggests.

In my excitement, I forget my shyness and frantically wave.

"Daddy, Yaz is coming over!"

My voice fails me when Yaz takes my baseball to sign. He smiles at me. I am beaming—I can't believe I have Carl Yastrzemski's signature.

Playing softball becomes a piece of my identity over the coming decade. I work hard, and I excel at it. Softball serves as part of my armor, like case-hardened steel protecting its inner flaws.

5

Secrets

Auntie Jackie's bright blue eyes sparkle under the wave of her short bottle-blond hair. Her perfume is so strong it takes my breath away. She reapplies her coral lipstick before we walk into Friendly's ice cream shop. Our thick coffee frappes arrive with their large straws, and we immediately vacuum the contents of our tall glasses into our bellies.

"Don't tell Nana we stopped for ice cream; we're already late for lunch. Okay, Kiddo?" she says, letting out a belch.

"It's our secret," I agree. I like secrets—they make me feel special.

We get on the Mass Turnpike, snarled with traffic.

"Jesus H. Christ!" my aunt yells, honking her horn at the driver ahead of us.

"What does the "H" stand for?" I ask.

"How the hell should I know. And don't share my *auntie language* with your parents. *Comprenez-vous?*"

"Got it," I say.

"If we go home the back way, will you let me sit on your lap and help you drive again?" I ask. Her lips curl up in a sly smile. We thrive in mischief.

On the way home from Nana's, we stop at the grocery store and head to the freezer aisle to get ice cream. "Pick out any frozen dinner you want. Nothing is too good for my fairy goddaughter," she says.

As we check out, she grabs a $100,000 Bar for herself and a Sugar Daddy for me. She quickly adds a box of Boston Baked Beans and Jordan Almonds to the conveyor belt. "Don't tell," she says. Eating candy together is one of our secrets.

Auntie Jackie is a fifth-grade schoolteacher in the Cambridge Public School system, so our school vacations coincide. I like to stay at her apartment. She lets me make "wine coolers" with sweet wine and ginger ale. I keep refilling my tumbler when I go to her kitchen. The wine dissipates my darkness and takes my sadness away. Drinking sweet wine together is another one of our secrets.

At night, we eat coffee ice cream sitting on her living room floor.

"Why can't we sit on the chairs?" I ask.

"Because they move out of place. I like them to be perfect for when guests visit," Auntie says. "Now shut up and eat your ice cream." *Aren't I a guest? My mommy says Auntie Jackie is "quirky." I think this is what she means.*

We watch *Quincy* on her TV. He is a medical examiner who solves mysteries about how people die. He lives on a boat. Auntie Jackie thinks he's handsome. "I need to marry a rich doctor who lives on a boat," she says with a wink.

"If I don't play for the Red Sox when I grow up, then I'll be a doctor like Quincy. You can live with me," I offer.

"Good, you can take care of me when I'm old. Don't ever put me in a nursing home, promise?" says Aunt Jackie.

"I will always take care of my fairy godmother," I say. This promise will haunt me later in my life.

Auntie Jackie takes me and Beth skiing for February vacations. We make the four-hour journey through New England to Vermont. We stay at a rustic ski lodge just a few miles from the mountain. When we step through the front door of the inn, the scent of burning wood from the fireplaces warms my heart. It reminds me of trees, and I find much solace in nature. The barnwood floors creak underfoot as we make our way to our room. We eat a family-style dinner in the dining room, then play ping-pong before heading outdoors for snowball fights.

In the morning, we quickly eat our breakfast and layer ourselves in our ski clothing. I am spellbound when I see Mount Mansfield, the highest mountain in Vermont. We start at Little Spruce, where Auntie Jackie enrolls us in the children's ski school. We quickly learn to maneuver around small moguls. As the week progresses, we easily acquire the skills to ski the little mountain.

Skiing is the one thing my sister and I do together. It melts away the competitiveness between us. Beth is brilliant, like our father, while I still struggle at school. At home, I constantly provoke her, my recalcitrant behavior masking my envy. Here, in the surrounds of the snow-covered mountains, we become aligned, and it only takes a few winters for us to become good skiers. We race each other down the mountain and seek out adrenaline-rushing trails. We drag Auntie Jackie through the woods and down parts of the mountain that she balks at; she curses at us and then sidesteps her skis down the slope until Beth and I nearly die of laughter.

Auntie Jackie tires long before we do. She waits in the base lodge, and we finally return to her after the mountain closes. At the end of each day, we pack up our ski gear and stop at a local bar for "après ski," where Auntie Jackie lets me sip her cocktails. She offers a sip to Beth, but my sister doesn't like the taste.

These ski trips are intoxicating, both figuratively and literally. I find myself in a molten state where my internal flaws and sense of darkness temporarily melt away.

In the summers, Auntie Jackie takes us to Long Beach in Cape Anne, north of Boston. We lug all of our beach paraphernalia across the hot sand. Jackie spreads out on her chaise lounge and reads her cheap novels under an umbrella. Beth and I ride the waves in the ocean and look for hermit crabs scuttling in the mossy rocks. At midday, we eat tuna fish sandwiches and Nutter Butter cookies while we play Crazy Eights. We wash everything down with sodas from her cooler. We go out for ice cream after a fried seafood dinner.

"I ate too much," Auntie groans, then belches loudly. I try to burp like Auntie does, but my sister tells me I'm gross. I smirk with delight. My sister rolls her eyes and then refocuses into her book.

"I wish I could throw up," Auntie says. "We need to stop at the store so I can get some ex-lax."

"What is that?" I ask.

"It's a magical chocolate that will help me not feel too full. Starting tomorrow, I'm going back on my diet. I'm getting fat again. It's all your fault; you make me eat too much junk food." She pokes my belly.

I feel her finger submerge into my rolls of tummy, which seems to have expanded over the summer. *Maybe I need magic chocolate too?*

6

Disordered Eating

The letters of the alphabet in block print and cursive writing adorn the blackboard in our third-grade classroom. We learn that penmanship is a practiced skill. Cursive letters are repeated with No. 2 pencils on lined yellow paper. Once we master cursive handwriting, we earn blue pens and white paper.

I drag my pencil through the lines of the yellow paper, seeking the beautiful loops that should live in the first letter of my name. It eludes me. Mrs. C taps the blackboard with her pointer, then bellows across the room.

"Lisa, get your hair out of your mouth and pay attention!" she orders.

I quickly drop the hair from my mouth. Mrs. C doesn't let up. She brings my bad habit to the attention of my parents, and ultimately my offensive behavior is resolved with scissors. I can't escape her scrutiny.

"Your penmanship is lousy. You are the only one in the classroom without a pen," she says. *Why do all of my teachers hate me?*

My palms sweat when Mrs. C calls on me to read a paragraph from the book. My brain and tongue refuse to cooperate; I mix the first letters of sequential words. I spill out meaningless gibberish. The class laughs. My inability to read aloud results in an onslaught of ridicule at recess. It will not be until much later in my life, after I am a professor, that I learn I am dyslexic—a term that has not yet made it into my third-grade academic world.

"Maybe you should spend more time reading and less time eating," one of the boys at recess taunts, making an oinking noise in my face.

My anger explodes like an overstressed pressure valve, and I punch him in the nose. I am called to the principal's office. I have no words and retreat deeper within myself. *Karen would not be at the principal's office.*

The ghost of my sister haunts me. I am eight years old and plagued by a sense of unworthiness. Karen appears in my thoughts when I make mistakes—when I can't learn, when I provoke fights with Beth, when I let my parents down. It is as though she sows my seeds of darkness. She has etched a deep groove in my self-sabotaging thoughts: *I will never be good enough. God took the wrong sister.*

When I get home from school, I immediately head to the freezer and grab our large container of ice cream. When the first spoonful hits my tongue, I feel the hurtful words of my day melt away. Within minutes, I consume a large bowl of my creamy friend. My emotional hunger seeks more. I am uncomfortably full.

In the bathroom, I look for the magic chocolate that Auntie uses, but we have none. I stand on the ledge of the bathtub so I can see myself in the mirror above the sink. I stare at my pudgy cheeks and my burgeoning belly. Hatred wells up within me. I slap myself in the face until I cry. I quickly wash my face. Big girls don't cry.

My mother calls us to dinner. We are having macaroni and cheese—again.

"I'm not hungry," I say.

"Eat your dinner," my mother intones.

"I don't feel good."

"Then you should go to bed," she says.

The option to go to bed early is not really a choice, so as soon as I tromp off to bed, I'm back at the table. The tension in the air is palpable. I don't want to eat my dinner, but I pour ketchup over my food and shovel it down quickly. Resentment builds within me.

Returning to the bathroom, I lock the door. My auntie once said she wished she could throw up after she ate too much. I hang my head over the toilet and push my belly as hard as I can, but nothing happens.

I turn on the water and fill the cup on the counter. I gulp down the cup of water, then another, and another. I try again. This time, I push harder on my belly. All of my dinner comes out into the toilet. I flush it down.

I wash my face and brush my teeth, feeling immediate relief but then merciless guilt. This is my first bulimic episode—a transformative event at eight years old that will consume me for the next three decades.

Over time, I create my rituals, learning which foods are easiest to throw up and those that won't budge. I use my bulimic behavior to numb my inner feelings of unworthiness and self-hatred. Mostly, I purge in toilets, but later in life, I also use the woods behind our house or trash bags that I keep in my closet. I master ways to hide my bulimia, and anyone who gets too close to my secret gets displaced in my life.

My eating disorder becomes an integral part of my protective armor, a deep-rooted secret that walls me off from meaningful relationships. I use binging and purging to create some semblance of control; ironically, it will ultimately take control of me. I have no sense of the psychological or neurological changes that can manifest in a body due to this life-threatening eating disorder.

In the decades to come, bulimia will cause heart palpitations, erode my enamel and gums, cause stomach ulcers, and render me prone to depression, shame, and guilt.

7

Religious Freedom

The sun beaming through the stained-glass windows dispels its rich colors across the pew. I am mesmerized by its beauty yet disheartened by the image of Jesus on the cross. The worst part of going to church is that I have to wear an itchy dress. The tights strangle my legs, and the patent leather shoes pinch my feet. Sometimes, my mom makes matching dresses for Beth and me. She wants us to look pretty, but I would rather play in the dirt and climb trees.

Church involves being quiet for a long time while a man in long green robes talks to everyone in the room. We call him "Father," but he is not my daddy. I only pretend to sing because I don't like the sound of my voice. I stare at the statue of Mary, my mind wandering to Karen. When my parents aren't looking, I make funny faces at my sister. Beth purposely nudges my mother, who gives me a very clear directive without speaking a word. *Church is not a time to play. I am nine years old, and I should know better.*

Confession is made so we can take part in communion. I dread sitting in the dark wooden closet, waiting to hear the judgment of the priest.

"I was mean to my sister this week. I ate all of her leftover birthday cake so she couldn't have any more. Then I took her hoppity hop that she got for her birthday, and I wouldn't let her ride it. She got so mad at me that she popped it. I lied to my parents when they asked what happened," I tell the priest.

"You must be kind to your sister and never lie to your parents," he admonishes. *What would the priest say if he knew that right after I ate her cake, I went and threw it up?* That must be a very big sin. *I am going to hell.*

My penance is one hundred Hail Marys. I always lose count. Each week, I fall into the same pattern, plagued by the guilt of my sins.

We not only have church service on Sundays, but we also have Bible study at a neighbor's home. I despise church studies. The woman who teaches the class is as mean as my schoolteachers. The only good thing about church school is that I get to ride my skateboard to Mrs. Holy's home. (I don't remember her name, so I created a private nickname for her.)

At the appointed time, I grab my blue skateboard. I push hard with my right leg and then coast over the bumpy pavement as I ride past tall pine trees along the streets to the teacher's house. Mrs. Holy invites me into her living room, where I sit on the floor behind the other children. I get distracted by the worn shag rug that looks like the inside of an aged avocado and smells like a dog.

My mind drifts to King. He, too, lives in the all-elusive heaven. I will never see him again. Sadness wells up. I feel "Karen's mantra" stirring. I quickly stuff a piece of candy in my mouth and hope the sugar will dissolve the assaulting thoughts. I try to focus on the day's lesson.

"Today, we're going to talk about the Ten Commandments. We need to follow these to get into heaven," the teacher intones.

I am never getting into heaven, so why bother to pay attention? My mind wanders to science class earlier in the day. We learned that the Earth is 4.5 billion years old and that dinosaurs roamed the Earth beginning 245 million years ago. Mrs. Holy tells us the Earth was created in just five days. I muster my courage and raise my hand.

"Lisa, do you have a question?" she asks with a roll of her eyes.

"Today in science, we learned about dinosaurs. On which day were they created?" I ask with true scientific curiosity.

"Lisa, you are being irreverent," she says sternly.

I don't know what "irreverent" means, but it doesn't sound good. The other children glare at me. I feel stupid, again.

I still have lots of questions about how evolution and creation work together, but I don't dare ask anything else. *How is it possible that every-thing was formed in five days?* Questioning seems to be a sin unto itself. I smuggle another piece of candy into my mouth and hope the sugar quells my scientific curiosity.

In order to mitigate my irreverent behavior, I decide it's best to skip church school the following week. I have my black Timex watch strapped around my wrist. I have one hour to kill. I ride my skateboard to a vacant grassy plot surrounded by tall pine trees. I grab hold of the roughened bark of a low-lying limb and scale the tallest reaches of my chosen tree. I place my hands on her, as though asking permission: *May I climb you today? Will you let me soak in your essence? Can I safely hide amongst your beautiful cone-filled branches? Will you protect me from the human world? Yes, she says.*

I take hold of the low branch and quickly elevate myself to her upper branches. From my perch, I can see the extended neighborhood. The rich scent of pine fills the air. I am transported elsewhere. Dreaming. Flying like an owl, silent in the air, above the onslaught of cruel children and teachers.

The sound of the children leaving Mrs. Holy's house awakens me back to this world. I quickly descend the tree and skateboard home. *This is the perfect solution!* But my plan has a fatal flaw.

"How was church school today?" Mom asks.

"Good," I reply. My sappy palms begin to sweat.

"Really? Because the church school teacher called a few minutes ago to ask if you were sick."

My father learns of my antics when he gets home from work. "I'm disappointed that you lied to your mother," he says. But he is not disappointed that I asked about dinosaurs or evolution.

Tears fill my eyes. My words catch in my throat. I offer no defense. My father doesn't know that I tell lots of lies because I don't like to get in trouble.

I try to explain my confusion between religion and science. In some semblance of a truce, we agree that I will take a break from religious studies.

"This is not something to share with your grandparents," he says.

"Which ones?" I ask.

"Both sets. This can be our secret."

Another secret. I'm getting good at keeping secrets.

8

Metamorphosis

A dolescence brings a complete physical metamorphosis—I am no longer a pudgy child. I limit the amount of food I eat to stop this monstrous transformation, but womanhood is hijacking my body.

My body does not resemble my twelve-year-old peers, who still retain some semblance of girlhood. No clothing or undergarment can conceal my buxom figure. I try to hide beneath heavy sweaters, but the taunting from the boys is merciless. I have developed a mean right hook—yet, I feel nearly defenseless against the onslaught of sexualized attention.

Hormones rage through my body; I constantly seek to numb myself to try and chase them away. I find comfort in bulimia. I limit my food at breakfast and lunch, eating a minimal amount of sustenance. In the afternoons, I gorge on ice cream and sweets before my mom gets home from her shift as a nurse. My sister is home, but she is always engrossed in a book. *Does she even notice how much food I eat?* I vomit all of my food and stuffed emotions before dinner.

My father often has a stiff drink when he gets home from work, before dinner. "May I have a sip?" I ask. The bourbon burns my throat and warms my empty belly. I offer to refill my dad's glass and sneak a large gulp before returning it to him. I feel my anxiety ease away. The magical properties of hard alcohol settle in my body. This is no wine cooler that slightly numbs my inner pain; instead, this fiery liquid provides a fast-acting injection that temporarily fills my inner void and dispels my shyness. My ongoing burden of unworthiness can't seem to take purchase in the realm of inebriation.

Alcohol finds friendship alongside my eating disorder. I begin to steal alcohol from the liquor cabinet. Each night, I drink down the seductive liquid, quelling my feelings of unworthiness and lulling myself to sleep.

Middle school is brutal. The boys taunt. The girls dissect each other. I have been babysitting across the street, and as a result, I was introduced to a cousin of that family—she is one of the "cool girls" at school. I am hanging with her on a Monday morning before classes start. My friend Sharon approaches, but the cool girl snickers. I quickly walk away before any connection is made between us. I pretend that I don't see Sharon, but she knows I did. I toss Sharon to the wind like a dried dandelion seed leaving its stem. She has been my sole friend through elementary school. But this is middle school. This is about survival. Sharon is not one of the cool kids. More importantly, she recently asked how I keep myself so thin. No one can get close to my secret. I abandon her to my addictions.

I am moody and quick with my mother and relentless with my sister. My sister and I look nothing alike. She is tall like my mother and likely will not carry the burden of a curvy figure. I seem to have inherited my frame from Nana. My sister is brilliant and will go on to become a national scholar. She reads at a college-level, while I barely read at all. My envy of her is masked as cruelty.

The torment of my sister worsens when my cousin Laura and I are tasked with babysitting our younger siblings while our parents go out together. Laura is thirteen, and I am twelve. Beth is nine, her brother Danny a few years younger, and Leeann is merely a toddler.

My mother and Laura's father are first cousins—they both come from a long line of Canadian farmers. Our parents get together on weekends, often involving large quantities of alcohol. Laura and I take great satisfaction in taunting our siblings when we babysit.

"We're in charge. You have to listen to us," we say sternly to Beth, Danny, and Leann.

If our parents actually go out to dinner, then we find even more ways to push the limits. We thoroughly enjoy being in charge—even if only for a short while. Our parents refer to us as "Laura-Lisa," as if we are one.

Any misbehavior reported by our siblings earns "Laura-Lisa" the task of cleaning up the kitchen. But we don't mind since we quickly realize we are rewarded with a treasure trove of alcohol left out on the countertops. Laura and I soon find our rhythm as the lubricious fluids soothe us and the antics of our siblings no longer bother us.

My parents notice that I have shifted my friends in middle school. "They are not a good influence," my parents say. *Do they know that these kids drink and smoke?*

"They are just people I hang out with," I say defiantly.

"What happened to Sharon?" my parents ask.

"She has new friends too," I lie.

My rebellious behavior helps motivate a relocation from our little ranch house in the suburbs of Boston to a colonial saltbox in the country-side. Our new home sits atop a grassy hill surrounded by woods and swampland. The town of Mendon offers long, winding roads leading nowhere. Main Street is home to a pizza parlor, post office, and general store. Expansive farms spread out across the rural community. Lowell's restaurant and the Miscoe Springs soda manufacturing plant round out the offerings. There are no movie theaters, bowling allies, or shopping malls. I'm counting down the days until I can leave this town and find some semblance of the life I seek. *Maybe when I'm a successful doctor with a fancy car? Maybe then I will be worthy of this world?*

I dread the thought of a new school, but I hope this will be a fresh start and the boys will have their eyes on their farms and not on my body. As I step into the classroom, the wood floors beneath my feet alert everyone to my presence, as all eyes of the small class turn to me. Blood rushes to my face.

"Class, this is Lisa Pruitt. She has just moved to our town, and I hope you will make her feel welcome," says Mrs. Rhodes.

I lower my gaze to the floor and quickly take my seat. Within minutes, a small folded note lands on my desk. I carefully unfold it, dreading its contents. I scan the words. "You make my Italian blood boil," it reads. I wish I could vomit right then. I rip the note into shreds and stuff it into my pocket. Someone of Italian descent will be wearing my right fist after school.

One thing is certain about this school: I will no longer feel stupid. As I navigate my new classes, I realize that I am well-prepared to be under-challenged. The fruits of my father's academic tutoring have finally paid off—I will no longer have to burden him with my academic idiocy. An inner smile lurks within.

The best part of this move is that I have my own room. My sister and I sequester ourselves on opposite ends of the house. I imagine she enjoys the respite from my steady torment. Her room is filled with Breyer horses and sketches with an equine theme. She is horse crazy. Beth constantly begs my parents for a horse. They finally compromise with riding lessons.

"Why do I have to go too?" I grumble.

"Because you're not old enough to stay home alone," Mom responds. I glare at my sister.

At the stable, we are introduced to our instructor Lyndsey. "These horses are quite safe, but they require a lot of leg," she says.

Soon we are out in the dirt arena astride our horses. Beth smiles brightly while I frown. Within minutes, my sister and her horse are well ahead of us in the arena.

"Good, Beth, you're doing a great job," Lyndsey encourages. "Lisa, squeeze your legs." I squeeze hard, but nothing happens.

"Kick!" Lyndsey yells.

I kick. Nothing. My frustration grows as I watch my sister move easily on her mount. I scowl, jealous—Beth is a natural. *Maybe I'm more suited to softball?* I leave the passion of horses to my sister, though later on, they will cast their spell on me too.

As I enter high school at the age of fourteen, I am afforded a great deal of freedom at home as long as I maintain good grades. This is an easy task—perhaps too easy. I complete all my homework by the time the school bell rings at 2:30 p.m. I play three varsity sports to occupy my time and my mind: field hockey, basketball, and softball. I no longer carry the burden of feeling stupid; instead, I am now teased for being too smart.

"Who is smarter—you or your sister?" one of my classmates asks. It's not asked out of kindness. There is mockery in his tone and hatred in his eyes.

"My sister," I reply. I walk away before I can land my fist in his face.

On the weekends, as he sips his drink, my father shares stories of his life as an engineering student at MIT. He offers me a small glass. I repeatedly fill my glass when he leaves the room. My father has a plethora of humorous anecdotes of pranks and antics with college friends. They all involved large quantities of alcohol. *Does one need a strong drinking ability as well as math proficiency to be an engineer? Perhaps I do have the requisite skills to be an engineer.*

My father continually pushes me to consider a career in engineering. It feels so far away—maybe he sees something in me that I don't yet see in myself. But my aspiration is not engineering; rather, I find myself drawn to medicine. I want to be a forensic pathologist, like Quincy on TV.

My eating disorder and alcohol abuse keep me numbed from my inner sense of unworthiness, lurking beneath my patina of protective armor. I am always asking: *Did God take the wrong sister?* Perhaps my sense of unworthiness will be nullified if I can create a successful career for myself. My pursuit of academic success becomes just as addictive as my other coping tools.

9

Deep Darkness

Boys are my nemesis. I wish I could be done with school, safely protected in my medical examiner's lab coat, working quietly among the dead, without probing eyes or rude comments about my fifteen-year-old body.

There is an exception to the ceaseless harassment: an upperclassman in my Spanish class. Tall and handsome, Dean has dark curly hair, deep-brown eyes, and a grin that makes me melt. I try not to stare. Dean sits behind me in the classroom, and when he passes by me, he offers a warm smile.

"Hola Lisa, cómo estás?" Dean says.

"Muy bien," I reply, my heart aflutter. I see the teacher glare at me, and I quickly open my Spanish book.

At my first high school dance, this handsome young man walks over to me. I am prepared for a quick exchange in Spanish, but not the extension of his hand.

"Would you like to dance?" Dean asks.

My feet feel like lead. My palms sweat as I offer a meek nod of my head. I don't know how to dance, but giddiness overtakes my body. He leads me to the dance floor, and I nearly float away with joy.

I soon discover the protective qualities of having a boyfriend, as the relentless teasing and pursuit from other boys quickly disappears. My armor has gained an impenetrable ballistic coating.

Dean drives a little sports car. In winter, he comes to the house, and we skate on the frozen pond next to the woods. In the spring, Dean asks me to his prom. My mother adores him. My parents let me go to the prom as long as I agree to be home by midnight. Auntie Jackie warns me that boys are not to be trusted, even if they are wearing tuxedos.

As my boyfriend approaches graduation, he suggests we continue our relationship when he heads off to college. His statement prompts a wave of terror in me as I realize I will no longer have his protection in high school. I can't imagine my life at this school without Dean's chainmail to protect me.

After drinking a tall glass of social bravery, I call Dean to break off our relationship. My words nervously stammer as I pitch that this is best for him since he will soon be heading to college.

"Dean, I don't think we should continue our relationship when you go to college," I say with a stammer.

"Why? We can still see each other. I can come home on the weekends," he says.

"No. You should date other girls," I say. In truth, I know that he can't protect me from the onslaught of sexualized attention at school if he is off at college. I need to find another bodyguard.

Deep down, I feel sadness. Much as I had when I tossed my friend Sharon to the wind. My inner voice at the ready: *I was never worthy of him anyway.*

As my sophomore year begins, I'm once again plagued by relentless provocation. Having a boyfriend is the simplest solution to this challenge. My eyes settle on one of the "punk rockers." He's not clean-cut like Dean—practically the opposite. He's one of the "bad boys" known for rebellious behavior. He goes by the nickname Spike. My parents do not approve of this new boyfriend.

I am drawn to Spike like a bee on honey. He speaks to the inner part of me held behind my façade. He represents some great irony of my life. I am clean-cut on the outside but a bad girl on the inside. I am brilliant on the outside yet unworthy and sad on the inside. He is yin to my yang.

When I turn sixteen, my dad gives me his old car to drive, a column-shift Ford Maverick, and this blue beauty offers me independence. I soon discover my womanly physique gives me the ability to buy alcohol at the liquor store. I use my babysitting funds to buy small nips of vodka. I keep them hidden inside tall boots in the back of my closet and use these highly concealable bottles to enhance my social prowess. I am essentially a highly functioning addict—balancing alcohol, bulimia, sports, and work. I feel invincible, but this will soon change.

I am losing my moral compass. I lie to my parents constantly. I am evasive about how much time I spend with Spike. I continually break my curfew and fabricate some story to justify my tardiness. I seem to be living under the philosophy of "It's better to ask for forgiveness than permission." My addictions tighten their stranglehold on me.

My mother's patience with me grows thin. "Every gray hair on my head is owed to you," she tells me on a night when I stagger in at 2:00 a.m. I am definitely a daddy's girl, and he affords me some leniency, but the anguish I cause my mother is draining his goodwill.

As my relationship with Spike evolves, I find myself drawn more deeply into his group of friends. They smoke pot and pressure me to join them, but I promised my father I would never do drugs, and I honor this vow. The punk-rocker clan taunts me.

"You're such a goody-two-shoes! Take a smoke," they pressure.

"No, I promised my parents I wouldn't do drugs."

My boyfriend joins in the taunting. "Do you think being a smart jock makes you too good for us?" Spike challenges.

I glare at him. I can't believe I'm being bullied by my own boyfriend.

"Let's just drink like we have been," I plead.

"I'll quit using drugs if you quit your stupid softball team," he challenges.

I feel my heart rip in two. Softball is the one passion that is good in my life. I should just walk away, but I am under some romantic spell as well as a "thread" of self-destruction. I should know that addicts think nothing of telling lies. Unfathomably, I agree to the terms.

I get drunk to work up the courage to tell Coach S that I am quitting the softball team. He is devastated.

"I need to quit the team so I can work more to save for college," I say.

"You could get a college scholarship with your athletic abilities," he counters.

I can't hold his eye contact. He stares right through me.

"Lisa, you can do better than this," Coach S says.

I don't know what "this" refers to anymore—my behavior, my boyfriend, my addictions? Does he know the depths of my despair? I stand firm in my decision but not without deep regret. My inner voice taunts: *I am not worthy of a softball scholarship. Karen would be an all-star athlete—she wouldn't be in this jam.*

A few weeks later, I'm looking for Spike after school. My punk-rocker boyfriend is not in our usual meeting spot near the student parking lot.

Then I see him with his clique of friends off in the woods, a cloud of smoke floating above their stiff mohawks. With mounting fury and fists clenched, I approach. My boyfriend is stoned.

I'm angry at him for breaking our agreement and livid with myself for being so stupid. I reach into my armory of *auntie language* and tear him down in front of his friends. "We're through!" I announce with visceral anger.

Seething, I walk away. A rock whizzes by my head. A second stone lands at my heels. The third nugget finds its target: the back of my head. Hot tears well up in my eyes—I never look back.

The breakup does not sit well with Spike. He spreads sexual rumors about me at school. His friends yell degrading names as I pass them in the hall; one even spits in my face. I am humiliated daily. My heart pounds with anxiety every time I have to change classrooms. Our high school is small—too small. There is no avoiding them.

The bullying escalates. I get threatening letters in the mail. Spike calls my home at all hours of the night. I begin carefully unplugging all the phones in the house each evening and restoring them in the morning. His continued assaults reveal weaknesses in my armor.

The inner defect of perceived unworthiness that took root in my early childhood now expands like a rapidly propagating flaw. I feel like an utter failure. I am sixteen years old and see no way out of the mess I have created in my life.

I try to numb myself with alcohol, but the liquor only magnifies my pain. I binge on huge quantities of sugary foods until I am ready to burst. I manage my way to the upstairs bathroom next to my bedroom and vomit repeatedly, hoping I can throw up the very emotions I have stuffed down: anger, unworthiness, and sadness. It is a violent purge. I wash the vomit from my face. My eyes bulging and bloodshot, I spew self-hatred into my reflection in the mirror. *How is it that no one has ever caught me in a bulimic episode? Am I that good at hiding it? Or is it just too harrowing for anyone to actually call me on it?*

You wasted a life. It's Karen who deserved to live. God took the wrong daughter. You're nothing more than an addict, I tell myself. I box my ears repeatedly until tears spill down my face. *I don't deserve to be here. I am worthless. I will never be good enough. Life would be better for everyone if I were gone.* Karen's mantra has become louder, and it continually expands in depth: *I am not worthy of this world.*

Alcohol and pills seem like the easiest escape from my pain. Mom has sleeping pills for her insomnia in the medicine cabinet. We have plenty of alcohol in the house. I wait until my parents are out of the home. Beth is either in her room reading or at church school. Like many in this small town, she is preparing for confirmation in the Catholic Church. I lost my spiritual compass long ago. *The question is whether I want to keep living the hell on earth I have created for myself or the eternal hell that is my destiny?*

I find my chosen bottle in the liquor cabinet and grab the bottle of sleeping pills. I pour a tall glass of 151 rum. Then I count out twenty pills—this still leaves some for my mother. I put four pills on my tongue and take my first swallow. It burns. Then I finish the pills and my drink. For good measure, I fill my glass again and gulp it down.

I lie in bed and prepare for eternal slumber. My head spins as regrets flood my thoughts. Then guilt erupts—this is an utterly selfish act. I have no note prepared. A deep numbness begins to wash over me. *Will I end up in hell? Or will I just be part of the dirt?* I've always wanted to know what happens in death.

I do not think about the devastation this will cause my family if I succeed. I am too deeply entrenched in my own shame to consider the consequences. Suicide is a permanent solution to a temporary problem, but I am so engrossed in my darkness that I can't reason with myself.

I wake up in the morning feeling like my head is in a vice. I've even failed suicide. My father is already off to work. Mom is just getting home from her night shift and is still in her nursing uniform. She looks exhausted. I tell her I have a migraine—I often get "migraines," but in truth, they are just hangovers. Mom agrees to let me stay home as long as I remain quiet.

Something stirs within me later in the day when I see my mom heading out the door to see her therapist.

"Mom, can I go see a therapist sometime?" I ask.

"Why?"

"I'm just feeling stressed."

"I'll ask Paula if you can meet with her," Mom says. Perhaps she hopes a therapist can quell my rebellious behavior.

My parents do not have a sense of my inner despair.

On the appointed day, I find myself alone in the room with the psychologist. I hope she can prescribe some medication to take away my gloom. My heart pounds as we make small talk.

"Lisa, is there something specific you want to talk about?" Paula asks.

I don't know where to start. My hands are cold, my body trembles, and I am drenched with sweat. I know that anything I share is protected by doctor-patient confidentiality.

"I tried to kill myself with alcohol and sleeping pills," I say.

"Lisa, stop. I am required by law to tell your parents."

"Please don't tell them! This is supposed to be a confidential conversation."

"The law is very clear in the case of a minor. I am legally obligated to disclose this information. I must tell your parents."

I am so stupid. How could I have not known this? I failed suicide, and now I am failing when I ask for help. I grimace at the thought of sharing these details with my parents. *How will I ever find worthiness in this world? How many A's will I have to earn to offset this disaster? Karen would not be in this situation.*

My parents are wrought with emotion when they hear of my attempted suicide. I never imagined the pain I would cause them if they lost another daughter—though we never speak of Karen. I am filled with remorse. I lose my privilege to drive until I am mentally stable.

My father puts the therapy under his name so my medical records will not be tarnished. He is protecting me. Clearly, this is another secret I am meant to keep. I don't tell anyone.

I am required to spend the next six months in therapy with Paula. It is torture—I have lost trust in her. I stuff down my fury. I sit on a sofa in her therapy room. She has a white-noise machine so others in the waiting room can't hear us. I no longer care. I have no intention of saying anything that will make my life any worse than it currently is. I answer personal questions in a way that I think will terminate therapy the quickest.

"Lisa, teenagers who attempt suicide often have other addictions. I sense that you have a problem with alcohol. Do you also have an eating disorder?" Paula asks pointedly.

"No. My father lets me have a few drinks with him on weekends. Once in a while, I blow off steam with alcohol. It is perfectly harmless. This was just a bad breakup," I lie, quickly covering over the question probing at my deepest secret. I feel my protective armor hardening under this duress. I stare directly into her eyes, unwavering. If I tell her the truth, then she will send me away to some treatment program. She is the only thing standing between me and freedom. For the remainder of therapy, I play the role of the perfect patient, and she is seemingly none the wiser for it. I am released within months and deemed "cured."

I am determined that no one will ever hurt me in the same way that Spike hurt me. My anger strengthens my protective armor, but the flaws still lurk beneath. Feelings of shame and unworthiness fester under my mask of confidence.

I immerse myself in school and work. I need to get to college. I need to become a doctor so I can find some semblance of worthiness in my life.

10

College Bound

Election to the National Honor Society at the end of my junior year marks the first mile on my arduous path toward worthiness. The ceremony is held in the small auditorium of our high school. The metal-backed chairs assault my spine, and my dress shoes pinch my feet. My mother bought me a new dress for the occasion, but it's hidden beneath my induction gown. The inductees are called up on stage one by one. It is dreadfully boring. I should savor the honor, but instead, I am anxiously awaiting one of the hidden vodka nips in the back of my closet at home. My father looks proud, and for that, I am grateful. My mom looks relieved.

I feel my mom nudge me. "Aaron is a handsome boy," she whispers.

Is she trying to help me wash away all memories of Spike? I've hardly spoken to Aaron in my three years of high school. I know he's boy genius, and the teachers love him. He can seem to do no wrong at school. He has always been too much of a "goody-two-shoes" for my liking. *Perhaps if I date him, I can find clemency from my mother for my behavior when I dated Spike?*

After the prompting from my mom at the Honor Society ceremony, I decide to pursue Aaron. I pay more attention in class and offer a few smiles in the hallway, and within a week, he is interested in earnest.

"Do you want to go to a movie sometime?" he asks.

"Sure," I say with a shrug.

Within the month, I have my new parent-approved beau. Aaron is super-smart and athletic. He is a clean-cut kid and college bound. His redeeming qualities are my quickest path to achieving forgiveness from my parents for my blunder involving Spike.

Aaron's family owns a beautiful pick-your-own blueberry farm on the other side of town. I can lose myself at the farm with its tree-lined paths, open meadows, and variety of animals. Aaron has an older sister and two younger brothers. His mother is an artist, and his father is an MIT-educated physicist. I join them in their weekly Sabbath dinner and enjoy the easy banter at their table as the wine flows liberally into our glasses. His family seems as comfortable with these social libations as mine. *Are we the only two families in town who let their seventeen-year-old kids drink?*

I help with the blueberry picking at the farm. My magenta-stained fingers deposit berries into the overflowing pails. The purple spheres hold the sweet nectar of spring. The townspeople arrive in droves to buy the best blueberries within miles.

I find ease at Aaron's home, feeling as though I'm part of some well-oiled machinery when I spend time with his family—maybe because his mother always has alcoholic beverages at the ready. I don't have to wait for a weekend like I do in our home. But it is more than that. Even when the banter at Aaron's home becomes cantankerous, the conversations continue to flow. In my home, I feel like the gears of the machinery get stuck and a deafening silence follows—I spend my time working or in sports to avoid it.

Aaron is handsome with the strong body of a farmer. I have grown out of my pudgy days and now have voluptuous curves. It doesn't take long for us to realize that the foundation of our relationship is a physical one. We both carry inner burdens and seek to numb ourselves continuously. Once the alcohol takes effect and our bodies have been exhausted by carnal pleasure, emotional abuse follows.

"If you ever get fat, I'll leave you," he warns as he makes a demeaning comment about the women in my family. Ironically, his own mother is overweight, but Aaron sees no flaws in her; it is as though she has him under some spell. I am seventeen years old and losing myself yet again in another abusive relationship—my inner darkness reminding me that I am not worthy of a loving relationship.

Aaron's mother offers praise to him, but his father cuts him down through elegant prose. I savor the hurtful words and embellish them at the appropriate times when we are both inebriated, returning his emotional abuse in earnest. At times, our abuse becomes physical. *Why would I expect more?*

On the outside, we look like a bright and loving couple. Yet, when we drink and are left alone with our own insecurities, we tear each other down. Like all addictive behaviors, we repeat the pattern. The emotionally charged banter is the binge; the dispelled anger and physicality of our relationship is the purge. The circular elements of our dysfunctional relationship call to some piece of both of us.

We both live in some strange façade—appearing to the world as intelligent, confident, and athletic beings—yet, we each carry inner demons. Aaron seems to be able to appease any and all adults with his shallow flattery, but beneath the surface, he is mean and cunning. I wear the burden of his emotional insecurity, and he wears the burden of mine. We are cruel and cutting to each other. Yet somehow, there is comfort in the routine of it.

Aaron carries hidden flaws. It takes me time to piece it together. He always has money—too much money for a boy of his age and upbringing. He always buys expensive jewelry for his mother and presents it to her in front of me. *Where does he get the money?*

I sharpen my eyes. I listen more carefully. He seems to have an affinity for expensive items that somehow always fall into his possession. He is quick and methodical with his stories. It takes time for me—years, in fact—to figure it out. He is a kleptomaniac. I try to unsee the truth. I push the thought away just as I push down the fact that I am bulimic and an alcoholic. *If I don't see his flaws, maybe he won't see mine.*

At the start of our senior year, Aaron and I explore college options together. We visit the University of Rhode Island first. URI is a state away but only an hour from our small town in Massachusetts. The campus is located in Kingston, a coastal town near the beaches of southern Rhode Island. As we walk across the expansive quadrangle amidst the old stone buildings, something resonates for me. We stop by the student services office as part of our campus visit to ask about pre-med and engineering options.

"URI doesn't have a pre-med program, but we offer chemistry and pharmacy majors," the campus recruiter tells us. "We have a number of engineering programs," he says, addressing Aaron. "I must also add that we have a world-renowned program in ocean engineering."

The recruiter reads through our transcripts and standardized academic test scores. He looks up with a smile. "Why don't you two start your studies with us in January?"

"Don't we have to graduate high school first?" I ask.

"You have everything you need. The only remaining requirement is an English writing class that you can either place out of or take here," he replies.

I welcome an early departure from high school. I can't wait to get home and share the news with my parents, armed with a stack of bright and shiny catalogs to help pitch it to them. But my idea of starting college in January of my high school senior year is not well-received.

"We're not in a financial position to send you to URI. We weren't planning for you to go to college until next September," Dad says.

I am not one to take "no" for an answer. I retrieve my savings book.

"Dad, I've been saving all of my money from my jobs during high school. We can use all of this. I'll work every summer and contribute to the cost of college. Please let me go."

"Let me think this through," Dad responds.

My father reads the URI catalogs and discovers there is a reciprocity agreement between states in New England. If I elect a major not offered by the University of Massachusetts, then the tuition would be the same as for a Rhode Island resident. Ocean engineering meets that criteria.

"The curriculum for chemical and ocean engineering requires the same chemistry classes needed for medical school," Dad says.

I grimace at the thought of majoring in engineering, but I am hungry to leave high school and get on with my life. "I promise to work every summer and contribute my earnings to the cost of my education."

"Okay. You can start in January. Let's celebrate with a margarita."

"Thank you, Dad!" I'm convinced that this is my path to medical school and a career that will bring me happiness. I gulp down my icy tequila-laden beverage.

My dad and I always shared drinks—perhaps it was the engineering connection or the mechanism by which we could best communicate. I always promised that I would abstain from drugs and I would work hard in school. Ironically, the same held true in Aaron's home. I don't think this was the norm for most seventeen-year-olds in our town, though it was the roaring eighties, and alcohol was more commonplace.

Our parents drive us to the campus in January. Aaron and I each have a single suitcase and backpack. We will live in the dorms on the south side of campus. In reality, we have no academic stamina, coming from a small rural high school where our classes had been relatively unchallenging. We are seventeen years old and away from home for the first time. The freedom of an unchaperoned academic life feels euphoric, and we will soon find ourselves academically challenged in ways that neither of us has ever experienced.

My declared major is chemical and ocean engineering, while Aaron is pursuing electrical engineering. Students are not admitted into the College of Engineering until sophomore year, after they have successfully passed calculus, physics, and chemistry. My freshman "weeder courses" are enormous, with nearly six hundred students in the physics lecture hall. I feel invisible, sitting in the back row with Aaron. We make a pact: if we already know the lecture topic, then we quickly make an exit. Sometimes we head to the library. We start skipping classes, thinking we can study on our own, but we are gravely mistaken. The weekly homework assignments are demanding and time-consuming.

The fraternities and sororities host parties on Thursday nights. We aim to have all our homework done by eight o'clock and then embark on a night of partying. Free-flowing alcohol holds sway over us, and once the "switch" is triggered, we can't stop. We find ourselves staggering back to our dorm in the wee hours of the night, falling further behind in our classes with each passing week. This is not like high school.

The open-access, all-you-can-eat buffets in our dormitories fuel my eating disorder. I find myself binging and purging at all meals. I start adding large amounts of caffeine to my addictive medley to keep up with my academic workload. I get no more than four hours of sleep each night. The hopefulness and excitement that accompanied me to campus quickly wane.

Several weeks into the semester, Aaron becomes gravely ill. Diagnosed with spinal meningitis, he returns to his family home. He will manage to complete his courses from there. I am petrified at the prospect of being alone on this large campus. I remain introverted and shy by nature. Making friends has never been a strong suit. I focus my attention on academics to cope with my mounting anxiety.

I use the isolation to buckle down in my courses. I am well aware that I will not be able to transfer into the College of Engineering unless I successfully make it through the prerequisites. Chemistry is relatively easy, and physics is manageable, but calculus has me concerned. My calculus professor is incomprehensible. He walks to the blackboard at the start of each class and proceeds to fill it with mathematical equations. I had been managing to keep up until we hit triple integrals and spherical coordinates. I once went to his office hours, but he merely threw squiggles and Greek letters onto my sheet of paper.

Key concepts are evading my understanding. I am nearly as lost as I was in elementary school mathematics. If I don't reach out to my father for help once again, then I will not likely pass this course or be admitted into the College of Engineering. Any hope of going to medical school or of finding a path to worthiness hinges on my ability to master calculus. My inner voice pipes up amidst my anxiety: *Karen would not need a personal tutor, and she certainly would not need to call her daddy!*

A schoolmate offers me a ride back to Mendon for the weekend. I drag my wearied body home to visit my family and Aaron at his family farm. I have my calculus book and dirty laundry in tow.

"You look very thin. Are you eating and sleeping enough?" my father asks.

I dodge his question. I have been teased by Aaron for eating a lot and not gaining weight and have always quickly deflected his comments with "I have a good metabolism." Fortunately, I have always been able to

49

purge when Aaron was deeply inebriated, and he has never suspected my bulimia. Other than my therapist, no one has ever directly asked me if I have an eating disorder. I can't relinquish bulimia now. She is an anchor in my anxiety-ridden academic life. I need her to succeed.

"Can you help me with calculus?" I ask my father.

"Did you bring home your textbook?"

"I have my textbook and homework with me," I answer, already feeling immense gratitude.

We embark on an intensive tutoring weekend. In a short time, he uses simple explanations to make clear to me the deeper concepts that I've been missing in the large auditorium. Ironically, he grabs an orange so we can work in spherical coordinates. The same fruit that we used to learn fractions.

Emanating from his ever-ready mechanical pencil, integrals flow onto the graph paper. His mathematical magic captures my thoughts, and I imagine my father in high school. As a high school senior, he had applied only to the Massachusetts Institute of Technology (MIT), considered the best engineering school in the world. Like many aspiring engineers, my father wanted to use his academic rigor to contribute meaningfully to the field of space exploration.

At that time, society eagerly followed the trials and tribulations of NASA, as its engineers, mathematicians, and scientists worked tirelessly to win the great space race. Brilliant minds around the world sought opportunities to use their mathematical prowess to put a man on the moon. My father was one of these brilliant people.

He had begun to immerse himself in his graduate studies at the time of my birth. Eventually abandoning his doctorate to support his family, he never gave up on his dream of using engineering in aerospace, nor did he ever lose his passion for lifelong learning. My father would have made a great professor.

A twinge of guilt sparks in my body and brings me back to the present moment. I cannot fail. My father gave up his PhD to support us. I owe him my academic success and an advanced degree to balance this equation and to help annihilate my inner flaws of unworthiness.

I visit Aaron while I am home. There is a sweet bitterness in it. He has been thriving from afar, while I have had to drag myself home to be tutored in calculus. What would have happened if he had stayed at URI this semester? Would he have thrived in calculus while my ship sank? Some part of me misses having a passionate drinking partner and a study mate, but I do not miss his emotional abuse. I am able to dole that out to myself without any bolstering from him. As I head back to URI, I am not sure if I want him as my boyfriend any longer. Time will tell. For now, I have to focus on my academics.

At the end of May, I return home after having completed my first semester of college. It is surreal to attend my high school graduation after being away for several months. I receive scholarship funds and money from relatives that will help offset my educational expenses in the coming year. I know my education is a financial burden to my family, and in just three years, my sister will be heading off to college as well. I must find a summer job.

My father helps me compose a cover letter and a simple, one-page resume. My work experience to date includes babysitting, packaging at the local machine shop, cleaning houses, and making sandwiches at D'Angelos. Somehow, my father makes me sound employable, and I secure a summer job at a computer company.

The position offers good compensation, but my tasks are painstakingly tedious. My duty is to stuff floppy disks into their sleeves before they are sealed and packaged. We use the same storage disks for our home computer. I enjoy the paycheck but despise the work, convinced I will die of boredom. This job incentivizes me to study harder in the coming year.

In the summer, I spend most of my free time at Aaron's farm. He is fully recovered from his spinal meningitis. Now that we have had a respite from each other, an attractive magnetism is drawing us back together. It's blueberry season; his mother makes blueberry pies, jams, and cordials. We drink her homemade liquors. Her magical purple syrup soothes away all of my anxieties.

"You know I was only seventeen when I got married," his mother comments. I quickly swallow my drink and ask for another.

There is clearly an expectation that Aaron and I will get married. Later in the evening, while feeling the jubilant effects of liquor coursing through our veins, we find ourselves engaged. *Did she cast a spell on us? Give us a love potion?*

His parents are delighted. Mine are not so enthusiastic—I am barely out of high school. Mom feels that I am far too young to be engaged. Dad believes I must complete my college education before considering marriage. My mind is overwhelmed with emotion. *Am I excited? Seeking approval? Afraid?*

My fairy godmother, who has never been married, states her opinion quite boldly. "Lisa Anne Prune-Pit, pack your bags. Your high school graduation gift from me is a whirlwind tour of Europe. We're going to London, Paris, Lausanne, and Rome. Perhaps this will shake the irrational thought of marriage out of your head." I don't know how she can afford this on her modest schoolteacher salary. Auntie doesn't seem to be very good at saving money, so I presume my parents have fronted the cost. I don't dare ask. We don't discuss such things in our family.

My international travel has been limited to visiting my mother's extended family in Canada, where her parents were born, and a family trip to Mexico when my dad spent the summer working at NASA. I have never been on such a long flight. Jackie and I get giddy with the complimentary nips of alcohol served on the plane.

In London, we tackle every tourist attraction accessible by foot or the tube. The Tower of London, Big Ben, and the castles are magical vistas bestowed upon my simple eyes. I have never seen such splendor.

At night, we find outdoor pubs for dinner and drinks. My aunt flirts relentlessly and earns us free drinks. We sit for hours, drinking our cocktails and growing silly as the night wears on. Eventually, we find our way back to our hotel while we can still remember where it is.

I always make certain to purge before we leave the pub. I have become quite adept at purging—it's all about the balance of fluids and food. I make sure to drink a large amount before vomiting. It's as though I can will the reversal of food through some defiance of gravity. I can get the task done within minutes. My efficiency helps keep my eating disorder a secret. The greater challenge is assuring that the local plumbing cooperates.

Bulimia is a part of me now; she is like an anti-anxiety drug. When my anxiety heightens, she is at the ready to quell my emotions with food. I don't question her judgment. She thrives in the presence of food, but she is a secret friend. If she were to be discovered, the magic she offers would evaporate from my life.

Each binge allows emotions to be stuffed down, and each purge offers a release of anxiety or stress. The frequency of my bulimic episodes corresponds to my stress level. I find a binge-purge cycle to be especially useful to quiet my inner voice, often triggered by some threshold level of fear or anxiety. Once awakened, this voice conjures statements of unworthiness that can send me into a deep emotional spiral. I keep the inner critic numbed with alcohol or stuff down the hurtful words alongside my food and then vomit them up together. This inner voice seeks to unrail me into a life of total unworthiness, always trying to convince me that God took the wrong daughter.

I naively believe that my eating disorder is a temporary coping tool I can relinquish once I achieve my academic worthiness. I underestimate the stranglehold it has over me.

Each night, we pour ourselves into our beds. I am exhausted, but sleep eludes me when my aunt turns into a grizzly bear. Her snoring is loud and disruptive; there is no rhythm to the madness of it. I finally resort to sleeping in the bathtub.

Within days, we're off to Paris with a ferocious schedule. We manage to see the Eiffel Tower, the Louvre, Notre Dame, and Versailles. Auntie Jackie claims she learned French in high school, but the only phrase she remembers is "*merci beaucoup.*"

"Clearly, you didn't pay attention in French class," I joke.

"Shut up. We'll see how you do in Italy," she retorts.

"I took Spanish in high school, not Italian," I reply.

We complete our trip with outlandish tales to tell when we get home. Jackie's favorite is when I inadvertently paid our bar tab in Italy with the wrong currency. "Oh, my beautiful Americano woman, I pay the rest for you," says the bartender with a wink. I don't realize my mistake until I figure out I gave him currency worth only a fraction of the bill. I am too mortified to say anything.

My auntie is thrilled there has been no further talk of marriage. She need not worry—I didn't have time to think about Aaron while we were in Europe, and I am about to be consumed by my academics.

11

Breaking Bonds

Seemingly innocuous letters connected by dashes, dots, addition signs, and arrows fill the blackboard. Professor Kaufman looks like a mad scientist in his long lab coat, goggles resting on his bald head. He points to the board and expects immediate answers, consulting his clipboard for a list of our names. He bellows out only last names. If you are absent, he marks your nonattendance; if you don't have the answer, then he makes a note of your stupidity. The lectures are agonizing.

Organic chemistry may be the course that derails my dream of medical school. This is the only chemistry class that does not inspire some intuitive understanding for me. One student in the room knows all the answers; he is both the most envied and disliked student in class. Matt is the only student called upon by his first name. I always sit behind him and hope I hear "Matt" before I hear "Pruitt." I dread that this is a year-long class.

Aaron is back on campus and enrolled in his electrical engineering courses. We take our studying more seriously this semester. We don't skip class anymore, and we keep up with homework sets. Our social activities are still centered around alcohol. In our inebriated states, our tongues grow sharp and we cut each other down, yet we keep finding ourselves back together. This relationship is an addiction in itself.

Aaron and I both seek to satisfy a deep need for intimacy and emotional abuse, and it has become just as addictive for him as it is for me. It's the chronic cheating that drives us apart; he has meandered a number of times after being inebriated at fraternity parties. With each incident of infidelity, I toss him to the curb and retaliate. Ultimately, I become hardened by these experiences, and it causes me to give back the engagement ring. My inner voice of unworthiness lurks: *Karen would not be in a relationship like this.*

At the end of the fall semester, I set up a meeting with the guidance counselor to process my transfer into engineering. At the appointed time, the door opens and an older gentleman in a worn tweed jacket pokes his head out.

"Come in, Ms. Pruitt."

I sit down in his small office. He scans my College of Engineering application form, a frown forming on his grim face. "So, I see that you want to major in chemical and ocean engineering."

"Yes," I whisper. *Where is my voice?*

"There are not many women in engineering," he states.

I nod my head, not entirely sure of his implication.

"Engineers need to be good at math. Are you good at math?" he asks.

"Yes," I reply. I omit the detail that my father tutors me in calculus.

"Do you even know what an engineer does?"

I simmer underneath my calm demeanor. "Yes. I know what engineers do. My father is an MIT-educated engineer who has worked for NASA."

I'm about to embellish and say he was an astronaut, but that would be pushing it. My hands make tight fists. I hope I don't punch him.

I'm met with a blank stare. My transfer is approved without another word.

"Thank you," I offer. I leave the building, my blood still boiling.

I make my way to the dining hall to get lunch, my emotions driving my hunger. I stuff down a huge amount of food from the buffet. The dormitory buffets are a bit like the large lecture halls; I feel invisible. Alongside the food, I push down my anger over the comments from the cantankerous old fart calling himself a guidance counselor. I then go to the bathroom and purge my lunch and the words of the obtuse advisor. I wash my face and take a stick of gum from my backpack. Once purged of my emotion, I head to the library and pull out my O-chem notes. My tenacity triggered, I am determined to successfully earn my degree in chemical and ocean engineering.

There are nearly twenty students in chemical engineering, and only seven have the ocean engineering specialty. I'm assigned to an eclectic team in the chemical engineering laboratory. I immediately recognize the organic chemistry wizard—Matt is returning to school after several years of military service. My other teammate is John, a returning student who manages a movie theater to support his family. The group is rounded out by Bob, a witty young petroleum engineer who is sharp with his words. As a foursome, we work well together, and by the end of our first lab, we are chums.

"We're going to happy hour. Do you want to come?" Matt asks. "Actually, are you even old enough to drink?" he adds with a chuckle.

"I am nearly nineteen. No one will card me," I say confidently.

We order our first round of margaritas and enjoy the free food. As the alcohol takes effect, I find my wit and humor. By the third margarita, I've earned their respect as a drinking buddy. These men become my friends and study partners.

I have my new protectors. Now I can actually decide if I want or need Aaron in my life. For now, he is another layer of safety in this male-dominated world of engineering.

12

The Gift of Mentorship

The tangy metallic aroma awakens my olfactory senses as I step into the metallurgy laboratory—hardness testers and heat-treating furnaces fill the surrounding walls. My eyes are drawn to elaborate three-dimensional models of crystal structures found in engineering alloys that sit on the lab benches. Upon the walls are posters depicting phase diagrams of iron-carbon and copper-aluminum systems. I don't know how to read them yet, but that will soon change. In this lab, we will study the mechanical behavior of metals and their alloys. I feel a deep inner calling to the scientific realm of metallurgy.

Physical metallurgy is not only my favorite course; it's the best course I've ever taken in my life. Professor Rockett gives inspirational lectures through the prose of storytelling.

"I learned about melting point depression in eutectic alloys the hard way when I accidentally melted a $2,000 crucible. You learn best from your mistakes," he offers with a smile. His pipe dangles from the corner of his mouth as he laughs at the memory. His story draws me into the magical science of phase equilibria.

"Anyone seen a good movie lately?" he asks.

We sit in silence. We're engineering students with no time for movies. We spend all of our "free time" on homework sets or drinking.

Professor Rockett welcomes us into his enchanting lab. I am captivated by his hands-on laboratories. We cold-roll brass and heat-treat steels, etch and polish metals to study microstructures, make dislocation models to understand plastic deformation, and correlate mechanical properties with alloy composition. I'm in academic heaven—I never imagined that alloying and strengthening schemes could be so intoxicating. I soak in the richness of his tales and his passion for metallurgy. He sparks a love of engineering materials that will stay with me throughout my life.

In high school, I had become good at math, physics, chemistry, and anatomy. Much of my motivation had been to get good grades and make my parents proud, always seeking a sense of worthiness. I was never ignited about learning as I am now in the realm of engineering materials.

Immersing myself in metallurgy, I excel in homework, exams, and labs. I read every word of my textbook, soaking in its content alongside the wisdom of the lectures. My hunger for academic excellence is beyond the seeking of worthiness. It is a thirst for knowledge, a calling that beckons me onto a path of lifelong learning. Later in life, I will look back and realize how inspirational and pivotal Professor Rockett was in my life trajectory.

As the semester ends, I am devastated by the fact that this is the only materials course in our undergraduate curriculum. The remaining materials courses are graduate level for the PhD students in chemical engineering.

"Lisa, can I speak with you after class today?" Professor Rockett asks, as we take our seats for his last lecture of the semester.

I approach the board after he wraps up class, my heart pounding and my palms beginning to sweat. "Professor, you wanted to speak with me?" I say.

"Yes. Lisa, you clearly have a natural affinity and passion for metallurgy. You would do well in our graduate courses. In the fall, you could take corrosion with Professor Brown and semiconductors with Professor Gregory. I think you would enjoy the classes."

"But I'm just an undergraduate," I reply, fear rising alongside my excitement.

"That doesn't matter. I'm confident in your abilities. Start with those courses, and then you can come back and see me. We can decide which classes you should take next."

Outwardly, I'm incredibly excited and honored, but inwardly, I'm nervous. I can't let him down—Professor Rockett is the first academic to openly recognize something in me that I can't yet see for myself. Believing in others when they can't yet believe in themselves becomes foundational to the mentorship philosophy I will utilize when I become a professor. Mentorship is a gift that keeps on giving.

My passion for engineering is now kindled in a way I had never imagined possible. I call my father to share Dr. Rockett's recommendation. It becomes clear that I will need to take summer courses in order to make room in my schedule for the graduate classes in the fall. My father is enthusiastic.

"I work with a metallurgist. Her name is Dr. Doreen Ball. Let me see if there is a possibility of working with her as an intern this summer," Dad says.

"That would be awesome," I reply, excitement pushing aside my underlying fear and anxiety. I feel that deep inner voice taunting: *Who am*

I kidding? Am I really worthy of this experience? She needs to be quieted. Time for a binge and purge and then back to my books.

Summer arrives, and it's my first day at work with my father. My blue wool suit is stiff and hot, sweat already soaking my blouse. My heels click on the floor of the reception area of CTI Cryogenics. Dad signs me in at the front desk. I complete the requisite paperwork, and then my father brings me to Dr. Ball.

"Lisa, please meet Doreen Ball," Dad says.

"It is an honor to meet you, Dr. Ball," I say, grateful the words have not jumbled in my mouth.

"Call me Doreen," she says with a smile. "Follow me. I'll show you the lab."

She has a lightness in her step, despite the immensity of her build. I note her casual attire and decide not to repeat my formal garb the following day. Doreen's bright eyes sparkle as she guides me through her research lab.

"We have high-pressure liquid chromatography, gel permeation chromatography, and Fourier transform infrared spectroscopy." I don't yet know what any of these pieces of equipment do, but I know by the end of summer I will have soaked up as much of her knowledge as humanly possible. I am in academic heaven. "We have all the requisite equipment to characterize microstructures, composition, and mechanical properties," she says with a smile.

Dr. Ball takes me out for lunch with her research team. We peruse the menu and decide to share a large pizza. Then the issue of beverages presents itself as they mull over the beer choices.

"Are you old enough to drink?" Doreen asks.

"I'm nineteen. I am old enough to drink in Europe."

"I like your humor, kid, just like your father," she says. She then orders a pitcher of beer and fills my glass. She gives me a wink.

On the nights when I don't have evening summer classes, Dad and I play for the company softball team. I earn a position at third base, thanks to my strong throwing arm from years of playing fastpitch softball. The team drains beer from the cooler throughout the game. These engineers clearly know how to drink. I'm starting to wonder if all engineers know how to drink. *Maybe this is the best career trajectory for me?*

My dad and I leave home early each morning to beat the traffic. It seems that engineers not only know how to drink, but they also know how to get by on little sleep. I enjoy the time with my father on our drive to work. I hear more about his life as an engineering student at MIT. He obviously chose the right field of study—he remains passionate about his work. I see a deeper realm of his humor and brilliance. His reflections always stop at college. He doesn't speak much of his childhood, and I have a sense that painful memories lurk somewhere in his past. I don't ask, afraid he might probe more deeply into my underlying pain. I keep our conversations in the "safe zone."

Summer races by. I have learned how to use spectroscopy, chromatography, and microscopy for forensic metallurgy. My dream of medical school is getting sidelined by a love of engineering materials.

At the end of my internship, Doreen takes me out for a final lunch. We order our usual pizza and beer. She has a seriousness I haven't observed before—I hope I haven't let her down.

"Lisa, I'm highly impressed with your research skills."

"Thank you." I gulp down my beer to dull the awkwardness.

"You should go to graduate school. Engineering needs more women—don't lose sight of your potential. You will have limitless possibilities."

"I need something stronger to drink to process all of this," I reply. How do I tell her she's my only female role model in engineering? That fear-kindled inner voice plays her reel: *I don't know if I have what it takes to be a pioneer.*

"You're definitely Gerry's daughter." She summons the waiter and orders us two margaritas.

I drink mine down in two hard gulps. The magic liquid quiets my inner voice and lets me savor this time with Dr. Ball.

If I could get a PhD, could I make up for the fact that my father never had a chance to complete his doctorate? Perhaps then my inner voice would be silenced, my inner flaw of unworthiness annihilated, and my addictions dissolved. I don't yet realize that striving for academic honor is becoming a compulsion for me.

13

Engineering My Future

I sit in the front of the classroom, mesmerized by the topic of corrosion in metals. Often the process involves an electrochemical reaction with oxygen that can deteriorate a structural metal. Corrosion generally puts metallic structures at risk for failure. I am immersed in Professor Brown's lecture.

"Consider the Statue of Liberty. Her patina protects the underlying metal. Yet, loss of passivation or surface pits can become precursors to cracks that can render a structure susceptible to failure," he states.

Am I such a statue? Does my academic façade merely serve as my protective patina against the flaws beneath? Is my perceived unworthiness the very flaw that is susceptible to chemical attack? I am usually immune to these intruding dark thoughts when I am immersed in my academics. But today, my inner thoughts bubble through—perhaps triggered by the large coffee and three donuts I ate and then quickly rid myself of before class started? Are my bulimic episodes and alcohol abuse the corrosive mechanisms that may lead to intergranular failure or stress corrosion cracking? I push my negative thoughts away and focus on scribing the wisdom on the blackboard into my notebook.

Professor Brown brings his British humor into his graduate course. He jokes that most mechanical engineers use paint to mitigate corrosion. I find myself lured into his world of electro-chemistry. Dr. Brown is not only a professor at URI; he also works at the Army Research Labs (ARL) in the Corrosion Sciences Division, a place where I will later vest considerable time.

Professor Gregory teaches my other graduate class. He's a young professor who received his PhD from Brown University only a few years ago. He provides me with a contagious passion for semiconductor materials. In his course, we learn that some materials have conductivities between metals and insulators. I am drawn again into the magical world of engineering materials. Like with Dr. Rockett's course, I find some inner part of myself ignited. Nothing else pulls on my thoughts when I am deeply immersed in the science of engineering materials. My mind imagines the atoms and substructures as though I become one with these materials. It is a deep inner pull, and I follow it like a magnetic current.

"The average is high because one student has aced the exam," Professor Gregory comments as he returns our blue exam booklets. My palms sweat as he approaches with my booklet.

"Lisa, can you see me after class?" he asks as the paper meets my hands.

What if I haven't mastered the material? What if I've failed like I did in first-grade math? My father won't know the material to tutor me on this topic. I bite my lip hard to stop my mental spiral. I carefully open the booklet: I have a perfect score—my first in college. I make my way to the front after class. *Is he going to think I cheated?*

"Lisa, would you like to work as a research student in my lab?" he asks.

"I'm not sure if you know I'm not a graduate student. I'm still an undergraduate," I respond nervously.

"I realize that you're an undergraduate. Professor Rockett speaks highly of you. Are you interested? You clearly understand the material," he says with a laugh.

"Yes, I would be honored to work with you." My response doesn't convey my excitement. I try to stay composed, but I'm so excited by the prospect of doing research I can barely find my words. I am nearly twenty years old and about to embark on the path of academic research.

Professor Gregory puts me at ease, and I blossom in his lab. Under his direct mentorship, I work on a semiconductor project involving wet chemistry and surface characterization of germanium oxides. My academic trajectory is forever changed when I fall in love with research. Like with lectures, I become aligned with the very materials I study. Just as I had felt the life of the pine trees I climbed as a child, I find some life force from within the materials that I characterize. I am ultra-focused in the lab, fully present in the now, and free of anxiety or depression.

Professor Gregory personally trains me on wet chemistry methods. I learn new characterization tools and discover the joy of reading archival journal papers. I find immense solace in the realm of research. He brings me to Brown University, where I also learn ellipsometry under the guidance of a collaborating physicist, Dr. Chrisman. They treat me like a graduate student, and I expand my research prowess under their mentorship. These extraordinary mentors imprint me with critical thinking skills and a love of inquiry-based learning.

The mastery I obtain in the graduate corrosion course earns me an invitation to work at the Army Research Labs in the coming summer under the supervision of Professor Brown. I will be afforded the opportunity to study surface treatments of alloys that can mitigate corrosion of the pitch links used in Apache helicopters.

For a girl who didn't want to study engineering, I find it ironic that I am being seduced by the depths of engineering materials. *Perhaps research is my path to worthiness?* My dreams of medical school are growing dimmer with each passing day. I no longer care as I am drawn into the research opportunities focused on structural materials.

The ongoing praise from my father further motivates me to excel in engineering. I don't yet see that my love of research and my love of academic praise are two distinct things. The former is a true divine calling, while the latter becomes as dangerously addictive as other behaviors in my coping toolkit.

In the spring semester of my junior year, I am invited to meet with the dean of engineering. His office feels formal. Dean Rose wears a dark suit and a burgundy tie. I fear that he is going to tell me I am taking too many graduate courses. I am enrolled in the graduate course on phase equilibria with Professor Rockett and engineering ceramics with Professor Gregory. I'm prepared to tell him that I plan to take summer courses while working with Professor Brown at the Army Labs. I plan to carry a full course load in the coming year to make sure I graduate.

"Ms. Pruitt, I understand that you have been taking quite a number of the graduate courses in chemical engineering," Dean Rose begins.

"Yes," I say weakly.

"I have a proposition for you. URI is putting together an undergraduate degree program in materials engineering. If you're willing to complete all of the required courses along with the remaining graduate courses, then you would meet the requirements to receive two engineering degrees next spring. Would you like to be the first graduate of our materials engineering program?" he asks.

"Yes. I want to do this. I am honored. Thank you!" I reply.

Later that night, I go through my usual routine of stuffing myself with sugar-laden foods while I study and then unburdening myself when I feel like a pressure vessel about to burst. In that post-purge moment, my inner darkness seeps in and plants her words: *What would the dean think if he knew I was a bulimic and alcohol addict?*

After my conversation with the dean, I lay out curriculum plans with my dad when I am home for a visit. I need to carry two heavy semesters in my final year of college. In the span of nine semesters, I will have earned two engineering degrees. My pursuit of medicine has been replaced by my love of research, and materials engineering specifically. After we outline how I will complete my two engineering degrees in the coming year, my father offers to make margaritas. We are sitting at the dining room table covered with my course catalogs. He clears his throat—his prelude to a serious discussion, a signal I have seen throughout my childhood as far back as when Karen passed away. I take a long swallow of my margarita in anticipation of his words.

"Lis, I have some news to share with you."

"Is everything okay?" I ask, my heart racing.

"I have accepted a position at Hughes Aircraft, on the West Coast."

"Congratulations!" *Does he see the tears welling up in my eyes? Does he sense my fears of what my life will be like without my anchor?*

"When will you move?" I ask. I try to smile, yet beneath my protective veneer, my fears fester. Dad has always been my academic anchor, and I'm afraid of my life in the tumultuous seas without him nearby. We celebrate with another round of margaritas. I drink until my fears melt away.

I lie awake in the middle of the night, riddled with anxiety, my head spinning. Beth is heading off to study mechanical engineering at MIT in the fall. I will be carrying a daunting workload in the coming year. My study buddies are graduating in May. My relationship with Aaron has been rocky, at best, over this past year. Though I had ended our engagement, a few months later, we crossed paths at an engineering party, and with alcohol coursing our veins, we found ourselves reunited. It is an addictive cycle I desperately want to break. His family has just sold their blueberry farm, and they are relocating to Pennsylvania. He will follow once he completes his electrical engineering degree. I have no idea how I will anchor myself when everyone leaves.

Over the summer, after my junior year of college, I focus my energy on corrosion science research at the Army Research Labs. My studies on the Apache helicopter components require the synergy of metallurgy, surface treatments, corrosion, and mechanical testing. I learn techniques for assessing the stress corrosion cracking in structural alloys. I become fascinated by the fracture behavior of structural alloys in corrosive environments.

The literature focusing on fracture mechanics draws me in—I intuit what it must feel like to be at the tip of a crack, where the stresses become mathematically sharp and hydrostatic stress states can rip a material apart. I feel a kindred alignment with these flawed structures. At this juncture of my life, I, too, feel various stresses trying to pull me apart.

Perhaps if I learn more about how to prevent fracture in an engineering material, I can utilize the same philosophy to improve my own resilience?

I have found my calling. I want to get a PhD so I can have a research career aimed at improving engineering materials for structural applications, and I want a life that renders me worthy.

I am twenty-one years old when I return to URI for my senior year. Aaron and I are dating, but we are both facing uncertainty as our families get ready to leave New England; the comfort of the known outweighs the uncertainty and fear of the unknown. Aaron assumes we will eventually wed and live on the farm, adding a large number of children to the workings of the family business. I can't imagine such a life. *Why do I keep finding myself back with Aaron—is it my need to always have a protector? Or my fear of being alone now that my father has relocated to California?*

In my final year of undergraduate study, I rent a small room in a campus home owned by a liberal arts professor. The quietness of my room is deafening—no study buddies, no dinner pals, no drinking partners. My longtime academic friends graduated the previous May. Because I started in January of my senior year of high school, I had been taking courses with the engineering class a year ahead of me. Now I am alone on campus. Aaron is living in Pennsylvania, and I won't see him again until Christmas.

How will I ever make it through this final year? I am carrying a challenging technical course load, and my self-doubt rises as I walk across the campus. I soon find myself befriended by a fellow chemical engineering undergraduate. We cross paths at Dunkin' Donuts and make our way to Crawford Hall with large coffees in hand. I had so frantically wanted to buy a dozen donuts that I could use to stuff down my anxiety, but Jon's gregarious and lighthearted nature saves me from the dreaded binge-purge cycle. As we walk across the URI quadrangle, I learn that Jon lives in a rented room just around the corner from me.

Jon introduces me to his friends from this cohort of chemical engineering students. I quickly discover this group of engineers also enjoys the happy hours at the local bars. It seems to be a trait of chemical engineering students that we not only enjoy chemistry, but we enjoy drinking it. The social lubricant of engineers seems to be established during college. I soon find myself feeling at home with my new protectors.

Early in the fall semester, I learn that Professor Gregory has nominated me for a research award through the Chemical Engineering Society.

"Lisa, you have been selected as a finalist and will represent URI," he says.

"I've never given an oral presentation." *Fear bubbles up within.*

"You can give a practice talk to the students in the department."

"Do I have to?" I ask as my voice shakes.

"You need to learn how to give research presentations if you want to go to graduate school. I'll help you," he reassures me.

Maybe I don't want to go to grad school after all. I never anticipated having to give a talk in front of people as part of being a research scientist. *How could I have not known this?*

Professor Gregory works with me for weeks. He offers feedback on my slides and coaches me through my first oral presentation.

On the day of my presentation, I'm nearly frozen with fear and drenched in a cold sweat. My knees and voice literally shake as I look out into the audience. My heart beats explosively, and my voice quivers. My palms are sweating profusely. I don't have any awareness of what I actually say. With each slide, words spill from my mouth. I can't hear them. I look at the audience and only see bright light. I am in the midst of a panic attack, and I am completely unattached to my mind or body. How do the faculty stand up at the front of a room and give a lecture? *I never want to be a professor.*

When the last slide is done, the room applauds. *Are they clapping because I did a good job or because they are relieved that I am done?* Professor Gregory approaches. "Great job, Lisa," he announces and then assures me that it will get easier with practice.

With Professor Gregory's mentorship, I next present my research at the Materials Research Society in Boston and publish my first archival journal paper. With his continual nudging, I immerse myself in the graduate school application process. I am honored when I receive a URI undergraduate research award. I quickly add it to my resume and feel a little worthier in this world.

Consumed by my six technical courses and well aware that I will be shouldering seven courses in the spring in order to earn my two engineering degrees, I lean heavily into my addictive toolbox of bulimia, alcohol, caffeine, and work. I am in survival mode, and the abuse of my body is catching up with me. I find myself at the infirmary with migraines. I check in at the front desk and wait until I hear my name called.

A nurse wearing a stark dress greets me with her clipboard chart. "Follow me," she says, guiding me to a small sterile room.

"Roll up your sleeve," she instructs as she strangles my arm with the cuff.

"Your blood pressure is very high, 160/90. The doctor will be in to see you shortly." The door slams.

What if my migraines are due to my eating disorder, alcohol abuse, lack of sleep, or all of the above? I need these tools to succeed. I can't let my father down.

I begin to consider that maybe I should just leave before the doctor comes. The door opens before I can escape. Soon the cold stethoscope catches my breath as the doctor listens to my racing heart.

"Have you ever been diagnosed with a heart arrhythmia?" she asks.

"No, I've always been healthy," I lie.

"Do you have a family history of high blood pressure?"

"My mom has high blood pressure." *I need to get out of this room.*

"Are you under extreme stress? Do you get enough sleep?" she asks.

"Just normal stress." Another lie. Who possibly gets enough rest as an engineering student?

She gives me a prescription for my migraines and tells me to come back and see her the following week. I fill the prescription, but I never go back.

14

The Runaway Bride

A massive wreath adorns the colonial saltbox, aglow with holiday lights, nestled among the snow-laden trees. The picture-perfect image could be straight out of Dickens's *A Christmas Carol*. It's a façade, just like me. This is our last Christmas in the family home. Dad is visiting from California, and Beth is home from MIT. Mom still lives in our house because it hasn't sold yet. Auntie Jackie will be joining us for Christmas dinner, likely arriving late, as usual. Aaron is also visiting from Pennsylvania, where his family recently purchased a bed-and-breakfast and dairy farm. I try to keep my emotions in check. I am not sure what I feel.

This past semester was personally grueling but academically successful. I submitted graduate school applications to several East Coast schools, but only one truly appeals to me. Brown University beckons not only because of its familiarity but also because it's known for its academic strength in fracture mechanics. Aaron advocates for Penn.

We have been on such tumultuous ground over the years; it seems inconceivable that I could succeed in graduate school while maintaining any semblance of a steadfast relationship with him. He still serves as a protector of sorts—keeping others at bay, allowing me to focus on my studies. I am certain we want different things from life. I am continually striving for academic recognition, as it quells my inner sense of unworthiness. Aaron wants a family; more disconcerting is that he wants a subservient wife. That is not a cloak I can wear.

Once all the gifts have been opened, Aaron takes out a tiny box from his jacket pocket. My stomach lurches—I fear that the contents of this package will bind me to a future I do not want. I am dreadfully sober. I carefully open the box. My face forms the requisite smile, but my outward expression clashes completely with my inner feelings.

"Lisa, will you marry me?" Aaron asks, kneeling in front of my family.

I want to vomit, but there's nothing in my stomach. I so desperately want to say "No!" Instead, I mumble, "I guess so." *What have I done? How can I bind myself to this life?* My heart is racing as my angst builds. My dark reel is sparked: *Karen would never marry Aaron. I am not worthy of real love.*

Out comes the champagne. I need a glass, a very big one. Actually, I need the whole bottle. I quickly down my first glass of champagne. Then another. My outward self smiles while my inner self is riddled with anxiety.

Dad approaches when I am alone. "You don't have to say yes if you don't want to. You're about to go to grad school. You can wait until your graduate studies are done. I tried to balance both family and academics, and ultimately, I abandoned my PhD."

"I know." In truth, I don't know what I know anymore. My life is heading into a spiral. Aaron will never agree to let me go to Brown. I feel like a caged animal. I feel a deep sense of desperation, but I have no one to rescue me.

Aaron's family throws us an engagement party over New Year's weekend. They had known he would propose at Christmas, but how had they known I would say yes? I scramble to shelter myself during this weekend. I invite some friends from chemical engineering, including Professor Gregory, because he has family in Pennsylvania. Aaron has invited friends from our hometown, and I will drive with them.

I have every intention of spending the entire weekend fully inebriated. I pour myself into the back seat. Already numb with alcohol, I make witty small talk all the way to Pennsylvania. My inner self listens in anxious silence.

Aaron's family is exuberant when I arrive at the bed-and-breakfast inn. Everyone is already drunk. I quickly help myself to more alcohol. Their inn is just minutes from the Pocono Mountains, and the plan is to ski during the day and party in the evenings.

After a night of partying, we're all a bit slow to rise. Everyone dons warm clothes, and we pack into three cars and drive to the ski resort. Aaron is a rank beginner, while I ski black diamond trails after my years of skiing with my sister and Auntie Jackie. We divide ourselves by ability. Aaron's family friend Frank becomes my ski partner. He's the only other person who can ski the advanced trails. We split off from the group, head over to the lifts, and make small talk on the chairlift ride.

"What do you do, Frank?" I ask, polishing off one of my vodka nips and offering him one.

"I own my own construction company," he says.

"That is impressive," I say.

"What about you?" Frank asks.

"I graduate this spring with two engineering degrees. I plan to spend my summer working as an engineer at the Army Research Labs before I start graduate school in September." *Am I bragging? Maybe I've had too much vodka already.*

"Wow. A big brain. Where will you go?"

"I want to go to Brown, but Aaron wants me to go to Penn," I admit with ease, buzzed from the vodka.

"You should go where you want to go." Frank's supportive response ignites something within me. My inner desperation takes notice of his affirming words.

In the evening, everyone feels the effects of the free-flowing alcohol. We are myopic. I'm laughing with my university friends at ridiculously stupid engineering jokes. Then I spot Aaron out of the corner of my eye, flirting with a young woman. *Is she a family friend?*

I watch her touch Aaron's arm. *I know that touch.* This calls for sweet revenge. I see Frank across the room. My shyness washed away by the alcohol, I make a beeline for Frank and give him my full attention. I ignore my fiancé, yet I know he is watching—we exchange glances from across the room.

Why does Aaron want to marry me? Why would I choose to marry him? Is it because we're so comfortable in the depth of our conflicts? Is this what our life will be like, always needing to have a buzz so we can tolerate each other? Will our marriage be a lifetime of deceit and lies? I stuff these thoughts down. A binge and purge is imminent.

At the end of the long weekend, we all pile back into our respective cars and start our journey home. Aaron stays behind with his family. My mind starts drifting toward my newfound friend.

Within the week after returning home, Aaron starts pressuring me toward a summer wedding. I see a way out of my current predicament, and it isn't going to sit well with anyone. I'm about to repeat the pattern of my past—running away from one relationship headlong into another. I don't have the moral strength to tell Aaron the truth; instead, I pursue the easier path. I seek the possibility of a new relationship, hoping to find my next protector. The universe must be reading my thoughts. Frank calls to see if I want to go night-skiing.

I have three weeks left in my winter break. I meet up with Frank after my days of work at the Army Research Labs. We run the slopes until the mountain closes and then continue our friendly banter over drinks. I find myself spending more time with him over winter break, entering dangerous territory.

Before I begin my final semester, I call Aaron and break off the engagement. I explain that we want different things, but he's furious and blames his friend. I arrange to return the ring. I am heartbroken because I have hurt him and his family, but I know I can't move to Pennsylvania. I can't marry him. I seemingly have it together on the academic front, but I am personally consumed by shame and guilt. I feel the pull expanding on my inner flaw of unworthiness.

In my final semester at URI, I take seven technical courses and do everything possible to master my courses while simultaneously numbing my emotional pain. I grow thin from my extensive binging and purging. I have dyed my hair red, black, brown, and now blond. No color masks my inner turmoil.

Frank starts sending me cards and flowers. He invites me skiing. He comes down to URI to take me to dinner. It doesn't feel like too much or too soon; instead, it feels like another way to numb my pain. I soak it up like a sponge.

In early March, a crisp white envelope with the Ivy League insignia of Brown University arrives. I already have fellowship offers from University of Pennsylvania and Penn State, but this is the envelope that will keep me on my path to worthiness. My hands shake as I pry open the glued seams. I scan the letter. I see "Congratulations" and "Presidential Fellowship." I call my parents to share the good news, then I lure my friend Jon to the bar so we can celebrate.

Frank suggests a celebratory ski trip to Steamboat Springs in Colorado over spring break. I eagerly agree and also coordinate a visit to see my father.

My dad observes that I seem to be spending a lot of time with my new friend. "Is this more than a friendship?" he asks.

"No, we're just friends." *Does he know this is a lie? Why don't I tell him the truth? Do I fear his judgment? Or maybe I don't want to hear a lecture about how I just ended a five-year relationship and I need time to heal and focus on my graduate studies?* I'm too ashamed to admit I've traded one relationship for another.

Having a protector seems to be another tool in my survival kit. It will be decades before I can process the depth of hurt that I am causing with my behavior. For now, I am just trying to survive and hoping that my academic accolades can somehow absolve me onto a path of worthiness.

April rolls in quickly. I only have one more month as an undergraduate. Frank presents me with a small box on my twenty-second birthday. My stomach tightens when I open the gift—it's a ring with a sapphire set between two diamonds. *This can't be happening again.* I force myself to smile.

"It's a friendship ring," he says.

I try to fit the ring on my right hand, but it only fits my left ring finger. I feel deep dread.

"Thank you," I say. *What have I done? I only want a protector.*

With a herculean effort, I manage to ace all of my courses. I have completed the requirements to earn two engineering degrees. I am figuratively and literally drunk with exhilaration.

After several rounds of margaritas, Frank asks, "Will you marry me?"

Silence overtakes me. I have no words.

"I will support you fully in your endeavor to earn a PhD."

"I don't think you understand. I intend to have a research career. I do not plan to have a family," I say.

"I can't have children. It is a long story related to my service in the Coast Guard," he offers.

I don't question his reasoning. I desperately want to succeed in graduate school. I need a protector. In a drunken state, I find myself engaged, yet again.

"Yes," I say.

I'm about to drag another soul into my tangled web of a life. I share my news with Aunt Jackie, and she is supportive but not pleased. I can only imagine how this will land on my parents.

In May 1988, I graduate with two bachelor's degrees, one in chemical and ocean engineering and the other in materials engineering. Aunt Jackie throws a spectacular graduation party. I am safely inebriated.

"Mom and Dad, we have news to share. Frank asked me to marry him." I feel his hand on mine. I can only imagine how cold and sweaty my hand must feel. My heart is pounding ferociously.

"We are getting married this August," Frank adds, "before Lisa starts graduate school."

The look on their faces says it all. My parents are beyond less than pleased.

"Lisa, you hardly know this young man. You need to focus on your graduate studies," my father advises.

"Dad, I won't let you down. I will complete my PhD, I promise," I say. He has no sense of the depth of my inner despair or the consequence for me if I don't finish. If I don't achieve this for him, then I can never be worthy. My inner darkness throws in her mantra: *God took the wrong sister.*

My mother is furious with me. "Lisa, you're being selfish and unreasonable." She had liked Aaron, and now I have traded him in for a new model. She can't accept my behavior.

In truth, my action is an impulsive grasp for stability in my life. I'm making decisions based on my fears and insecurities, but I have no words or mechanism to explain my actions. Instead, I numb myself further with another drink.

I am ignorant of the realms of a committed marital relationship. The only things I seem to be able to commit to are academics, research, and work. I have no real friends—that is, no friends who are aware of my inner struggles, fears, or insecurities. My prowess in the realm of academia is counterbalanced by my lack of people skills.

After the URI graduation, I'm back at the family home with Beth and my mom. The real estate market has been slow, and our house has yet to sell. I will be working at the Army Research Labs until graduate school.

I do my best to avoid confrontation with my mom, but I have crossed a line. When asked if I will delay the wedding, I rebel and announce a wedding date. When my parents state that they don't have funds to pay for it until the house sells, I boldly push back, "Frank will pay."

Frank and I find an apartment on the East Side of Providence, Rhode Island, a few blocks from the Brown campus. Fueled by my anger, I move out of my family home when no one is around. I leave a simple note: "I have moved to Providence with my fiancé." My father calls immediately to tell me that my callous action has deeply wounded my mother. It will take years to create any semblance of healing between us. I bury my shame in my addictions.

August brings heat and humidity and a small garden wedding. My sister has graciously agreed to wear a peach-colored silk gown as my maid of honor. With no close friends, I have rallied women from our hometown to be bridesmaids. Drenched in sweat, we squeeze ourselves into our cumbersome gowns. I maneuver my sticky arms into the white lace wedding dress.

Residual alcohol from the previous night still exerts its effects, and I'm grateful to be numb. My aunt and sister are the only close family members who are not openly upset with me. My mom isn't speaking to me. Dad assures me I can come back home if this doesn't work out, but I don't think this is actually true.

As I walk through the rose garden—accompanied by my father and witnessed by my mother, aunt, and sister, as well as my cousins—toward my awaiting fiancé, it all feels wrong. My fate is sealed like a chemical swept into an irreversible reaction.

PART
TWO

Journey to
Rock Bottom

15
Navigating the Ivy League

Brown University abuts the historic East Side of Providence with its many colonial homes. I never considered myself worthy of an Ivy League education, and my doubts are paralyzing. My anxiety stirs the voice of the inner critic: *I am not Ivy League material. I am a nobody from a little rural town who needed her daddy to help her pass first-grade math.*

I quickly eat four bowls of cereal and vomit it back up, temporarily dispelling my fears and my sense of unworthiness. I gulp down a large cup of coffee and savor the caffeine as it pulses through my veins.

I pace our apartment, trying to muster the courage to go to campus. Frank left for a construction job early in the morning. This is not like my undergraduate experience where I arrived with boyfriend in hand or my father just an hour away. I have a husband now, but he is not trained in engineering or the sciences. I will have to find my own way in graduate school.

I finally gather up the nerve to pedal my way to the Barus and Holley engineering building. The thought of stepping into the unknown stirs up tremendous anxiety. I freeze at the entrance. Exhaling loudly, I pull the heavy door open, step into the lobby, and look for my classroom. The decor feels more austere at Brown than at URI. *Do I really belong here?*

Crystallography is my first class. I sit in the front of the room with pens in hand and quickly transcribe everything from the board to my notebook. The course is steeped in theory, unlike the hands-on engineering materials classes at URI. I remain intrinsically hardwired as an introvert and fail to muster the courage to introduce myself to anyone before I leave the room.

Applied mathematics is next on my schedule. The classroom is nearly full by the time I find the room. I sit in the back. It takes no more than a few minutes for me to realize that I have no idea what mathematical language is on the blackboard. I have taken six semesters of mathematics as an undergraduate, but I have never had a course in complex variables. Fear engulfs me—I feel like an impostor among the elite.

I am also enrolled in continuum mechanics because it is the prerequisite for all the other mechanics courses I will need for my doctoral studies. I sit in the front of the room. I am in awe when a woman approaches the blackboard—she has a skip in her step and a brilliant sparkle in her eyes. Janet Blume is an assistant professor who earned her PhD from Cal Tech. She is the sole female professor of my engineering education.

Professor Blume serves as an inspirational role model to me. I quickly realize that I need to hone my skills in tensor calculus to succeed in her class. I make a mental note to find the library after classes are over. I will become well-acquainted with the mathematics section of the library. Failure is not an option. I am certain that success in grad school is my meal ticket to worthiness.

My graduate studies are funded through the Presidential Fellowship. I know from my work at ARL that I want to study fracture of engineering materials. Several faculty members at Brown specialize in fracture mechanics, their expertise spanning dynamic fracture, fatigue fracture, experimental fracture, as well as theoretical modeling of fracture. I had no idea that the field of fracture mechanics was so vast. The choice of PhD advisor is overwhelming.

Professor Gregory earned his PhD from Brown. I call him to get advice.

"Professor Gregory, can you help me choose a PhD advisor?"

"Call me Otto. You've graduated," he says with a light laugh.

"I can't possibly call you 'Otto.' How about Dr. Gregory?" He laughs louder.

"You want a PhD advisor who's not only a good research mentor but also a lifetime mentor. Someone who will always have your back," he offers.

"Who would that be?" I ask. I am starting to grasp the weight of my decision.

"I think the best mentor for you would be Subra Suresh. He's world-renowned for his expertise in fatigue fracture of engineering materials, and much of his work is experimental. He's also known to be an exceptional mentor."

"Thank you, I'll let you know how it goes," I reply. *Should I have stayed at URI and pursued a PhD under Dr. Gregory's direction?*

It is nearly dinnertime. This meal is no longer a solo event serving as my transition into an evening of homework sets. The reality of married life sets in—I will be expected to have dinner and a conversation with my spouse. Culinary skills are not my specialty. When my husband gets home,

I have pasta and wine on the table. I make small talk and shovel the food down and gulp my wine. After dinner, I head to the bathroom, lock the door, turn on the water, purge, wash my face, and brush my teeth. Done. My eating disorder is merely part of my day-to-day routine, and now she is merely a part of my married life.

I see the look of confusion on Frank's face as I get ready to head to the library after dinner. Since morning, he's seen me for all of thirty minutes.

"Can't you study here?" he asks.

"No. I can't be distracted," I say, annoyed by the question.

With a cringe of guilt, I grab my backpack. I stop at the convenience store near campus and pick up a pound of candy and several cans of soda. I shove these in my backpack to smuggle them into the library. It is a routine that served me well as an undergraduate, and I hope it works in graduate school. I will purge when my homework is done—it is my reward.

I have a long night ahead to work on applied mathematics, continuum mechanics, and crystallography. I set myself up in a quiet corner of the library. It's time to make friends with applied mathematics.

When I return home after midnight, my husband is already asleep. I pour a tall glass of Maker's Mark and gulp it down. The hot liquid satiates my hunger and calms my nervous system. I crawl into bed quietly and read my crystallography book until my eyes get heavy. I will manage four hours of sleep and rise when Frank gets up for work.

This becomes the pattern of our marriage. We live estranged without any sense of intimacy. Marriage to me is the safety of the gold band around my left ring finger. Now I can focus solely on my academic pursuits.

Frank occasionally gets angry about the amount of time I spend on the campus. "Why do you have to stay at the library until it closes? Why can't you do some of your studying here?" he pleads.

"I get distracted here. I need to focus, or I will never master complex variables and the tensor mathematics I need for continuum mechanics," I muster.

"What? I have no idea what you are talking about. Why can't you speak in plain English?" he says in frustration as he walks away.

I know he is heading for his bourbon, and soon his mood will soften.

Frank's mild outbursts are nothing compared to the emotional abuse I have sustained in the past. I am well-trained to weather any passing word of frustration. Frank rationalizes that our relationship will get better once I settle into graduate school or once I graduate. He is wrong—it will never get better.

I have my first meeting with Professor Suresh. I stand outside his office and work up my courage to knock on his door, my hands cold and clammy. A welcoming voice invites me into his academic abode. Prestigious degrees from the Indian Institute of Technology and MIT decorate the walls. My eyes are drawn to his vast collection of prestigious awards. Professor Suresh has an enviable library of books. Wearing a bright smile, a crisp shirt, and an elegant tie, everything about Professor Suresh exudes wisdom.

I suddenly feel minuscule, like Alice in Wonderland when she ate the crumb that made her shrink. I need the other crumb that lets me grow so I can find the courage to speak. I have never been in the position of asking to join a lab. I feel the words jumbling around in my mouth just as they had when I was in elementary school.

I get straight to the point. "Professor Suresh, my name is Lisa Pruitt. I just started at Brown. I have a Presidential Fellowship. I would like to work in your research lab."

I am grateful that I do not muddle my sentences, though I may have just achieved a speed record for words.

"Call me Subra," he says. "Tell me more about your background."

I share my educational trajectory as well as my research experiences. I begin to relax as I note the sparkle in his dark brown eyes.

"I recently acquired a project funded by the Office of Naval Research that involves fatigue fracture characterization of polymeric composites. This might be a good match for you," Professor Suresh suggests. "You will need to take fracture mechanics and all the requisite mechanics courses for the research."

"Thank you, Professor Suresh. I won't let you down." I feel like a child not wanting to disappoint her academic father.

With that, I am invited into the magical kingdom of the Suresh research group. Some students will graduate during my first year, while others have years remaining in their PhD research. Almost everyone in the group works in the realm of fatigue fracture mechanisms within advanced alloys, intermetallics, or structural ceramics. I am the sole student working on polymeric materials. My sheltered eyes open, as I see not only women but also a vast span of ethnicities. Our lab hosts scholars from India, China, Japan, Spain, the Netherlands, and the United Kingdom. I soak in the multicolored richness of life.

My classes are challenging, but I enjoy the opportunity to master the requisite knowledge for my research. I am in the lab every day shadowing the graduate students in the Suresh group. I hone my mechanical characterization skills and learn how to run the servo-hydraulic systems for fatigue testing. I use the transmission electron microscope for microstructural characterization, the scanning electron microscope for fractographic analysis, and optical microscopy for crack growth measurements.

Each night, I spend time in the library working on applied mathematics. With each passing week, I gain improved mastery of this elegant scientific language. Then, I continue my materials and solid mechanics homework sets at my desk in the lab while the fatigue tests are running.

I take comfort in the hum of the servo-hydraulic system. I'm often in the lab until late in the evening and have a drawer that I keep filled with candy for my nightly energy.

On one particular night, the lab phone rings around midnight.

"Suresh lab," I say, secretly hoping it is Professor Suresh so he knows how committed I am to research. Alas, it is my spouse.

"Are you coming home? Why did we rent this expensive apartment if you were going to live in the lab?" he spews.

I sense he has been drinking again. Once he passes his alcoholic threshold, his mild-mannered personality escalates into anger. I know this transformation all too well.

"I will be home when this fatigue test is done," I offer.

"When do these eighty-hour weeks stop?" he asks.

"When I finish my PhD," I offer, as I hear the click terminating the phone call. He can't possibly understand. Academic success is my only path to absolution.

16

A Parallel Universe

Our marriage is dysfunctional at best. In a nutshell, I fail to show up. Marriage has become my alternate universe, the alter ego of the person who appears at the university. At campus, I am alive, engaged, and drawn into the theory of mechanical behavior of materials. At home, I am always being questioned: Why do you have to work so many hours? How long until you graduate? When will we have a normal life?

My parents live in California, while Beth studies mechanical engineering at MIT. I see my Aunt Jackie once in a while for dinner, but I have no obligations to pull me from the rigor of my doctoral pursuit. Frank's family lives only an hour away. We are invited to dinner every Sunday, but I am "too busy with work."

Initially, my husband grumbled mildly in protest, but as the months accumulate, he is less tolerant of my work habits.

"Would it kill you to take an afternoon off to visit my family?" he asks.

"I have too much homework."

"Well, we wouldn't want the big brain to shrink, would we?" he says as he slams the door. I wear the guilt like a heavy cloak. *Why can't I find it within myself to make time for his family on the weekends?* I quickly head to the store. Perhaps two bags of candy are in order today? I numb myself with sugar and mathematics.

Frank's parents make the journey to Providence each month. We dine at the little Italian restaurant around the corner from our apartment. I empty my wine glass quickly to quell my nerves and prepare myself for the inevitable question.

"Lisa, how long until you graduate?" they ask.

"I plan to graduate in May 1990 with my master's, but it will likely be another three years to complete my PhD," I explain. I gave this same answer the previous month. I drink more wine to dispel the awkwardness of the silence.

"Visit when you can," my in-laws say.

I nod and smile, feeling a bitterness welling up. I don't want to visit anyone; I just want to work.

November brings blustery air and fallen leaves that were held so vibrantly by the trees just weeks ago. I feel like a fallen leaf myself as I process my husband's words.

"My company is not solvent, and I owe back taxes," Frank states bluntly, with an empty bourbon glass in hand.

"I thought you had a successful construction business?" My armor stiffens.

I soon learn this is no trivial matter. We will need to sell his truck and use all the money that we had received as wedding gifts to start paying down the owed taxes. Frank will need to find a job. Until then, we only have the income from my graduate fellowship.

I simmer with my thoughts. I am twenty-two years old, and I have never had any financial debt. I saved up my money from the time I was a babysitter at eleven years old until I worked as an engineer at the Army Research Labs. I came into the marriage debt-free, but now I legally share this immense financial burden.

I stuff down my anger and vomit it out, repeatedly. I am furious with Frank and angry at myself for getting into this financial mess. I immerse myself more deeply in academic work. My visceral anger wakes my inner dragon: *I will never get a PhD or be worthy now.* My perceived unworthiness gains traction and expands beneath my rigid armor, threatening to burst out like the very flaws I study in the laboratory every night, moving closer to their critical length just before rupture.

Frank finds a job as a surveyor. It doesn't pay well, but it enables us to keep up with our basic living expenses—until we get our first heating bill. Our historic East Side apartment has charmed us with its wide floorboards, built-in cabinets, and antique windows, but now that winter is upon us, we discover its one defect: there is no insulation. We put plastic up over the windows to combat the heat loss, but the seams in the floorboards open to an uninsulated cellar. We keep the thermostat to a bare minimum and burn wood in our old fireplace.

Some nights are so cold that we burn the pine furniture we inherited just to keep warm. I spend as little time at home as possible so I can remain productive at school. I get home well after midnight and then drink enough bourbon to numb my mind and to get warm enough to sleep.

To the outside world, we pass as a happily married couple. Now that I have become part of the Suresh group, I have made friends with a few of the other graduate students. Yuki and I are contemporaries in the lab. She lives with her boyfriend just a few minutes away from campus. They enjoy cooking and often invite us to their home for dinners.

We spend many Saturday nights with Yuki and her boyfriend, Doug. They cook us extraordinary meals, then joke about my huge appetite. Frank laughs. "Yes, Lis has a great metabolism. She gets to eat whatever she wants and never gains weight. I prefer my love handles," he says with a laugh as he grabs the rolls at his belly. Frank holds the dinner conversations with ease. When we leave, I feel my anxiety rise up—a purge is imminent. I have homework sets and research to do—fun time is over.

Underneath this smokescreen, we blame each other for our financial predicament. Frank seems to believe that our relationship would miraculously improve if I left academia. I counter that he should find a higher-paying job that would enable him to pay off our debt. We have no communication skills. I continually numb myself with alcohol, food, and work. He grows increasingly infuriated with my extensive absences from our home. *What have we gotten ourselves into?*

In the dead of winter, I come home and find Frank in an emotionally devastated state, sipping a tall glass of bourbon. I can tell by his expression he has disconcerting news to share—he was given a pink slip and is now unemployed. His income will be limited to whatever unemployment offers. Filled with anxiety and simmering rage, I find myself in need of the same beverage he is drinking.

I blame him for our financial crisis, yet I cannot outwardly express my emotions to him. Our home is stifled by my silence. It's easier for me to cope by reaching into my toolbox of addictions than to have an honest conversation with him. He suggests the unthinkable.

"Could you go back to ARL and work as an engineer?" he asks.

I run out of the apartment without a word, slamming the door behind me. I have nowhere to go except back to the campus. I stop by the store, buy several bags of candy, and find a remote place in the library where no one will find me. I need to be alone. I try to numb my pain and ingest as much sugar and mathematics as I can possibly contain. Then I purge until my raging emotions are exhausted. As the library closes, I head back to the lab, where I know it will be quiet. I find some semblance of calm that comes with being deeply embedded in my research. I start spending even more time at the lab in order to avoid the looming crisis in my home.

I call my parents. I know I have estranged myself from them through my selfish actions, but I don't know where else to turn. I need to borrow money, or I will end up having to drop out of graduate school. My father asks how much we need to get through this year until our lease expires. My parents generously offer to help us out financially, and I thank them for their help. I am also eternally grateful that they haven't stated the obvious: "You brought this on yourself."

My husband again hints that I should finish with a master's degree so that I can earn a "real income" as an engineer. I deflect these conversations and bury myself in my studies. I don't want to let my father down. My need to complete my PhD feels necessary to offset the deep inner sense of unworthiness I still carry. Quitting is not an option.

My studies and research consume me. I return to the lab every night after dinner, armed with a large bag of candy and caffeinated beverages to sustain me through the night. I use sugar and caffeine to muster up a round of false energy to work well past midnight. When I return home, I drink alcohol to try to calm myself enough to get some sleep. A few hours later, I load myself up with caffeine and return to the university for classes. I am caught up in my façade of academic achievement, hoping somehow these accomplishments will offer me some sense of value in this world.

Frank has taken a part-time job as a land surveyor. It pays poorly, but it is a cash income and helps us make ends meet. It is clear that Frank has some of his own sense of inner unworthiness around education and income. We never openly discuss it, but he often teases me about being a "big brain." I don't make a lot of money yet, but he is clearly in tune with my earning potential as an engineer or scientist.

As we struggle with our finances, he is starting to process that there may be enhanced income with a PhD over a master's degree.

"How much more could you make with a PhD?" he asks.

"I think I have far more earning potential with a PhD," I say, making a case for the extra time in graduate school.

Frank never went to college. Frank served in the Coast Guard and then established his own business serving the construction industry. When his business failed, he lost his sense of self. Now it seems that my academic success is the path of worthiness for both of us.

The universe must sense our misery. We are so deeply embedded in our financial despair that she must think we want more of it. One evening, shortly before dinner, I come home from the university and see my in-laws pacing in front of our apartment. The look on their faces indicates that something is dreadfully wrong. I feel a sense of dread as I approach. "Lisa, there has been an accident," they say.

At the hospital, the halls are abuzz with nurses. I feel an urgency in the air. When I walk into the hospital room, I see that Frank is heavily sedated. I learn from the nurse that he had been working with a machete, clearing brush for his survey work. He cut through his knee and is fortunate that he has not lost his leg. Bile fills my mouth. The pure uncertainty of the situation overwhelms me.

I have no idea what this injury means for our future. It will be months before he can return to work, but this will not stave off the arrival of medical bills. We have no other option but to move in with his parents until he recuperates and we are financially solvent again.

I am hanging on by a mere thread. Now I drive my in-laws' car an hour each way to get to campus. I should be filled with empathy for my spouse's injury and gratitude for the generosity offered by his family, but instead, I wallow in resentment.

We now live upstairs in his family home. Each day, I get up early and return late. There is always a prepared dinner waiting for me. I ungraciously stuff the food down, then purge for emotional relief. I am starting to wonder whether I should quit graduate school after I complete my master's degree and return to ARL as a research engineer. This option feels like failure, and I hate to openly fail at anything. I must focus on my academics to get myself out of this crisis.

When Frank is finally healed enough to work, he finds a job as a draftsperson for a construction company in southern Rhode Island. Each morning, we leave his parents' home early, and he drops me off at the university by 6:00 a.m. Frank picks me up in the evening, impatiently waiting until I'm ready to leave.

"How long until we can move back to Providence?" I ask.

Every day the answer is the same. "When our bills are paid."

It takes us the summer to get the medical bills paid. After what feels like an eternity, we find a less-expensive apartment in Providence a few miles from campus. I will bike to the university, and he will drive his parents' car to work.

I am making good progress on my research and plan to take my preliminary oral exam early in the spring semester leading up to the completion of my master's degree. The preliminary exam proves to be my most difficult academic task, not for lack of academic knowledge but because it is an oral exam. I remain burdened by my introverted nature and intrinsic shyness. Like my first oral presentation, I enter a black hole when I am speaking. Words leave my mouth, but I feel disconnected from my body. I can't feel my feet. My heart pounds in my ears. Sweat drips down my arms and across my palms. Somehow, I answer all the technical questions, and I am greatly relieved when I pass the exam. My PhD advisor likely makes a mental note of my need to improve my oral speaking skills, but he says nothing but "congratulations, well done."

I feel a deep sense of gratitude as I complete my master's degree at the end of my second year of graduate school. With this milestone complete, Frank begins to see the light at the end of the tunnel—only three more years until we have financial freedom. I am twenty-four years old and under an academic spell, feeling that, with a PhD in hand, I can redeem myself in this world. For me, redemption is worthiness, yet for Frank, redemption is prosperity. These bifurcated beliefs will drive a stake into the undoing of our marriage.

17

A Journey with Horses Begins

My lab mate at Brown rides for the equestrian team. I'm not only fascinated that she rides with such a high level of mastery but also that she has time for any outside activities. Maybe it's because she is nearly done with her graduate work?

My husband crosses paths with my equestrian colleague at one of our lab dinners. By the end of the evening, he has found out the name of the farm where she rides and has learned they offer lessons.

"We should take riding lessons together," Frank suggests.

"I don't have time to ride. I have to focus on my research and classes."

"Will you just try one lesson with me?" he asks.

"Okay," I grumble.

Although I choose not to disclose any of my thoughts with Frank, his invitation leads me to consider my past relationship with horses. These creatures have always had a majestic, if not mystical, quality for me. We lived next to horses when I was a child; our neighbors up the street used them as therapy for disabled children. I admired that the horses never cast judgment on these children, and I often wished that they would take me into their herd and heal me.

My sister was consumed by horses—they were her passion, and because of that, I didn't take any outward interest. As children, I had considered us to be yin and yang; if something was hers then it couldn't be mine. Yet, inwardly, I felt a deep connection with these sentient beings.

Merely ten miles from the Brown campus, the drive to Hawkswood Farm is stunning. I absorb the bright cherry, pumpkin, and mustard foliage that makes autumn in New England so delicious. Captivated by the beautiful farms that appear with each turn of the road, the sweet fragrance of hay and horses intoxicates me.

Carol Franco, the owner of the farm, greets us with release forms in hand. She is well-worn with hay blended into her wiry hair. Her smile assures us that she loves her life. She has nearly forty equine companions, including docile creatures for beginners as well as advanced steeds for dressage and jumping. Hawkswood Farm is expansive with outdoor arenas, pastures, and fields, with vast offerings of obstacles for jumping. Her house and a little cottage sit across from the massive barns.

Carol lives and breathes all things horse. She exudes mastery in the barn. She asks us about our riding experience. I had my riding lessons with my sister when I was younger, and Frank states that he had owned a horse years ago. His answer surprises me. *How is it that I hadn't known that about him? How did he afford it?* Our horses are chosen accordingly. Irish, a speckled Appaloosa, is assigned to me, while Bucky is chosen for Frank.

"Don't worry, Bucky has no bucks left in him, and Irish is more likely to unseat a rider by lunging for grass," Carol says with a hearty laugh.

Carol shows us the tack room where we collect our saddles, bridles, and grooming supplies. Carol shows me how to tack up Irish. She breathes out a heavy sigh as she senses that her poor horse must accommodate another clumsy beginner. I pay close attention as she saddles and bridles my horse. When I finally manage to mount, she sizes me up and tells me I have the body for riding—long, muscular legs and a strong core.

Carol has us warm up the horses at a walk and then asks us to squeeze our legs into the horse to ask for a trot. My body quickly finds the two-beat rhythm. My biggest challenge is keeping Irish from lunging at the hay as we navigate the indoor arena. He has twice managed to secure himself a snack.

"Hold your reins like you're holding ice cream cones," she yells across the arena as I try to keep Irish from lunging for the hay on the ground.

I'm smitten by the end of our first lesson. I ask if we can arrange for another lesson in the coming week. Frank smiles. Our riding lesson seems to have temporarily dispelled the tension between us. *Perhaps horses can provide a foundation for a shared life?*

An equine spell has been cast over me. The horses nourish my soul, muting some of my internal defects. With each passing week, I quickly progress in my riding. Carol has a different horse for me to ride each time. I revel in the beautiful movement of these majestic creatures.

Frank is handy, and Carol lets him trade farm chores for riding privileges. He selflessly does this for me so I can continue riding, and of course, it's the only time he has me away from the university. As the months pass, my husband no longer takes lessons but goes out for occasional trail rides. For this generous act I am eternally grateful, but I can't seem to find the words to openly express this to him.

I have been actively working on strengthening my protective armor, and while it protects me from outside attacks and negative emotions, it also seems to create a barrier against expressing positive emotions. I am becoming as unyielding as structural steel, shielding its knight from external dangers.

A few months into our riding immersion, Carol approaches us with a proposition. She has a little cottage next to the upper barn that's about to be vacated and asks us if we would like to live on her farm. The rent is half the price of our apartment in Providence.

"You could trade chores for riding privileges," she offers.

I don't hesitate. "When can we move in?"

"I think you're forgetting that we only have one car, and I need to be in southern Rhode Island each day," Frank says.

"It's only ten miles. I'll ride my bike to campus each day," I offer.

As I hone my riding skills, Carol gives me free rein to ride one of her young horses. Nicholas is a six-year-old appendix quarter horse and an exceptional jumper. His bay coat glistens like molten chocolate.

Notoriously naughty, Nicholas is known around the farm as Bad Boy Nick. We are kindred spirits. While I may be building a protective armor, my inner defects fester. At some level, I still see myself as a bad little girl. Nick's mischievous antics bring me great humor, and he serves as a healing balm to my own inner darkness.

With Nicholas as my mount, I pick up the sport of three-day event-ing, the equestrian equivalent of a triathlon comprised of dressage, show jumping, and cross-country jumping. This experience plants another seed for me. Someday, when I have my PhD in hand and financial security, I will have my dream horse with whom I can compete in three-day eventing at the highest level.

The adrenaline rush of galloping and jumping over solid obstacles fully captivates me. I embrace the training, and Carol invites me to show Nick at local shows. I work harder at the university to ensure that I don't fall behind in my engineering studies. My only time with Frank involves being around the horses. He seems appeased, and he, too, finds enjoyment around the horses. *Perhaps there is some path toward happiness for us in this type of life?*

With winter upon us, my husband is laid off from work again. It seems that the construction business in New England is seasonal at best. I have made it painfully clear that I am not moving again, and I will not yield on this point. I love living on the farm, riding Nick, and navigating the back-country roads to campus on my bicycle. I can't fathom leaving all of this.

I inform my PhD advisor that my husband is unemployed and ask if I might pick up extra work. Subra can't offer me more money as a research student, but there is a possibility of earning extra income as a teaching assistant. The thought of teaching petrifies me. In the near term, he kindly helps my resourceful spouse find part-time work at the university as a draftsperson.

Frank is hired for twenty hours a week to help prepare ink drawings of professors' manuscripts and book projects. He supplements this job with afternoon work at a local sandwich shop and then an evening position at Home Depot. I ride my bike to the university by 9:00 a.m. each morning. Frank picks me up at two o'clock the following morning after his shift at Home Depot. We throw the bike in the back of our vehicle and drive the rural roads back to the farm. We often find Carol out in the barn, checking on the horses. Her hours are as insane as mine. I usually help her and then find my way to bed by 3:00 a.m. For me, this is an idyllic life. For Frank, exhausted by holding three menial jobs, this is just a means to an end. He is counting down the days until I have my PhD and my high-paying job.

At some level, we both hope that this type of life could be ours in the future, a life where we own a horse farm, and he uses his handyman skills to run the day-to-day operations of the business. Presuming I take a job in New England or at a location where the cost of living is low enough to live this dream, it seems like a life where we could both be happy. But the universe has other plans waiting for us.

Each morning, I am up by 7:00 a.m. I down my coffee, then quickly pull on breeches and riding boots. Once in the barn, the soothing sound of horses eating their morning hay absorbs me. Nick juts his head out over his stall door and whinnies when he sees me. I step into his stall and breathe in the nectar of his muzzle, an intoxicating aroma of soft leather and sweet grass.

Riding Nick is the highlight of my day—depending on the weather, we might ride in the indoor arena or outdoors. I love the feel of this horse beneath me, and I feel the immense power of his canter carrying us together with ease over the field or arena. I hear only the soft, rhythmic sound of his hooves as we canter. My mind is nowhere else. My interaction with Nick fills my well, and then I am ready for a busy day at the university.

I cycle to school and arrive ready for classes by mid-morning. Later in the day, I eat with Frank at the sandwich shop and then head back to the lab to do research while he goes off to Home Depot for his night shift. Our days are long, but I wouldn't trade it for the world. I am in both academic and horse heaven.

Living at the horse farm, riding horses, and cycling the back roads to the university provide me with great solace. I wish I could say that these outlets are enough to break me free of my addictions. Alas, bulimia, alcohol abuse, and work addiction remain active parts of my daily toolbox.

I continue to naïvely think I will leave these addictive coping tools behind once I complete graduate school and have less stress in my life. Little do I know what lurks ahead.

18

The Making of a Professor

In my third year of graduate school, my PhD mentor does the unthinkable and asks me to be a teaching assistant in our large undergraduate course in materials science. Unbeknownst to me, I am being shaped into a professor. Subra offers his students continuous opportunities for professional growth and is quick to observe what they need to reach their academic potential. He knows when to be the wind against or beneath my wings.

Teaching will not only enable me to make extra money but will also provide me with the requisite skills to pass the rigorous oral PhD qualifying exam. As a teaching assistant, I am expected to hold office hours for student questions, lead experimental labs, and teach a weekly discussion section with the students.

"This will be good for you," Subra encourages. My advisor states this with ease, just like he effortlessly delivers extraordinary lectures in engineering. When he lectures on how most structural materials have some type of defect that will render them prone to failure, I resonate with these flaws. My advisor likely does not see my internal defects because I keep them well-protected beneath my academic armor.

I am a confident experimentalist—teaching small groups of students in labs and in office hours will be enjoyable. However, I remain highly introverted, and the thought of teaching a large class fills me with dread. I still struggle with an extraordinary fear of public speaking, prone to jumbling my words when I become anxious. Palpable memories of being teased in elementary school fill my thoughts, my inner critic always at the ready to throw me a self-limiting thought.

I spend an inordinate amount of time preparing for my first discussion section with the undergraduates. I invest nearly twelve hours in a derivation involving X-ray diffraction. My notes are complex; I am incredibly proud of my thoroughness. It never occurs to me that the lecture will be well beyond the understanding of a sophomore in their first materials science course.

On my first day of teaching, I walk into the large classroom and scan the expanse of chairs filled with eager young minds. My heart is pounding, my hands blue with coldness, and my clothes soaked with anxious sweat.

"My name is Lisa Pruitt; I am a doctoral student of Professor Subra Suresh. I will be teaching you each week," I say, quickly pivoting to the blackboard.

I write every aspect of my notes onto the board for forty minutes straight, my chalk quickly converting to dust. As I reach the end of my notes, I feel a great sense of relief. I then turn around to ask if there are any questions. I am horrified when I see a room full of blank faces staring, uncomprehending, at the blackboard. I have failed to teach them.

When the first question finally comes from a brave student, I focus on just answering that single question. Then another. I manage to salvage the hour one question at a time. This is going to be a dreadful semester. I am relieved that I have no intention of becoming a professor.

As the weeks pass, I grow more at ease with the students. I learn their names and make the recitations more interactive. I engage them with questions and work out practice problems. I still get butterflies, but I no longer feel as though I am at risk of heart failure.

By semester's end, I actually enjoy teaching. Subra asks me to help teach his advanced metallurgy class in the spring, and I enthusiastically agree. With each passing semester, my love of teaching will continue to blossom. Although it's likely obvious to my PhD advisor, I do not yet see that I am setting a trajectory into the realm of professorship.

With Subra's prompting, I submit the findings of my polymer fatigue work in the form of an extended abstract to a prestigious international conference entitled Deformation, Yield and Fracture of Polymers. My work is selected for a podium presentation. I'm both ecstatic and panicked at the thought of giving this talk. Subra works with me to polish my oral presentation. My audience will be nearly two hundred international scientists with expertise in polymer mechanics. My advisor tells me how important it will be to give a high-level presentation and to "schmooze" with the scientists at this meeting. Just the thought of "schmoozing" makes me nauseous.

By the time I arrive at Cambridge University, I have my presentation committed to memory. I am less worried about my twenty-minute presentation than the five minutes of questions that will follow. The conference is held at Churchill College. We are housed in the dorms and will eat all of our meals together. As I sit in the audience on the first day, I am in awe as I listen to the presentations. These speakers are the authors of the research papers that I have consumed in pursuit of knowledge related to micro-mechanisms of fracture in structural polymers. I soak in every word from these world-renowned scientists. What will happen when I give my talk? My visceral fear kicks in, and with it, my dreaded sense of unworthiness and insecurities rise. *Do I belong here?*

Subra introduces me to the scientists he knows, including the preeminent Ali Argon from MIT. I wonder if he knows my sister. Beth will soon graduate with a degree in mechanical engineering. As the conference unfolds, I observe that Professor Argon has a pointed question for every speaker.

On the morning of my talk, I'm up early after a fitful night of sleep, filled with nightmares of various questions posed by Professor Argon. I don't show up for breakfast. I pace my room and recite my talk over and over. I feel like a parrot.

As my talk is announced, I step up on stage, look out from the podium, and see a fretful sight: my PhD advisor sitting in the front row next to Professor Argon. I suddenly feel nauseous. I am grateful that I have no food in my stomach.

I have practiced my talk so many times that the presentation itself feels automatic. My heart pounds fiercely, and I'm drenched in sweat, but the words flow from my mouth automatically.

Time stands still when I finish. The moderator opens the floor to questions, and Professor Argon stands up. I feel my knees buckle.

"How do you explain your observed crazing in your compression fatigue tests?" he asks.

"Crazing is evidenced by the fibrillation of the polymer ahead of the crack tip. This mechanism requires a tensile component of stress. I interpret crazing to be evidence of residual tensile fields upon the unloading portion of the fatigue cycle," I respond. *Did that just come from my mouth? That sounded like a scientifically sound answer!*

At our coffee break, several scientists come up to me to talk about my research presentation. I am nearly dizzy—the love of my academic work soon eclipses my shyness. I have the opportunity to speak with many of my academic icons. Dr. Greg McKenna from the National Institute of Standards and Technology (NIST) encourages me to apply for a postdoctoral fellowship lab. I explain that I am only in my third year of graduate school, but he encourages me, nonetheless. Professor Ed Kramer invites me to Cornell in the coming summer to learn their method for staining and imaging polymeric crazes with their TEM (Transmission Electron Microscopy). Professor Henning Kausch invites me to come give a seminar at the Swiss Federal Institute of Technology (EPFL) in Switzerland.

By dinner, I am nearly overwhelmed with emotion. I enjoy the banquet dinner, and as the alcohol flows, I hold my own in witty conversation with these academic geniuses. I am twenty-five years old, and I finally feel some semblance of worthiness.

It never occurs to me to call Frank, because I am consumed by my academic world. When I return home, he is angry at my oversight.

"Lisa, did it ever occur to you to call me while you were in England?" he asks, deeply hurt and immensely frustrated.

I quickly pivot and lie. "There was only a single payphone, and the time difference made it impossible to call when you might be home."

Upon my return to Brown, I prepare for my PhD qualifying exam. I must demonstrate my expertise in fracture mechanics and materials science, as well as my outside minor in structural geology. I put together a large three-ring binder with notes compiled from all of my courses, even the graduate courses that I had taken as an undergraduate at URI.

Each day, I spend hours studying, and each week, I meet with one of the postdoctoral fellows in the department for an hour of rigorous questioning. The interrogations get more grueling as the exam date approaches. I learn to weather the academic inquisitions with ease, all the while abusing my body by reaching deeply into my addictive toolbox.

At this stage of my life, I consider my addictions to be useful tools to help me succeed in life; I don't yet see that they are weapons of self-destruction.

The day that will decide my fate as a doctoral student finally arrives. "This will be the smartest day of your life," Subra says with a lighthearted tone. I don't know whether to take this as a compliment or an insult. Later in my life, I will say the same thing to my PhD students, knowing that this is the day we hold all of our knowledge at the ready for cross-examination. In truth, our wisdom continues to blossom, but it feels empowering to think about having such knowledge at an early stage of one's life.

The examination room feels claustrophobic. I feel the intimidating presence of the four faculty sitting at the table before me. It seems like I'm in a time warp, and I have no sense of whether minutes or hours pass. At the end of the exam, the professors ask me to step outside for a few moments. Subra opens the door and invites me back into the room. I can see by the sparkle in his eyes that the news is good. My heart beats faster.

"Congratulations, you are officially a candidate for the doctoral degree in engineering," they say. Inside, I am giddy with joy. My ability to express my emotions is hindered by my armoring. Outwardly, I am fully composed and can't seem to find words beyond, "Thank you!"

I immediately call my parents and my Aunt Jackie to share the news. Then I celebrate with the graduate students in the Suresh lab. Frank is the last to learn of my success. I cannot find it in myself to include him more deeply in the inner realm of my academic world.

After completing all my required courses, I am drawn to a biomaterials class in the medical school. This course rekindles my passion for medicine. I share my enthusiasm with Subra, and within a short time, a collaborative opportunity with the Hospital for Special Surgery (HSS) in New York presents itself.

Dr. Clare Rimnac serves as my mentor from HSS. She has her PhD in materials engineering and uses her knowledge to improve the performance of orthopedic medical devices. Our collaborative project investigates the crack growth in ultra-high molecular weight polyethylene, the primary polymer used in the bearing coupling of total joint replacements.

Through her mentorship, I see an opportunity to make contributions to the medical field through my engineering training. My academic path is coming full circle as my forgotten love of medicine finds a way back into my life.

19

Faculty Search

As I begin the final year of my PhD, my dream of returning to the Army Research Labs as a research engineer is being displaced by my newfound love of teaching. Subra brings a number of faculty advertisements to my attention. I scan them quickly—there are big-name institutions like University of Michigan, University of Southern California, and UC Berkeley. But the universities in rural locations where I could have a horse attract my attention. I am especially interested in the polymer program at the University of Massachusetts. I had never considered a career in academia, but now the prospect of becoming a professor intrigues me. *Such a prestigious career would certainly earn me worthiness in this life.*

I compile my curriculum vitae and cover letter along with copies of my publications. I mail off my faculty applications to several academic institutions. I also apply for both the National Institute of Standards and Technology (NIST) and the Hospital for Special Surgery (HSS) post-doctoral fellowships. I don't expect to hear back from the prestigious universities, but the universe has other plans. I am in for quite an adventure.

I don't discuss my career plans with Frank at this juncture. It seems as long as I earn a good income, then he will be happy. It never occurs to me that some of the positions I have applied for could be problematic for him or could make any semblance of life-balance elusive.

My first interviews are with the Polymer Mechanics group at NIST in Maryland and the Hospital for Special Surgery in New York City. In a matter of weeks, I have two post-doctoral fellowship offers. Subra is confident that faculty interviews are forthcoming. "Don't accept any post-doctoral offers yet," Subra advises with a smile. When I mention my offers to Frank, he shudders.

"Do you know how expensive it is to live in New York City or outside DC? Would your salary cover our living expenses?" Frank asks.

"This is just a post-doctoral opportunity. It would only be for a year, and it merely serves as a bridge to a faculty position," I counter. I realize at this point that he is banking on me earning a good salary.

"Won't you be working?" I ask.

"Of course. But you are the big brain ... you are the one who has the earning potential. I am limited by how much I can make as a draftsperson," he counters.

What happened to the successful businessman I married? Is he gone? Was he ever really successful? Am I the sole breadwinner now?

I am nearly overwhelmed with the depth of uncertainty that this career choice brings into my life. I am saddened to think of leaving Hawkswood Farm and Brown University. I focus on writing my PhD thesis and rely on my artillery of coping tools. My bulimic episodes scale in direct proportion to my stress level. My gums are now raw and bleeding from continuous purging.

I'm finding myself both excited and apprehensive about a path in academia. I love teaching, but I remain innately introverted. I still can't fully imagine myself as a professor. I love my life with horses, and I don't see how an academic path allows room for this passion. I also can't imagine a path on which Frank and I will find happiness. I can't fully process these thoughts, so I stuff them away.

The first academic response arrives, from Texas A&M University. I hold the crisp envelope in my trembling hands. I look for the telltale phrase, "We regret to inform you …" but the words are not there. Instead, I am being asked to contact the Aerospace Department to arrange my interview in the coming weeks. Trepidation rises up, and anxiety quickly follows. My eating disorder is intensified; she is always at the ready to help me cope with my stress.

I schedule the interview. It will not be a one-day visit like I had at NIST or HSS. Instead, they have asked that I spend three days so I can see the campus and its surroundings. I am throttled with fear. I work with Subra on my presentation so it is polished. He offers his paternal advice as my academic advisor. He thinks that this will be the first of many academic interviews. This is a location that has appeal for Frank. He is certain that I will have a higher salary as a faculty member than as a post-doc and that the cost of living in Texas will be substantially lower than those of my other offers.

When I arrive at College Station, the department chair of aerospace engineering greets me. He shows me the surrounding area and expansive homes that could be afforded on a faculty salary. I notice a number of horse ranches within close proximity to the campus. I am intrigued as I see an opportunity to blend my passions.

I have two full days of interviews with various faculty in the department, leading up to my seminar presentation. When I arrive at the engineering building, a young cadet in the lobby offers to be of assistance.

"Excuse me, may I help you?" he asks.

"I'm here for a faculty interview," I say.

"Ma'am, this is the engineering building. Maybe you're in the wrong place?" he replies.

I feel my hands becoming fists. "I'm interviewing for a faculty position in aerospace engineering." Now I am irked.

I arrive at the chairman's office and see Society of Women Engineers magazines spread out on a table outside. *Why are these magazines here?* I have two full days of one-on-one meetings with faculty. There are no female names—this does not feel promising. *Are they trying to make me feel welcome? Are they hinting that they want to hire a woman faculty member?*

The individual meetings feel like a replication of my qualifying exam. I am repeatedly asked to derive various equations from fracture mechanics. I can do this with ease, but it becomes exhausting as the day progresses. It feels as though my gender or youth is a concern for them. I am only twenty-six years old and do not yet have my PhD in hand. I sense their apprehension, and the feeling is mutual.

My seminar goes well, and the chairman is enthusiastic when we have our final meeting before my departure. He shares typical start-up packages for assistant professors. The salary is well above what I would receive as a post-doc, and he assures me I would have ample space and resources to set up my experimental lab. He then adds that I would be the first female hire in the department. I enjoy being competitive, but I'm not sure what life would be like as the sole female professor in the department.

"We wouldn't expect as much from you," he adds. *What does that mean?* There seems to be some undertone that the bar for tenure would be lowered for me because I am a woman. Swallowing my fury, I smile and calmly ask for clarification as to the expectations for tenure. I listen to him fumble an answer about the need to publish archival journal publications and leading research programs.

"I assure you that I am well on my way to meeting your expectations," I say. On my plane ride home, I can't shake the comments from my mind, nor the messaging of the magazines. I sense that they desperately want female faculty, but it is not clear to me that they believe women are as capable as men in the field of engineering. I can't imagine coming to a place where I would not be certain that I had earned tenure with the same academic rigor as my male colleagues.

A week later, I have an offer in hand. I can't imagine this could possibly be the case—yet, by the time I schedule my PhD thesis defense, I have five academic offers and an invitation for two more faculty interviews.

My last interview is at University of California, Berkeley. Subra was a post-doc at Berkeley, and he clearly has a soft spot for this institution. He suggests that I decline my post-doctoral offers and inform the other institutions that I need to complete my interviews before making a final decision.

All of this negotiating is extraordinarily stressful, and I become more deeply entrenched in my addictive behaviors. My marriage is strained to its limits. For Frank, the answer is clear: take the offer at Texas A&M, where the pay is high and the cost of living is low. The nuances of quality of students, academic reputation, and opportunity for academic growth are lost on him. He simply wants a life. I want a career.

When I arrive at UC Berkeley, I am taken by the beauty of the campus and the majestic campanile tower glowing against the night sky. The sweet scent of star jasmine permeates the air as I find my way to the Women's

Faculty Club, where I will spend the night before a day of interviews.

My first meeting of the morning is with the chairman of Mechanical Engineering, Professor Bogy. He describes the tenure process, and it is clear that the expectations for tenure at this world-class institution are high. Ironically, the very high standard puts me at ease—if I am granted tenure at Berkeley, I know I will have earned it.

Professor Dave Dornfeld is my faculty host. Kind and jovial, Dave shares with me what a great place Berkeley is and how much he has enjoyed his time here. "The atmosphere is much more relaxed than some of the East Coast schools. The dress code is more casual," he says with a smile. Dave is comfortably dressed in a polo shirt, khakis, and Birkenstocks, while I am stifled by a wool suit and heels. He also assures me that there are plenty of places to ride horses near the Berkeley campus. He then mimics the whinny of a horse. I laugh. He offers a warm smile.

I have an enjoyable day at Berkeley with the extraordinary mechanical engineering faculty who work in design, materials, and manufacturing. I also make note of a highly successful woman, Professor Alice Agogino. World-renowned for human-centered design and engineering education, she is an impressive force. I feel certain I have found a path to be a successful professor here.

As I complete my PhD, I have offers from every institution where I interviewed. My anxiety stirs up as I consider making a life decision of such magnitude. My inner critic chimes in: *How is this possible that they see potential in me as a professor? How will I ever get tenure at these institutions?*

My PhD mentor advocates for UC Berkeley. "Lisa, this is your best offer. You will have access to superlative research students, and you will be able to do your best work at this prestigious university."

I feel a pang of guilt and uncertainty as I decline my other offers. Equally excited and petrified, I accept the position of assistant professor in mechanical engineering at UC Berkeley.

Frank is beyond disappointed—he is angry. He has no interest in living in California. "Why can't you take the position at U Mass or University of Michigan?" he pleads. He has had little say in my decision, and he is furious with me. "Why are you so selfish?" he questions.

I don't know how to express to him that UC Berkeley resonates for me at a visceral level. I promise him that I will only stay until I am tenured, and then we can move back to the East Coast. This is a promise I will later regret making.

The most difficult part of leaving Brown is leaving Hawkswood. I have come to love the farm, the horses, the people, and the riding opportunities. On the morning the moving van arrives to take our possessions to California, I stand in Nick's stall with tears streaming down my face. Carol comes out to say goodbye.

"Nick and I will miss you," she says through her own tears.

This is too much for my body to hold. I sob as I wrap my arms around Nick's neck. I am heartbroken.

What have I done? I don't want to leave. I stuff down my deep pain alongside the loss of my baby sister Karen and my childhood dog, King. Grief is a beast that I fear will swallow me whole—I have never learned the skills to process such emotional loss.

20

Publish or Perish

My success as a professor will hinge on my ability to build a world-class laboratory and to publish high-quality research papers. I know from conversations with my PhD advisor that tenure is awarded to faculty who demonstrate excellence in research and teaching, with an emphasis on the former. Assistant professors are typically allowed up to seven years to earn tenure, although some universities make the decision after ten years. The earning of tenure is notably one of the most stressful periods in an academic's life. I will not be relinquishing my coping toolkit anytime soon.

I pull open the heavy doors that lead into my assigned lab space. My eyes are assaulted by archaic equipment that once belonged to preeminent mechanical engineering faculty. I set my vision on the future, where this will be the home of my research group and we will have equipment for the characterization of engineering polymers used in medical devices. Humbled, I imagine the number of grants I will need to make my dream a reality.

Taking the elevator to the fifth floor, I find myself at 5134 Etcheverry Hall. I put my key in the lock, turn it, and slowly push the burgundy door open into my faculty office. It is stark with off-white walls, a steel gray desk, and a bookcase equipped with a sole textbook: *Shigley's Mechanical Engineering Design*. I thumb through it and groan. This is the book from which I am expected to teach my first class—there are no notable chapters on microstructure, dislocation plasticity, or fracture mechanics. Instead, chapters are devoted to thread design, bearings, and gears. I am a faculty member in the Department of Mechanical Engineering, but I own no degrees in this field. Fear bubbles up: *I am an impostor. How will I possibly succeed here?* I must keep this inner critic at bay—I stifle her down with work, food, and alcohol. I must succeed, or I will never be worthy.

The single window is nearly the size of a door; its glass panels swing wide open. *I can jump if things get too bad*, I muse. Stacked in the corner are cardboard shipping boxes filled with books collected throughout my engineering education, framed engineering degrees, and my distinguished teaching award from Brown. This office will be my home away from home. My husband will soon argue that this office is my home. Maybe it truly is.

I take my course syllabus to the photocopy room. As the light of the copier flashes beneath my paper, I hear the door open behind me. It's one of the senior faculty members, obviously approaching retirement.

"Are you the new secretary?" Professor O asks.

Inwardly, I groan; outwardly, I offer a smile. "No. I'm the new faculty hire."

"You look young enough to be a graduate student," he says with a chortle.

"I was one just a few weeks ago," I say with a bit of friendly repartee.

"I used to date a secretary when I was an assistant professor," he offers.

"How nice for you." *Is he serious?*

"Aren't you afraid to be alone with me in this little room?" he adds.

He must be joking. Besides, his comment is not the worst I've had to absorb in my professional career. There was that creepy professor who walked through the undergrad lab and looked me over before saying, "You must get good grades with a body like yours." I had wanted to throttle him. Instead, I pretended I hadn't heard him and walked away.

Over the coming weeks, Professor O stops by my office daily to offer his sassy statements. I offer quick counterattacks. He seems to enjoy the rapport. My younger days of being bullied have built up my armor, and years of undergraduate study groups have me well-versed in what passes for humor to some men. I quickly create a false bravado, and things settle into lighthearted banter. I can't be distracted from my tenure mission.

David Dornfeld has volunteered to be my mentor. He takes me out for lunch on my first day as an assistant professor. We eat at Nefelli's. He orders a croissant and cappuccino, while I have a spinach salad and an espresso. This is a meal I intend to keep.

"Did they give you the key to your lab yet?" he asks.

"Yes. It looks like a museum of ancient testing machines," I say in jest.

"That's how the university remodels its laboratories; they hire assistant professors," he chuckles. "There are lots of small grants on the campus earmarked for junior faculty. Apply to all of them; you'll be amazed at how quickly you can pull funding together."

Cheerful and lighthearted, Dave is world-renowned for his manufacturing research, but he also makes the academic life look fun. He jokes that in the game of tenure, you can do anything you want as long as you do it better than everyone else. "Just aim to be one of the top researchers in your field when you come up for tenure." He leisurely sips his cappuccino while I gulp down my espresso. Coffee will be a staple of my diet.

I work long days, logging eighty to ninety hours each week. My husband works at a Home Depot in the plumbing department. It never occurs to me the depth of resentment that Frank carries for my accomplishments or for the prestige of my work. Outwardly, Frank is supportive around my new colleagues. He even comes in on the weekends to help me move out the archaic equipment and to paint the walls in my research laboratory. Inwardly, he simmers over how I pulled him away from his family.

"I still can't believe you took this position at Berkeley over Texas. This job pays 20K less and yet the cost of living is twice as high. For a girl with a big brain, you have no common sense," he taunts.

I ignore him. I am on a mission to get tenure, and I will not be side-lined by his commentaries. The depth of my commitment to research and teaching will be an ongoing thorn in his side.

While gaining tenure is the most important professional weight on my shoulders, it is not the most urgent task. I need to build a world-class research lab and balance this with teaching. The old adage of "publish or perish" feels very real to me. I have brought a graduate student with me from Brown, but the transition feels sticky to both of us. We are both accustomed to a well-established lab. I have spent $50,000 to purchase a servo-hydraulic testing system from Instron, a piece of equipment used for fatigue testing and the most important acquisition for the success of my research. My start-up package is now nearly depleted—all the remaining equipment and expenses in the lab will need to be covered by grants.

I have reached out to Clare Rimnac at the Hospital for Special Surgery to rekindle our collaboration on medical polymers. We will examine the effects of sterilization and aging on the fatigue behavior of orthopedic-grade ultra-high molecular weight polyethylene. This polymer will serve as the foundation of my medical polymer group for the coming decades.

The juggle of grant writing, conference abstract preparations, labo-ratory research, and teaching is daunting. Each day blurs into the next. I am grateful for teaching, as it serves as a clear marker that it is a Tuesday or Thursday. Otherwise, all of my days feel the same.

Academically, each day comprises collecting data, writing papers, writing grants, preparing lectures, teaching, and meeting with students. I balance my energy with coffee, protein bars, and candy. Most of my binging and purging is done at night. I practically live in Etcheverry Hall.

"What type of life is this?" Frank asks when I get home at two in the morning.

"It will get better after tenure. I promise," I say. But that is a lie—deep inside, I know it will not get better.

I am one of six assistant professors hired in the department, and the only one with no post-doctoral experience, and the sole woman. My one female role model in the department is Alice Agogino; she is a full professor and the first woman to achieve tenure in our department. She is an icon in human-centered design. For all the women who may come behind me, I feel a heavy pressure to succeed. The weight of this need to succeed is bolstered by other obligations. I don't want to disappoint Subra or my parents. I need to succeed so I can have my life with horses—I intend to buy my dream horse and to return to three-day eventing after I receive tenure. I must stay true to my ever-meandering path toward worthiness. Failure is not an option.

It is Saturday morning. I hear a scratching noise outside my office. I open the door and am greeted by a playful golden retriever who leaps up to lick my face. Then I see Dave.

"It's good to see you working on weekends," he says playfully.

"Weekends? I practically live here," I retort.

"Untenured faculty are supposed to live here," he says with a chuckle. Then he makes his ridiculous whinny noise, and I realize he is joking.

Dave invites Frank and me over to his home for dinner. We meet his wife, Barbara, an artist who brings a calming energy to our conversations. When they learn that we are both animal lovers, they ask whether we would like to stay at their home and dog-sit when they travel. We become the official dog-sitters of Mike and Sophie. Spending time at their beautiful home in north Berkeley reminds me of how much I miss living on the farm.

We never broach the topic of our move away from New England. We lived an idyllic life on an expansive horse farm just miles from the Brown campus and a mere hour from his family and my aunt. Now, we live in a simple apartment on the south side of campus, an area riddled with noise and crime.

Frank lures me out of Etcheverry with the one enticement that he knows will work: horses. He has found a local barn that offers three-day eventing and lessons. It is an offer I can't refuse.

"I don't have time," I say, when Frank initially offers the riding lessons.

"I will pick you up at lunch hour. I'll drive you over ... just change in the car. I will have you back at Etcheverry before anyone knows you are gone. I think you can spare an hour for yourself each week. Somehow, you managed to ride every day at Brown. It didn't seem to slow you down." Something stirs within me, and I feel a life with horses beckoning me out of my academic world.

Frank picks me up at Etcheverry and takes me to my weekly lesson. It is the one time each week we spend peacefully together. The drive through Tilden Park to the horse farm in Martinez brings back fond memories of the backcountry road from Brown University to Hawkswood Farm. I feel dreadfully homesick. I can only imagine the emotions it stirs up in Frank. I am biding time until I can have some semblance of a life, and I hope my riding lessons will anchor me in the tumultuous seas of my academics.

"Why don't you ride too?" I ask Frank.

"We can't afford for both of us to ride. You need the outlet. I am happy just to be around the horses," he says.

I am relieved that he doesn't remind me we could have owned horses if I had chosen a different career path.

I am not entirely sure why we stay together. I don't have the sense that Frank is happy. He resents the hours I work, but he also knows that my success at Berkeley is our best path forward to prosperity. My father suggests to him that he return to school so he can find a better career path. Dad suggests engineering as a field of study. Of course, we have no disposable income at the time.

Later, after a glass of bourbon, Frank retorts to me, "Why does your father think engineering is the end-all? Look at our life. And I don't want to be a bloody engineer. Besides, I don't have one of the Pruitt big brains like your father, you, and your sister." He is reeling, and I acquiesce.

"What about taking some hands-on courses, like machining or welding?" I counter. "Maybe?"

In the coming months, Frank manages to find a machining certification program through the local community college. For this, I am grateful, as it relinquishes me from his constant questioning of why I have to work so much.

I am twenty-seven years old and too busy working to contemplate marital bliss. For me, joy is found in delivering good lectures, publishing high-quality research papers, and bringing in research funding. True happiness will be a successful academic life amidst a life with horses— much like I had at Brown, but without any inner demons of unworthiness and without a need for daily bulimic episodes and alcohol abuse.

During these early years as an assistant professor, alcohol and bulimia are my allies. There is never a day when I don't use alcohol. He is like a trusted friend: helping settle my nervous system, aiding my path to sleep, serving as a social lubricant, or easing a conversation in a room of esteemed colleagues at a conference. He helps quell my introverted nature and shyness. He also numbs my inner critic.

Bulimia takes a different role. She has been with me daily since I was eight years old. My relationship with her is built on secrecy. She is like a lover, offering guilty, temporary pleasure. She provides me with an outlet for emotions, and she helps me purge away hurtful words or thoughts, no matter their sources.

These two allies, alongside my need for work and achievement, are entrenching themselves into the neurological makeup of my body. They are no longer just tools. They are a part of me. I have no time to question their presence in my life. I presume they are helping me find my path of worthiness.

21

Papers, Proposals, and Presentations

Papers, proposals, and presentations consume me. I am working on proposals for the NSF CAREER and Office of Naval Research Young Investigator Awards. We have the orthopedics project with the Hospital for Special Surgery underway, and we need to get data in time to make the Orthopedic Research Society Abstract deadline. I'm also collecting polymer fatigue data for an upcoming presentation at Churchill College in England. I work seven days a week, and I'm usually in the lab or office well past midnight. Without data, I can't write papers or give presentations. Without funding, I can't sustain my research program or earn tenure. I am burning the candle at both ends.

I have recruited two graduate students and two undergraduates into my research laboratory. Including my student from Brown, I have three young women and two young men working for me. My gender ratio is an anomaly. Mechanical engineering is comprised of 20 percent women in the undergraduate and graduate population, and the percentage of women on the faculty is currently about 5 percent. Some things are slow to change.

When I arrive at Cambridge University in England for the Deformation, Yield and Fracture of Polymers (DYFP) conference, I feel an immediate sense of relief as I am greeted by familiar faces. I was only a third-year graduate student at the last meeting. Schmoozing is even more critical now that I am an assistant professor. I will eventually need a cohort of esteemed colleagues who can assess and hopefully champion my research when it comes time for tenure. I am one of only a few women in the polymer mechanics community. As was pointed out to me by my mentors, when one is in the minority at a conference, there is greater visibility, yet this distinguishability is often accompanied by more scrutiny. Good or bad, my presentation will be remembered—it must be stellar.

My talk entitled "Cyclic Near-Tip Stresses for Fatigue Cracks in Polymers" is well-received. With this burden behind me, I'm able to enjoy the conference. At the conference dinners, the liberal flow of wine enables me to engage confidently in scholarly conversations. Many researchers head to the bar after dinner, and I am quick to join them. I had never imagined that many of these esteemed scientists would drink the same way I have throughout much of my academic training. Perhaps my early assessment of drinking as an engineering skill is more widespread than I realized? With libations in hand, we discuss research well past midnight. Great ideas and collaborations are forged at the bar. I feel at home at this meeting, where I seem to have found a group of academic kindred spirits.

Immediately following my meeting at Cambridge University, I fly to Switzerland. Professor Henning Kausch has invited me to give a talk at his home institution, Ecole Polytechnique Federale de Lausanne (EPFL) in Lausanne.

My elegant hotel room has a beautiful view of Lake Geneva. Exhausted from my late nights at the Churchill conference, I hope that sleep does not elude me as I fret over the talk I need to give to the polymer group at EPFL the following day.

Henning Kausch greets me in the morning. "*Bonjour*, Lisa," he says in his soft-spoken manner. I feel awkward in his presence and don't dare speak any French. I can't recall whether the Swiss kiss the cheeks two times or three. My limited exposure to international cultures has me feeling like I don't belong here. Henning is a world-renowned macromolecular physicist and polymer scientist. I hear my inner voice knocking on the inside of my academic armor: *What have I accomplished in my life to justify being here?*

After breakfast, Henning and I head to the campus. I am riddled with anxiety. He introduces me to several of his colleagues who work in structural polymers. A chill sweeps through my body as I am introduced to give my seminar. My words seemingly flow out with ease because every word has been committed to memory. These talks are highly stressful for me—some people speak of "butterflies in the tummies"—mine is more like an adrenaline surge that might accompany "being chased by a lion." It will take me many more years of public speaking before my lion can subside into the realm of butterflies.

After my seminar, we head out to lunch with several faculty. I breathe a deep sigh of relief when I realize that wine will be served with lunch. The waiter has a generous pour as he fills my wine glass.

"*Salute!*" they say as we all hold up our glasses. Conversation flows, and my fear dissipates as the alcohol takes effect. My adrenaline levels retreat, and a sense of calm washes over me. The rest of the afternoon feels tranquil.

I am invited to dinner with Henning and his wife, Karin. They generously welcome me into their home surrounded by beautiful vineyards, and Henning shares the locally made wine with me. My fears melt away as I sip their white wine and pet their family cat.

On the following day, they take me for a beautiful drive into the Swiss Alps. Our timing coincides with a local festival, and cows wearing bells create a harmonious rhythm as they plod along their mountainous path. We dine at a mountain chalet, where we enjoy fondue, wine, and Swiss chocolate.

As I wrap up my trip, I am honored by a compliment I receive from Henning. "Lisa, I am impressed with your research. I am on the organizing committee for the International Conference on Fracture in Sydney. I plan to put forth your name as an invited speaker."

I am twenty-eight years old and nearly overwhelmed with excitement. Henning Kausch is another pivotal mentor in my life. Though there are decades between us, we will remain friendly colleagues throughout my academic career.

22

Engineering Is Elementary

I have been assigned an undergraduate class entitled Mechanical Behavior of Materials. I love the topic, but the required textbook written by Shigley has limited materials science content. I cannot align my passions with how the subject matter is expected to be taught. I am a materials scientist, and I feel a calling to speak in my own scientific prose. As a professor, I have the option to exercise academic freedom, though I need to be mindful of how much I push my boundaries before I am awarded tenure. If I alienate my senior colleagues, I could inadvertently disaffect their support for my tenure case.

I shift gears figuratively. I still cover the requisite design elements in the syllabus, but I change my focus into the realm of materials science. "Let's talk about how material structure affects its mechanical behavior," I say to my class.

I bring enthusiastic energy into the classroom with this new approach to my teaching. I pass around material models and test samples I brought with me from Brown. The students are ignited by this new framework where things move through their hands.

I couple basic materials science with mechanical behavior of materials lectures. The students are intrigued by structure-property relationships. Students seek me out in my office hours to discuss these concepts in greater detail. I have a line of students winding down the hall each afternoon. I am twenty-nine years old now, and my somewhat youthful age puts many of the students at ease. I savor this time with them, as it makes me feel useful and appreciated.

Although passionate about teaching, in the back of my mind, I ponder the advice I received about "research being the most important aspect of our tenure process." I push the thought away. The Berkeley students are incredibly bright and highly motivated. I cannot let them down. I will simply work harder to make sure that my research remains at the forefront of my field of expertise.

Reviewing my lecture on defects and how they can be used to strengthen or weaken a material, I decide that I am a complex alloy, using bulimia, alcohol, and work as her strengthening mechanisms. Once I am tenured, I imagine that my flaws will be annihilated, yet flaws do not simply dissolve into their microstructures unless they undergo elaborate heat treatment and recrystallization schemes. Engineering materials that have flaws are prone to failure under critical values of stress. I don't yet see that my flaws—perceived unworthiness, bulimia, alcohol abuse, and work addiction—will ultimately weaken my academic armor.

I am serving on a PhD qualifying exam committee for a student enrolled in my graduate class on fracture mechanics. The external member is a geology professor by the name of Ian Carmichael; he is also the director of the Lawrence Hall of Science (LHS), a public science center in Berkeley.

I have brought various hands-on demonstratives to the oral exam to pose my questions to the student. After the candidate successfully completes the exam, I pack up my things to leave.

"Lisa, would you consider coming up to LHS to meet with me and one of my team members at the children's museum?" asks Ian. "Perhaps there is a way that you can bring some of your engineering education prowess to the Hall?"

I meet with Ian and his colleague, Barbara Ando, at LHS. We discuss possibilities for using the final project in my undergraduate course as an opportunity to create interactive exhibits for kindergarten to eighth-grade outreach education on their main floor. They offer to provide funding and materials for the student projects.

This resonates deeply with me. I think back to my personal struggles in my own primary education—if I had not had my dad to teach me in a way in which I could learn, then I would not be here today as an assistant professor. Outreach is a way I can give back.

In collaboration with LHS, I work toward the creation of a number of exhibits. My first outreach teaching event utilizes my undergraduate class, Mechanical Behavior of Engineering Materials. The students create an interactive exhibit entitled "The Way Things Break" that targets K–8 learners. The undergraduate student teams come up with amazing projects that engage children to learn about brittle and ductile behavior, stress concentrations, and fatigue and fracture. The exhibit is a huge success.

I pioneer an alliance with LHS in which we leverage my courses to bring engineering into the children's museum as well as local schools. We successfully implement a series of exhibits associated with my pedagogy: Fantastic Plastic, The Human Body Shop, The Bionic Bear, Body by Design, How Things Break, and Think Like an Engineer.

My PhD students are instrumental in bringing experiential learning into the classroom. We will eventually present educational outcomes at the annual conferences of the American Society of Engineering Education and receive a number of awards from this prestigious society. Such recognition validates my educational outreach activities, but I'm not sure it strengthens my path toward tenure.

I have received a number of stern warnings from some of my senior colleagues who think my outreach activities could put my tenure case at risk. This unsettles me. I ask Dave about this at our next mentor meeting.

"How are your teaching evaluations?" Dave asks, sipping his cappuccino.

"My course evaluations are always high for both teaching effectiveness and course worth."

"It's people like you who make my teaching look bad," Dave chuckles. "Have these activities hindered your research?"

"No. The NSF CAREER Award seeks projects that merge teaching, research, and outreach."

"Have you created any new courses? They will look for that when you go up for tenure," he adds.

"I have created a graduate course on polymer engineering and an undergraduate course on structural aspects of biomaterials. I'm also teaching three of our required courses, one at undergrad level and two doctoral courses," I say with pride.

"Oh. Maybe you're spending too much time on teaching. Don't forget that tenure rides on research."

Panic runs through me as I process my conversation with Dave. I work tirelessly to balance my efforts across the academic pillars of research, teaching, and service. I can't imagine my life if I am denied tenure. My inner sense of unworthiness would win the battle. I can't fail. I have to have a successful case.

I have no sense of how to live a balanced life. Dave somehow seems to live a cheerful life. I naïvely believe this joy must come after tenure. After all, Subra also seemed joyous in his work as an academic. *Am I missing something? Will I be worthy and happy after tenure?*

I buckle down and work harder. My commitment to academia places an immense burden on my marriage, but I'm too busy to reflect on this compromise.

23

When the Teacher Is Ready, the Student Appears

Each of my doctoral students is a gift to me, stretching my boundaries into new realms of research and expanding my professional horizons. I am incredibly fortunate to have a cohort of exceptional students in my lab. They serve as extraordinary teaching assistants, and we work hard together on the research needed for publishing in archival journals. I understand now why Subra had said that I would have the best students at Berkeley, enabling me to do my best work. My students are the anchors in my otherwise tumultuous sea of life—they are my academic family.

One of the most influential students in my early academic life is Marni Goldman. In our email correspondence, Marni tells me she is a PhD student in the Materials Science Department. She has read a number of my research papers and is interested in working in my lab. Marni sends me her resume, and I am floored by her accomplishments. She was valedictorian of her high school and then went on to earn degrees in both psychology and materials science at the University of Pennsylvania. Currently the president of the student chapter of the Materials Research Society at Berkeley, she has already completed her master's. I am enthusiastic about having her join our research lab. We agree to meet in my office.

At the appointed time, I hear a loud knock on my door.

"Come in," I say.

This is met with louder knocking. I open the door and look downward—Marni is in a motorized wheelchair. I quickly scan my brain to see if I can recall this important fact. I do not. I am captivated by her mischievous smile. *Perhaps this is her test of me?* Immediately, my mind kicks into high gear. I remember from our correspondence that Marni specifically wants to do experimental work.

We spend the next hour discussing her research interests. Marni would like to incorporate transmission electron microscopy into her PhD work. She is also interested in studying the oxidation problem in ultra-high molecular weight polyethylene (UHMWPE), using Fourier transform infrared spectroscopy, small-angle X-ray diffraction, and differential scanning calorimetry. I share with her that I don't own this type of equipment. Marni reassures me that we can use the facilities at the National Labs. Now I am questioning whether I am smart enough to be her mentor.

We discuss her physical limitations, and she informs me she was born with a severe form of muscular dystrophy. The doctors hadn't expected her to live beyond the age of two. She has been a quadriplegic since childhood. I try to process her life journey. She has me in awe—my life challenges pale in comparison to hers.

We ultimately decide to assemble a team of undergraduates who she can directly mentor and who can serve as her hands for many of the experiments. Marni changes the trajectory of my research lab. From this point, there is hardly a time when we don't have a team of undergraduates in our laboratory mentored by our doctoral students.

Marni and I are nearly the same age—I am almost thirty, and she is just a bit younger, yet she is wise beyond her years. We have a resonance with each other. *Perhaps her physical challenges mirror the mental ones I face? Is she somehow showing me that I am capable without my addictive crutches?* I push my thoughts away. I have no time for self-analysis. It will be many more years before I can reflect on the abuse I subject my body to through work, food, and alcohol. For now, I have only one goal: tenure.

Marni pushes me to expand my research platform deeply into the heart of materials science. Soon our research takes on the legs of small-angle X-ray scattering, spectroscopy, and calorimetry. She is meticulous in her technical writing, and in a short time, we have accepted abstracts at the Orthopedic Research Society, the Materials Research Society, and the Society for Biomaterials. *Who is mentoring whom?* Her brilliance triggers my inner flaw of unworthiness: *Am I smart enough to mentor a woman like Marni? Do I even belong here?* I stuff down these debilitating thoughts and reach deep into my coping toolbox.

Marni accompanies me to the technical conferences, along with her parents, Micky and Michael. They serve as her caregivers, and we become fast friends. Marni is clearly on a mission. Foremost, we need collaborators to help deconvolute the X-ray data. I remain dreadfully introverted and still lack my voice in new venues without the social lubrication of alcohol. On the other hand, Marni is a force to be reckoned with. I follow behind, trying to keep up with her motorized wheelchair.

I watch Marni work her magic. She quickly identifies and targets potential collaborators. I soon find myself introduced to Dr. Anuj Bellare, a young polymer materials scientist with expertise in small and ultra-small

X-ray scattering. Marni quickly forges a long-term collaboration and friendship between us.

Marni is like having an academic fairy godmother, as she seems to sprinkle magic collaborative dust everywhere she goes. Soon my lab is overflowing with industry grants. Many high-level archival publications follow in short order due to her ferocity and attention to detail. I can barely keep up with it all.

I am honored to have Marni in my research lab. She is committed to having more women and disadvantaged students in engineering, and we work together on this platform. As my research team expands, I find that women make up more than half of my lab. My colleagues begin to joke that they can't get any women students in their labs because they are all working with me.

In the course of Marni's doctoral studies, she and I become good friends. Yet, I keep my inner struggles hidden from her as best I can. She has an intuitive sense about her, though, and quickly observes that I work far too many hours, drink far too much caffeine, and get far too little sleep. I think my issues with food and alcohol may be on her radar, but she never calls me out on them directly.

Marni entices me to the Oakland Zoo to see the new baby elephant named Kijana. We watch the playful antics of this orphaned creature, living on the generosity of volunteers who care for him round the clock. It is unlikely that he will survive, but I am reminded by Marni that she, too, beat the odds. We sit quietly together and watch the elephants. I feel that she is about to offer me life advice, transforming into my mentor, friend, mother, and grandmother all combined.

"Lisa, you work too much. You need to take better care of yourself," she says.

"How can I get tenure if I don't work long hours?"

She rolls her eyes. "You can't get tenured if you're dead."

I assure her that I will work on improving my life balance. *After tenure.*

24

The Academic Freight Train

I am four years into my assistant professorship. My "mid-career" review of research, teaching, and service went well the previous year, and my chairman has now recommended that I go up for tenure early. I am merely thirty-one years old when my tenure case is compiled. I am both thrilled and terrified.

I call Subra to share this news with him and to get his advice. Currently the chairman of Materials Science at MIT, he's highly knowledgeable about the requisite elements of a successful tenure package, especially an accelerated case like mine. He, too, was tenured early.

"An acceleration only amplifies the scrutiny of a tenure case," Subra notes. He advises me to continue giving high-level talks at international meetings. He emphasizes the importance of publishing as many high-quality, peer-reviewed journal papers as possible before my case is submitted.

I receive and accept invitations to speak at the International Conference of Fracture in Sydney and the International Meeting on Deformation, Yield and Fracture of Polymers in Cambridge. The meetings are a world apart, yet my talks are scheduled within a day of each other. I muster up all the energy I can find to pull off the Herculean feat of delivering both talks.

Frank is delighted that I am coming up for tenure early. He has already hinted about moving back to New England. He has made sure horses remain a mainstay in our lives. For that, I am immensely grateful. He even helped me find a horse to ride a few minutes from the condominium we purchased in the Oakland Hills through the assistance of a university loan. Horses provide me with a positive form of energy that enables all of my academic cogs to keep moving. I imagine that Frank thinks if I stay connected to horses, then it better assures the trajectory back east.

I am only four years out of my PhD when I compile my case for tenure. In his friendly manner, Dave Dornfeld reminds me that my "self-critical evaluation" is, in fact, not meant to be "too critical." My self-assessment includes a portfolio of my research, teaching, mentoring, and service. I include copies of all my journal papers and conference papers, as well as a list of respected academics in my field who can assess the merits of my research. My chairman, David Bogy, is confident about my case. Once the package is submitted, I try not to think about it. I distract myself with more work.

Marni sternly warns me that I cannot continue at this pace. I assure her that the crazy hours I am working are just temporary.

"I will ease up and focus on life balance when my tenure case goes through."

"I am not sure I believe you. I will be keeping tabs on you," she threatens.

Marni becomes my first PhD student to graduate. She then relocates to Stanford, where she will become the director of their STEM outreach program. Though I will miss her daily presence, I will be relieved that she doesn't see my inability to relinquish my work addiction after tenure. As I continue on my trajectory in the coming years, I will minimize in-person get-togethers with her so I can avoid her direct scrutiny.

During this time frame when my tenure case is under review, I am introduced to Dr. Michael Ries, a surgeon joining the Orthopedics Department at the University of California at San Francisco (UCSF). A preeminent specialist in total joint replacement surgery, he studied materials engineering at MIT before going to medical school.

We immediately find ourselves in the landscape of structure-property relationships of UHMWPE and their effect on the mechanical performance of this polymer in hip and knee replacement. Mike becomes a weekly fixture in our lab meeting, bringing us challenging clinical problems as we offer engineering wisdom. Mike and I collaborate on clinical case studies, offering insight into failure analysis of orthopedic devices. With our combined resources, we are able to perform synergistic studies that put us at the forefront of orthopedic biomaterials research.

At this same juncture, I am also introduced to scientists and surgeons in the vascular group at UCSF. In collaboration with some of the fluid mechanics faculty in the department, we work toward a successful NIH-funded project that seeks to investigate the vulnerability of atherosclerotic plaques. This becomes a mechanism for me to mentor several PhD students in cardiovascular tissue mechanics.

In parallel to these activities, I give fundraising talks for the College of Engineering. We are working toward the creation of a Bioengineering Department and a new building on the campus. Along with a number of mechanical engineering colleagues, I will serve as part of the initial core faculty to develop the Department of Bioengineering at Berkeley.

I am continuously sought after for research collaborations and talks, and I have no ability to politely say "no." I just keep working as I await the decision regarding tenure. I feel some inner prompting that this academic recognition is my path to worthiness.

After completing his machining training, Frank has picked up additional courses, enabling him to find more lucrative work. However, he is only biding time until we move three thousand miles east.

I feel like my head is about to implode. I don't know that I have ever felt this anxious or stressed in my life. My bulimic episodes are more frequent as I try to offload my stress levels. Nights are heavy with my somber alcoholic liquids as I aim to mitigate the anxiousness soaring through my neurological system.

I contemplate that how I feel is what academics must mean when they speak of the "stress of getting tenure." At this juncture, I would be devastated to not get tenure—it would feel like the ultimate failure.

I am greatly relieved when my chairman comes to my office to share the news of my tenure. He provides me with the official letter confirming my tenure and promotion to associate professor. "Congratulations! This is well-deserved. You may be the first in our department to be put up for tenure after only four years past their PhD," he remarks. I am beyond words, ecstatic, and deeply relieved.

This is my greatest life accomplishment to date, yet I still don't feel wholly worthy. I thought worthiness would wash over me and take away my inner darkness, yet it's still lurking within. *Perhaps my sense of worthiness hedges on full professorship?* I am sure I can sustain this workload a little longer. It will be many more years before I can see the insanity of it: the highly addictive aspect of seeking academic accomplishments to achieve worthiness and the inability to get off the academic freight train before it steamrolls over a cliff.

After I receive tenure, Frank and I go out for a celebration dinner. I am giddy with joy until he brings up the inevitable question.

"When are we moving back to the East Coast?" he asks.

"Everything is going so well here at Berkeley. I will likely come up for full professor in just a few years. Can't we stay a few more years? I am sure I can secure a far more lucrative faculty position back east with that level of credential."

The previous year, Frank and I purchased a one-bedroom condo with a university loan, within biking distance to the campus and near an equestrian center. For the past year, I have been riding a little Arabian named Port Boss. He is suited for trails but not eventing. In the back of my mind, I have etched a dream horse with whom I can return to three-day eventing, as I had done in graduate school. I promised myself that this would be my gift after earning tenure. It's time to unleash the new scheme that's been brewing to entice my husband to stay a little longer on the West Coast.

"What if we sell our condominium and buy land to build a ranch? Our condo is worth a lot more than we paid for it. We can get horses and start a life like the one we had at Hawkswood Farm," I suggest.

Frank's jaw drops. I see the disappointment welling up in his eyes. He says nothing but downs his drink quickly. I do the same.

This is not what I had promised him when we had relocated from Brown to Berkeley. *Will he agree to my idea?* It could offer a way to stay at Berkeley and blend my love of engineering research with the need to have horses back in my life.

25

Twin Eagles Ranch

The real estate values in the Bay Area have skyrocketed, and we stand to make a healthy profit on our condo. I am thirty-two years old when we find a real estate agent who specializes in horse properties. It soon becomes crystal clear that any land we can afford is over an hour's commute to Berkeley. We look at several overpriced parcels of land on the outskirts of the Bay Area. Nothing resonates. Frank is growing weary and frustrated with my antics.

"Why don't you just take a job somewhere else?" he asks.

"There are no suitable positions open right now."

In truth, I haven't looked beyond any openings that might exist at Brown. I don't think they would hire me back until I have spent ten years out in the academic circle establishing myself—at least that's what I was told at the time I originally was interested in applying for Subra's post when he relocated to MIT.

"I think I found something that will be perfect," exclaims our agent. We follow her in our Jeep up Mines Road in Livermore. It's a long, mountainous road with gut-wrenching switchbacks that seemingly go on forever. We finally arrive at a gated dirt road. Our agent gets out and swings open a rusty gate for us.

"Two more gates," she says with a smile.

Is she kidding? Then we see it in all its glory: a pristine forty-acre parcel of ranch land. Located on the backside of Mount Hamilton, the only access is through the series of gates on an unmarked dirt road. I see rolling hills dotted with oak trees. My imagination runs wild. I see horses and pastures—I see freedom.

"This is it!" we say in unison. Yet, our visions are, in fact, quite different. I imagine building an eventing facility like Hawkswood Farm. Frank sees potential for a simpler life. Our thoughts are interrupted by the cry of two eagles soaring above us against the deep-blue sky. We both look up. "That seems like an omen," I say. "What about Twin Eagles Ranch?" asks Frank. The name of our ranch is manifested.

The parcel is homesteaded property that carries a greatly reduced tax burden if we use it for ranch purposes. While we profit from the sale of our condo, we are nearly depleted of cash, as we must put the majority of our funds into securing a land loan and paying a debt I had not known about prior to financing the ranch.

"No, there must be some mistake," I said when the loan officer disclosed the amount. There was no mistake. Frank had taken a loan without my knowledge. I was seething.

I have no sense of the amount of money it will take to develop this property. Frank has extensive surveying experience and has a better sense of what we are getting ourselves into than I do.

Frank and I are of two distinct minds about the ranch, yet we never discuss it. He is thinking about the cost of grading sites, putting in drainage and water lines, septic and leach fields, power, and a house. Our ranch has no electricity, but it does have a well for water. We hire a local man who starts grading sites for us. Frank focuses on the site for a home.

I am only thinking about fencing, pastures, barns, the arena, trails, and jumps. At the top of my list is fencing in a set of pastures, creating an arena with good footing for horses, and procuring a barn with attached paddocks. My mom comes from a long line of farming, and my one intuitive belief is that animals come first. This is ironic, as I don't even own a horse yet, but I know he is out there somewhere—I just have to find him.

It quickly becomes clear that we can't afford to bring power lines into the property, nor can we afford to build a traditional home. We are burning through our cash reserves fast. My parents generously offer us some funds to get started on the ranch. My sister and her future husband, Matt, offer to help us with fencing. Beth is now working on her PhD in mechanical engineering at Stanford. Though we have never been close, I am grateful for their help. In the coming years, Beth, too, will enter into the realm of the professoriate. I still carry my childhood insecurities around her—I am convinced she is the real deal while I am still an impostor.

I take on consulting work so we have funds for horses and everything that goes with them—tack, feed, and a horse trailer. We create an engineering consulting business, and Frank manages the funds I bring in. He now sees that I have immense earning potential, and suddenly, my workaholic tendencies don't seem so problematic.

Frank and I find a used trailer home and have it trucked onto the property. We set up solar panels as our source of electricity, with a backup generator. We pump water from the well to a holding tank and then gravity feed it to the trailer. We are living like pioneer people. Frank seems in his element living out here in the simplicity of wilderness. I am just biding time until I have an eventing facility. I am imagining a profitable horse business.

We decide to have a small "ranch party" and invite a few of my engineering colleagues who are now mutual friends of ours. I hear them laugh after emerging from their cars—it has taken them almost two hours from their homes in Berkeley. Clearly, they think I have lost my mind. It will be a ninety-minute commute to campus if I leave before traffic starts. Dave jokes that perhaps the process of tenure has made me lose my sanity. I can't yet see the insanity of it all.

After my promotion, I bolstered my riding. For the past year, I have been taking weekly jumping and dressage lessons with a trainer in Livermore, with the goal of finding a three-day event horse. My trainer knows I now have a ranch and presents an opportunity to adopt a "free" ranch horse. Blaze is a beautiful foundation quarter horse, and we quickly adopt him into our lives.

"Now, we don't have to buy a horse," Frank comments.

"Blaze is a ranch horse; he is not suited to do three-day eventing," I say with a grimace.

"Why can't you just ride this horse on the local trails around our ranch?"

"I want to return to eventing. I need a horse and an arena," I plea.

"Do you have any idea how much it will cost to put in an arena on this property? Can't we do that when we move back east?" he taunts.

"It may be years before I am promoted to full professor. I want to event now, while I am young and athletic," I say.

"Will you really ever be willing to leave Berkeley? We should have relocated after you were tenured, like you promised. Better yet, we never should have come to California. You think the world revolves around you," he yells as I walk away.

My inner voice is triggered with my mounting anxiety. I stifle my thoughts, convinced I can solve my problems if I work harder and bring in more consulting funds. The friction between us is just beginning to reveal the true depths of our marital problems. We want very different things. He wants a simple life. I want it all. Unbeknownst to my husband, I have no intention of relinquishing the quest for my dream horse.

26

Unexpected Beauty

I have big dreams. Memories of my life at Brown and living at Hawkswood are burnished in my brain. I am convinced I can replicate that life on the West Coast and envision the creation of an eventing facility on our forty-acre ranch. I want to pick up the realm of a three-day eventing competition where I left off riding Nick during graduate school. I have managed to put away some cash—Frank does not know about it. He manages all of our finances, and he is not supporting my endeavor to buy an eventing horse.

I tell my trainer, Brenda, what I am looking for so she can help me with my pursuit. "I definitely don't want an inexperienced youngster or a thoroughbred who has raced," I add.

"Lisa, you don't have a hundred thousand dollars for a dream horse; let's focus on what we can find within your budget," she advises.

Brenda tells me she has a friend with a horse who might be perfect for me. We drive together to a remote ranch. We walk up a dirt road to the gate of a rocky pasture, where I see a tall woman dressed in her riding britches, tall boots, and an equestrian jacket. She looks like one of those women who can stay clean around horses. I have never been of that breed—once near the equine sort, I am a magnet for dirt, hay, and fur.

"Hi, Rhonda, this is Lisa," says Brenda.

"Brenda told me what you are looking for. I think JJ will be perfect for you."

I see a herd of horses on the hillside. *Which one is JJ?* Rhonda points to the emaciated thoroughbred with his half-eaten tail. *She must be joking.*

"JJ is four years old and a year off the racetrack. His registered name is JJ Luck. His sire is Geneo JJ from the Go-Man-Go line. His mother is Windy's Luck from the Seabiscuit line," she says, clearly motivating her asking price.

I don't want some neglected thoroughbred who didn't make it on the racetrack. My dream horse will have the athletic ability to excel in dressage, show jumping, and cross-country. JJ is most definitely not my dream horse!

"Let's try him," Brenda suggests. I glare at her. We take JJ to the round pen. I follow behind gloomily. *This horse can't possibly be the equine companion I seek.*

We set JJ free in the round pen. He moves out with surprising grace, his feet floating in the two-beat rhythm of the trot. He is sheer elegance. His chestnut coat starts to glow. I notice the spark in his eye as his charm penetrates the air.

Brenda pleads with me to try him, and I hoist myself into the saddle. JJ is quite tall, measuring seventeen hands, or five feet eight inches, from the ground to his shoulders (withers).

JJ has a huge trot and nearly unseats me. His canter is balanced to the left, but his right lead is clumsy and uneven. Even more unnerving, he continuously throws his head up and nearly clocks me in the face. Brenda yells out, "We can fix that!"

I thank Rhonda after my ride and give JJ a few horse cookies from my pocket. He gently takes them from my hand. I can't recall a horse with such a delicate touch. JJ looks at me with his large, knowing eyes. My heart melts, but my brain reminds me that I seek a seasoned horse for competition, like Hawkswood's Bad Boy Nick. My trainer asks if I want to take JJ on trial. My brain overrides my heart.

"No. Not him." We leave the ranch and drive home in silence.

Yet, I can't shake this bright chestnut thoroughbred from my thoughts. JJ has cast his spell on me. He manifests himself into my dreams, where I begin to see his unexpected beauty hiding underneath his external disguise. I sheepishly make the call to my trainer.

"Brenda, can you ask Rhonda if I can take JJ on trial for two weeks?" I ask. I sense a smirk on the other end of the phone.

JJ arrives at the facility where I board Blaze. I haven't told Frank about my new acquisition. I'll see where things are in two weeks—I only need to tell him if I opt to keep JJ. For now, it is best to keep the arguments at bay.

Within the first few days of my "trial," JJ has jumped me out of the tack or bucked me off a number of times. This horse can jump! The problem is that JJ jumps everything as though it's five feet tall. It is nearly impossible for me to stay with him when he decides to throw in an exuberant buck on the other side of a jump. My brain tells me to send him back, but something inside me connects to this horse with his exquisite, intelligent, and all-knowing eyes. I've never known anyone—human or animal—who could look into me the way he does.

Just trying to manage my life brings immense stress. I am teaching a full course load, overseeing a large research group with two distinct themes: orthopedic biomaterials and cardiovascular tissue mechanics. I am also serving as an engineering consultant and an expert in a patent infringement case—all to support my equine pursuits. I can't remember the last time I've slept more than four hours. Addicted to sugar and caffeine, I constantly seek external energy to handle my workload.

I'm so accustomed to hiding my anxiety and stress behind my academic façade it never occurs to me that JJ might sense my incongruencies. He always mirrors back to me what I am feeling on the inside. I can't seem to hide from him—when I am anxious, he is anxious. When I am frustrated, he is frustrated. It is as though he has X-ray vision into the part of me that lives beneath my academic armor: the little girl who wants to be worthy and loved. I feel a visceral connection to this horse. I know he is meant to be with me.

I successfully negotiate to buy him at half the asking price. JJ is officially mine, or I am officially his—I am not sure who owns whom.

My acquisition is not well-received by Frank. He is not at all impressed with my negotiating prowess, nor is he enamored of this horse.

"What are you thinking? Look at this emaciated horse. Are you an idiot? You have a perfectly good horse. Ride Blaze. Send this one back!" he shouts.

"No, I'm keeping him. I bought him with my money." *This is war.*

"Your money? I think you mean *our* money. We're married. All of our funds are pooled together. Do you understand?" he says venomously. Frank is furious. I am beyond furious. A rift grows between us that will never be healed.

I have no words to explain the spell this horse has cast on me. The seeds are sown, and unbeknownst to me, I have stepped onto a new path. My life will never be the same.

27

Journey to the Cowboy

Pure joy fills my body as we gallop over a large log jump. Sometimes it feels like JJ has wings. We are schooling cross-country jumps at the horse park in Woodside as we prepare for an upcoming jumping clinic. I am thirty-four years old, and I am completely smitten with this horse. He has ignited a love in me that I did not know was possible.

Whether jumping is natural for horses or not has been the subject of spirited debate. They offer natural dressage movements as they prance to impress each other in their herds, yet horses seldom jump obstacles in the wild. Most avid show-jumpers argue that their horses love to jump. I, too, would argue that JJ loves to jump.

I keep the horses boarded with my trainer, ideally located halfway between our ranch and the university. I get up at 4:00 a.m. and put in a full day, making time to ride on the way to campus or on the way back to the ranch.

I ride JJ six days a week, and I manage to ride Blaze three days a week. Frank has found a technical sales position in Castro Valley and is able to bring in more income. We take the horses out together for trail rides on weekends. Even with the horses, we find ourselves bristling against each other. Frank is a leisure rider, and I am competitive. I like to be precise with how I ride and handle the horses.

"Look at Blaze and me; we are counter-cantering," Frank gleefully says as we move out on the trail.

"You are bouncing all over the place, and since we are tracking right, you should be on the right lead. You are on the left," I say, cringing as I watch.

"Why does everything have to be a competition with you?" Frank scoffs.

We finish the rest of our ride in silence: a mirror to our marriage.

My case for full professor is imminent, and within the coming year, I plan to have the necessary elements—arena, barn, and pastures—ready to bring JJ and Blaze home to Twin Eagles Ranch.

I envision a highly competitive path with my limber steed, but these dreams are clouded by a dangerous head-throwing habit. I have never experienced a horse who could use his head like a weapon. The trainers have resorted to working him in draw reins or a running-martingale, yet he still manages to sling his head back when he is frustrated. I grow increasingly concerned that he is going to sling his head into my face. My fear is soon to be realized.

JJ and I are wrapping up our schooling session, having jumped nearly all of the training-level jumps at the horse park. All that remains is the water jump. JJ has never jumped into water. My jumping trainer, Anita, rides Blaze into the water so JJ will see that it is safe. I bring him around at the canter and feel his adrenaline surge beneath me. JJ launches early, and we land well into the water. I am thrilled that he jumped in and equally pleased that I have stayed on him.

I lean over to offer JJ a big pat on his neck, but in that same instant, he throws his head back. His skull smashes my face at full force, and I hear a loud crack. I slump over his neck, blood pouring from my nose and lips. I stare down at the water, watching the red swirls beneath me.

"Oh my god, Lisa! Are you okay?" yells Anita. Blaze whinnies.

JJ stands stock still. He offers a slow whinny back to Blaze, as though he were apologizing. We slowly make our way to the exit point by Blaze. I am still in the saddle and sit up slowly.

"Should I call an ambulance?" Anita asks.

"I'm okay. I think I just broke my nose," I say with false confidence. I hope I haven't fractured my skull. I have too much work to do when I get home.

I don't dare get off JJ until we are back at the trailer, fearing I might pass out. We make our way back to my horse trailer and load the horses. My shirt soaked in blood, I grab a disposable ice pack from my emergency kit and keep it compressed to my face as Anita drives us back to the boarding facility in Livermore.

Once we arrive, we unload the horses and return them to their pasture. JJ doesn't want to leave the gate—he knows I am injured and that he is the cause. I feel his remorse.

I keep ice on my face once I return home and start grading projects for my medical device course—ironically, I'm lecturing on facial implants in the coming week. I don't dare look in the mirror.

Frank knows something is drastically wrong when he sees me and insists we go to the hospital. I assure him that I am fine. Then I stand up and collapse from the pain. I grudgingly agree to go to the emergency room.

X-rays reveal that I have ruptured my eye socket and pulverized the cartilage in my nose. I decline the surgical insertion of a titanium mesh under my eye and instead agree to wear a faceguard while the bone heals.

I am sent to a specialist to have my nose surgically reshaped into some semblance of normalcy.

I can't ride until my face is healed. I relinquish JJ to a team of trainers, but he is being inordinately stubborn, elusive, difficult to catch in the field, and unruly under saddle. Eventually, they refuse to work with him.

"You need to sell him or take him to a cowboy," Brenda advises.

I know in my heart that the former is not an option.

I actively seek out a cowboy who can "cure" my problem horse. A woman at the boarding facility recommends Charles Wilhelm, well-known for problem-solving behavioral issues with horses. His ranch is in Castro Valley, essentially halfway between my ranch and Berkeley.

I trailer JJ over to Charles, expecting that he will "fix" my "problem horse." He laughs. Charles has a motto at his ranch: "The horse is always perfect."

"It's never, ever the horse's fault," he states.

I don't fully grasp what he means by this. Perhaps it's never the horse's fault unless he's a high-strung thoroughbred who breaks his owner's face?

Charles suggests that we take JJ into the round pen and do some flag work. JJ has no tack on, and Charles simply holds a stick with a small flag at its end. By JJ's response, one might think Charles is lighting firecrackers under his feet. The instant Charles waves the flag, my thoroughbred is off to the races, galloping full throttle in the round pen. Charles calmly makes a slight move. He switches the flag to the other hand, and JJ is now galloping in the other direction. Within moments, Charles has brought him from gallop to canter and finally to trot. With each iteration, the transition gets smoother. All the while, Charles speaks words of wisdom to me. He tells me what he is doing and why, yet I can't process what is being said. I just want the head-throwing problem solved, and it's not clear to me how any of this round pen work will solve that.

At the end of the session, Charles walks over to me.

"JJ is intelligent and athletic, but he is also highly spirited and emotional. This will take some time," Charles says.

I nod. At some level, I feel like Charles is describing me.

"Why don't you consider my apprenticeship program this coming summer? You can bring JJ along. I'll work with him and teach you my ground school methods. You will work with a number of horses using natural horsemanship techniques. These skills will help you with JJ," he adds.

"But I just want to fix the head-throwing problem," I reply in full ignorance.

"Lisa, there are no problems, just learning opportunities."

"Okay. I will devote time to this apprenticeship over the summer when I am not teaching," I say with excitement. My research programs run year-round, yet I am confident that I can make it work.

"It's a deal." Charles tips his cowboy hat and saunters off to the next "perfect horse."

I wait until Frank has finished his dinner and his tall glass of bourbon, hoping the drink has softened his mood. I gently spring the news that I will be boarding JJ with a cowboy this summer and working part-time as his apprentice.

"How are you possibly going to manage that? You already work eighty-hour weeks. Now you're going to work with a cowboy too? Your "bargain" horse is getting expensive. Maybe it's better if you just sell him," Frank says, his anger building.

"I'll just leave earlier in the day. Charles's ranch is halfway to Berkeley, and it's just a few minutes from Blaze. I can stay down there one or two nights a week to break up the commute. I have my summer salary. I will use those funds."

"Your summer salary is already allocated to building a barn and fencing in the pastures. You have no sense of how much money you're spending on creating this *dream* of yours!" Frank shouts.

"Then I'll pick up more consulting work!" I shout back. I down my own large glass of bourbon, not willing to take no for an answer.

"For a woman with a huge brain, you can be an absolute idiot!" Frank yells as he heads out the door, slamming it behind him.

I pour myself another tall glass of bourbon and wash the words away. *True marital bliss.*

As an apprentice for Charles, I learn how to work horses on a cowboy halter, a rope halter with an attached twelve-foot lead rope. I get light with my hands as I work the horse—much like a good dog handler working their canine companion on a loose leash. My timing and balance on the ground improve as I work various horses in the round pen. With a slight rotation of my shoulder, I learn to ask the horses to change direction. I absorb this knowledge viscerally. When I am with the horses, I am in flow, just as I am when I step into my engineering classrooms.

At the completion of the summer, I am feeling good about my ground skills with horses. JJ has softened significantly, although he still throws his head when he's anxious. I return him back to the boarding facility, where he will live with Blaze until the barn is complete. The pastures are nearly fenced.

I have burned through an enormous amount of money, trying to get the ranch ready for the horses to come home. It feels endless. My parents, as well as Beth and Matt, have helped us with various projects, trying to move us in the right direction. When my family is around, Frank is loving and supportive about my career and the ranch, but when we are alone, he is angry and bitter. I am guilty of the same. Our "happy marriage" is merely a façade: one of many façades for me.

It's a crisp autumn morning. JJ is back with Blaze and back in training in Livermore. We have a number of shows scheduled for the coming months.

"Let's go take the horses out for a trail ride and get them some exercise," I suggest, hoping it will ease the tension between us.

We make our way down the mountain road to the back of the boarding facility. Our horses have the pasture on the eastern end of the property, abutting the Livermore airstrip. We pull up to the gate. Something is amiss—Blaze seems anxious. He offers a high-pitch call, not his usual soft nicker. He wants us to see something.

I step through the gate. JJ stands solemnly with his hind leg cocked, haunches drooping, clearly in distress. He doesn't move or nicker as I walk up to him. Something is very wrong. He looks at me with his large fluid eyes. As I gently traverse my hands across his spine, I get to the point where his pelvis drops. JJ cowers in pain. I don't understand—there is no external wound. He was perfectly sound yesterday.

One of the ranch hands drives up and informs us they chased off people who were shooting BB guns at the ranch the previous night. JJ was crazed and running at full tilt when they arrived at the scene. *Maybe JJ flipped or fell somehow in the chase? Who would think it's fun to shoot at these magnificent creatures? Why didn't anyone call us?* Later, we learn that they never saw JJ get injured—they thought they had safely chased off the offenders.

I have to get JJ to a vet, but he won't move. I call Charles. He suggests that we give him something for pain and says he will come help us load JJ into the trailer so we can take him to the equine hospital.

Frank and I drive in silence—we are probably praying for vastly different outcomes. I want a path of full recovery, while Frank likely wants a quick ending to prevent long-term suffering. Metaphorically, this applies to both our personal and equine worlds.

When we arrive at the equestrian hospital, the veterinarian meets us. He administers a sedative then takes a battery of X-ray and ultrasound images. I learn that JJ has fractured his spinal process. He must have taken a fall in the midst of the BB gun chase. The vet gives me the grim prognosis.

"JJ will likely never be sound again. You might consider euthanasia."

"No, ending JJ's life is not an option," I insist.

Frank sees my eyes and knows not to question.

Instead, we agree to a pain management plan and an early retirement lived out in pasture. It's time to unveil Twin Eagles Ranch to our horses.

Within the coming week, we take the leap of faith to bring the horses home to the ranch. I am equally excited and fearful. We don't have the barn completed, but the pastures are fenced. More importantly, I don't have a set of ranch hands to help me. I will be feeding the horses at 4:00 a.m. before going to work. I will need to rely on Frank or a neighbor to feed the horses in the early evening. *Why haven't I thought through the details of keeping horses on the ranch while also working at Berkeley? Do I ever think through the details?* I am more of a visionary, "big picture" thinker. Frank packages my thinking as "stupid and lacking common sense."

A daily routine of having the horses at home starts to emerge. I start working from home one day a week. The respite to my soul is well-needed. I can see them from the bedroom window early in the morning, and I can watch them in pasture when I work out on the deck. With pain medicine, JJ seems willing to follow Blaze all over the hilly terrain of our ranch.

As the months pass, JJ looks sounder. I begin working JJ in long lines—two long leads attached to a bridle. From there, I can walk beside or behind him. Together, we navigate the trails and dirt roads connecting the local ranches. I meet several of our neighbors, who invite me to use their properties as well. One elderly gentleman offers to help me whenever

I need help with feeding or blanketing. This is especially welcomed when I work long days or travel to conferences. I offer to help him with his young horse in my round pen. I begin to ponder: am I a professor or a cowgirl? Can't I be both?

28

The Pendulum of Life

My pendulum swings between two distinctly separate worlds—academic and equine. My life with horses is expanding, yet I have not been able to cut back on my academic life. The only thing that continually yields is my sleep. I am confident that after I am promoted to full professor, I will be able to establish some normalcy in my life.

But is that true or even possible? I still have a three-hour commute. I still have teaching, research, and mentoring alongside service to both the university and my profession. How am I going to be a successful professor and live out my dream life with horses? Frank asks me this all the time. The answer is obvious to him: we relocate back to the East Coast or to an institution where work-life balance is possible. We have been married for nearly thirteen years, yet the chasm between us is ever-increasing. Somehow, Frank believes that moving elsewhere will lessen my workload and be the healing balm to our marriage.

My case for full professor has been submitted. I am merely eight years beyond my PhD and only three years beyond tenure, yet our chairman,

Karl Hedrick, feels that my accomplishments are worthy of this promotion. For non-academics, such accolades may seem trivial, but in the world of academia, recognition as a full professor is the end-all. Personally, it is my belief that this recognition is what I need to finally earn worthiness in this world.

A number of distinguished honors have bolstered my portfolio. In addition to the National Science Foundation CAREER Award and the Office of Naval Research Young Investigator Award, I have also received the American Association for the Advancement of Science Mentoring Award, a Congressional Citation for excellence in engineering research, and the University of Rhode Island Distinguished Alumni Award.

In order to create some semblance of a work-life balance, I will need to consolidate my research from two vast fields into one. Once my cohort of PhD students working on the vascular project graduate, I will limit my research to orthopedic applications. With this plan, I think I see a path toward more balance. As a full professor, I will finally be worthy and perhaps able to relinquish the tools in my coping toolbox.

Not a day has gone by since I was eight years old when I haven't had a bulimic episode. She has been my faithful companion, but she comes with a price. With each round of vomiting, my heart feels like it might explode, and my gums bleed. She is a compulsive friend who encourages me to do things I might not otherwise do; I don't think twice about stealing or lying when it comes to food. Alcohol is my other long-term friend. He has been in my life nearly as long. He is manipulative, and I can be myopic in his presence. I wonder, *Will I be able to let these friends go when I am a full professor? Can I ever truly be worthy with them in my life?*

I am thirty-five years old when my promotion to full professor is approved. I am ecstatic about the news but hesitant to share it with Frank. In his mind, this will be the signal that it's time to relocate back east. I am torn—a piece of me is hungry to return to my roots, yet my eight years at Berkeley have been an academic's dream. I have extraordinary students both in the lab and in the classroom.

Dave Dornfeld takes me out for a celebratory lunch at Chez Panisse. Over our meal, he suggests that I take over as the director of the Engineering Systems and Research Center.

"This position comes with summer support and teaching release. It would give you more time for your horses," he says as he quietly mimics the whinny of a horse.

I don't discuss my decision with Frank. I accept the directorship, not certain it's the best decision for me. I much prefer teaching to the mountain of administrative work that will come with this position. On a positive note, I am afforded the opportunity to spend two days a week working from home.

Back at Twin Eagles Ranch, JJ is feeling better. I noticed him cantering and rousting Blaze in the pasture the other day. He now seems jealous when I take Blaze out for trail rides. When I brought Blaze up to the barn to saddle him, within moments, JJ sauntered into the barn behind us. *Did I leave the gate open?*

I put both horses in the paddocks and walk back to the pasture gate. It is chained shut. The fencing is five feet high. I walk the perimeter—no breaks in the fence. There is only one possibility: *JJ jumped out of his pasture!*

Now that JJ knows he can jump out of the pasture, I can't take Blaze without him. We run a hotwire a foot above the fence line to keep JJ in the pasture, as he has also taken to jumping out on a whim. Then a realization occurs to me: If JJ can jump a five-foot fence, then he's ready to go back to work. It is clear that JJ is ready to go back into training.

I enroll JJ in a jumping workshop offered by a former Olympian. Under her tutelage, JJ is an impressive force. I find myself drawn back into the competition world with a new trainer. Initially, it's me riding JJ on the cross-country courses. Annie, our new trainer, soon realizes that JJ has the capability of competing at much higher levels in the hands of a professional. She proposes that she show JJ so he can realize his potential: I can still train him, but she will compete JJ at the shows. My inner critic awakens. *I will never be worthy or capable of riding this talented horse.* With a heavy heart, I agree to the arrangement, and we embark on a series of three-day eventing competitions.

I am spending money as quickly as I earn it. It never occurs to me that I could be pushing myself to a breaking point. In hindsight, this is a great irony. Many of my engineering courses are founded in the mechanical behavior of materials. There are common themes: strength comes at the expense of ductility; internal flaws render systems prone to premature failure; cyclic loads over time can cause the growth of an initial crack to a critical length, resulting in fracture. All of these failure modalities have the potential to bring me to the breaking point as I push my academic armor and my body to its physical limits. I use case studies for failure analysis in my classes, and we always look for the root cause of failure. I don't yet see that my abuse of work, food, caffeine, alcohol, and lack of sleep, compelled by an inner sense of unworthiness, is setting me on a course toward failure.

I have promised Frank that since I am now a full professor, I will begin looking for opportunities on the East Coast. In truth, I am not actively looking—I am too busy working and enjoying my competitive equine world, where I am actively training in three-day eventing. But my life in the competitive three-day eventing world is short-lived because all the behavioral issues we had sorted out with Charles quickly reappear for JJ in the realm of competition.

"JJ needs to go back to the cowboy. Just because he's the color of an orangutan doesn't mean that he gets to run around and behave like one," Annie says as JJ exuberantly bucks after his drop jump. No one seems to appreciate that JJ could have had a career as a bucking horse.

Serendipitously, a friend suggests that I enroll in a clinic with Dennis Reis, a world-renowned horseman. He is known for natural horseman-ship, a philosophy of working with horses that utilizes equine instincts. It is premised on communication that aligns with the body language used among horses in their herd environment.

Dennis can put horses in a classic dressage frame with the lightest of aids, sometimes called invisible aids because, to the outside observer, he seemingly does nothing. Elite riders like him are so well-connected that they can do "less sooner"—not "more later" like most amateurs. I aspire to have his skills.

I pull JJ from the competition world, and I sign up for a five-day clinic over my winter break. Frank rolls his eyes—he can't believe the amount of money I spend on this horse. Any and all free time I have is consumed by JJ.

"Why don't you just put a gold band around his hoof and marry him?" he spews as he slams the door. He gets in his truck; dust flies from his back wheels as he drives to the closest bar.

29

Natural Horsemanship

In the midst of my winter break, JJ and I arrive at Reis Ranch for the five-day clinic. The horseman who will forever change the course of my life greets me with his bright smile. Warm in his welcome, Dennis is tall, especially in his spur-adorned cowboy boots and cowboy hat. He exudes mastery of everything related to horses. I soon find myself entrenched in his method of working horses on the ground and carrying this softness into the saddle.

Charles Wilhelm had provided me with a number of basic ground-school skills, but Dennis Reis spent his early days in rodeo and working with the pioneers of natural horsemanship. Those elevated skills in the saddle are requisite to my ability to work through the challenges of JJ's bucking and head tossing when immersed in the stimulating world of jumping.

Over the course of a few days, I learn the basic cues of body language on the ground and in the saddle. I already see a change in how I communicate with JJ. Yet, what I truly seek is the mastery of the horseman. I am drawn into his magical touch with horses. My thirst for his knowledge is akin to my love affair with physical metallurgy. My quest for an equine education has been ignited.

Before I leave the winter clinic, I sign up for a nine-day clinic offered in the coming summer. I place the charge on my credit card, neglecting to inform Frank. I live my life by the philosophy of asking for forgiveness later rather than permission beforehand. It doesn't always work so well, but this way, Frank only gets angry once.

After completing another action-packed academic semester, I arrive for the nine-day summer clinic with both JJ and Blaze in tow. I will be living in the horseman's bunkhouse, and my plan is to put in time on academic matters before and after each day at the clinic. Fortunately, the horseman's ranch is within forty-five minutes of Berkeley. None of this is sitting well with my husband. Horsemanship has cast some sort of powerful romantic spell over me.

My love of horses is having the opposite effect on Frank. We have been married for fifteen years, and he is becoming insistent that we relocate back east. *Or what? He never threatens to leave.* We never openly discuss divorce, yet I know I have certainly had fleeting thoughts about dissolving our marriage.

Nearly two dozen horse-rider pairs from all over the country are in this horsemanship clinic. The group includes a bull-riding champion and his parents from Texas, a number of aspiring horsemen from around the country, and a small group of women from the local Wetzel ranch. Shirley, the matriarchal leader of these women, and her horse Tristan have worked with Dennis for many years. Tristan is also a chestnut thoroughbred—our equine companions will forge an unyielding bond between us.

Each morning, we have a lesson in the classroom before summoning our horses. This is not like any engineering course I have taken or taught—there are no theories or equations. Instead, lectures are steeped in understanding equine behavior. Dennis is not only a master horseman; he is also a philosopher of life.

"Everything that your horses teach you will apply to your lives," he says.

My journal fills with his words of wisdom—I have not been so enraptured by a topic since my materials engineering education. Something stirs my soul.

"At the start of this course, you will be unconsciously incompetent; you will be unaware of the mistakes you make. With practice and self-awareness, you will become consciously aware of your mistakes," he professes.

My goal is to become unconsciously competent in this equine philosophy—to have such a deep knowledge that I no longer have to consciously think about it. I have this mastery when I teach engineering courses, but I aspire to it when working with JJ. His philosophy resonates with me at a visceral level. Dennis inspires us to have a state of awareness where every gesture means something and where we are fully aligned with our horses.

I am adept at using my cowboy halter and lead rope, but unlike many others in the clinic, I am still using my jumping saddle and my flimsy English bridle. Others have large stock saddles and Western bridles. I am called out on this immediately and then educated on the benefits of well-made Western tack.

"Western saddles offer more leather and 'real estate' when working with horses, especially those horses who are prone to startling, bucking, or other behaviors that can unseat their riders. The Western bridles use slobber straps and simple sweet-iron snaffle bits that enable one to create a horse who is lighter on the aids," says the horseman. I realize I may be parting with more money in the not-too-distant future.

I am overwhelmed with emotion when I watch Dennis work with JJ. I see how light JJ can be and how much potential he has. A select group of us are invited to stay for the horseman's ninety-day course, and I opt in to this special opportunity. I still haven't solved JJ's "head up in the air" response without using some form of mechanical leverage. Dennis assures me that we can work through this if I stay for the summer. I know I can make this work—it's summer, and the campus is only forty-five minutes away. I am certain this decision is right for JJ and me. My soul is beckoning for this opportunity.

I am deeply enthralled by the process of natural horsemanship. Dennis instills in us an understanding that our horses will change only when we change. Perhaps Charles was telling me the same thing, but I wasn't ready to hear it the previous summer. Something finally reveals itself to me: we are not here to "fix our horses" but rather to "fix ourselves." I spend hours with JJ each day in the horseman's clinic, learning the natural ways of working with horses.

When we start jumping obstacles, JJ shows his capabilities as a jumper and also reveals the "head in the face" issue. Dennis asks to ride JJ. His apprentice quickly swaps my tack for a balanced Western saddle and a bridle with a simple sweet-iron snaffle bit and slobber straps. Dennis uses no mechanical leverage, and he merely laughs when JJ offers a buck. Within moments, he teaches JJ to put his head down when he applies pressure from both legs. Every time the head goes up, the legs go on. Soon the behavior transforms itself. No other person has been able to solve this issue. My heart swells with gratitude.

Dennis talks me through the process of getting JJ to put his head down when I apply leg pressure, how to release quickly, and how to be soft in my aids. I practice until it's second nature.

"You need new tack, cowgirl," says the horseman. I order a custom saddle and bridle for JJ.

"Lisa, this has to stop. I just got the credit card bill," says Frank, bitter with my equine endeavors.

"Just use my summer salary," I offer in protest.

"You have no clue how much money you spend. We have a ranch, but you are never here. Now you are living at the horseman's ranch for the summer and throwing away your summer salary," he spews over the phone.

"I will take on another consulting job in the fall," I counter.

"You don't have enough time for another consulting job. Something has to go. We need to sell Twin Eagles and move back east, as you promised. Or does your big brain not remember that?" he says, then hangs up in anger.

I am already numb with alcohol and will soon purge his words away. I know his pattern. Frank gets angry and throws around some hurtful words, then he buys himself some new tools or ranch equipment, and it all dissipates.

I try to remain blissfully unaware of our financial state. I know my salary, and I have a rough idea of what I spend, yet I have no sense of how much he earns or spends or the amount of debt we are accumulating. This is a fatal flaw.

Over the course of the summer, JJ becomes my liberty horse. Such is our trust that I now can ride him without a bridle or halter. We jump picnic tables and stacks of barrels. In his element, JJ jumps obstacles at liberty and then jumps back over them to return to me. There is a sparkle in his eyes, and I'm sure there is a sparkle in mine as well. JJ follows me wherever I go in the arena and plays canter tag with me. It's as though I am part of his herd. Perhaps I have always been part of his herd, but I had been too inept to speak his elegant language.

The natural horsemanship work deeply transforms my relationship with JJ. We are kindred spirits. I see now that JJ is my mirror—when I soften, he softens. As I relax, he relaxes. When I trust him, he trusts me. My earlier challenges with JJ resulted from my thinking that he needed to change, when all along, it was me who had to change. His unruly behavior was merely his protective armor; he was simply mirroring the armor I had created to cope with my inner pain.

I am thirty-seven years old and have entered into a truly magical realm of my life where I get a glimpse of what worthiness can taste like. My thick unyielding armor that has kept my inner unworthiness locked deep inside dissolves away in the presence of JJ. We develop a beautiful partnership when we realize that we no longer need our armor with each other. We can now see the grace we have within each other, without judgment. Just love. I have never loved anything or anyone so deeply in my life. We are in the midst of an equine love affair. Feeling fully alive and in a flow when I work with JJ, I am aware that he ignites a passion within me I never knew existed. My relationship with him is like no other I have ever experienced. A residue of worthiness warms my heart in his presence. It will take me many more years to find any semblance of this in any other aspect of my life.

The clinic comes to an end in August. JJ and I are invited to spend a week at the Grand National Rodeo in Las Vegas with the horseman in December. I agree to the invitation without blinking. This gives me something to work toward over the coming months.

I feel great sadness on the day I load JJ and Blaze into the horse trailer. I say my farewell to Shirley, yet I know we will see each other often to continue this work. I have had my eyes on one of the Wetzel horses all summer, and I plant my seed with her. "Shirley, please let me know if Juan ever comes up for sale. I would be interested in giving him a good home."

Juan is a magnificent gray Azteca—a cross of Andalusian and quarter horse—with a flowing black mane and tail. Juan looks like the type of horse one sees in fairy tales. I don't know how I would afford him, yet I sense that Juan has a place in my life. I don't dare mention Juan to my husband—I have to choose my battles carefully. For now, the only battle I must win is the journey to Vegas in December.

30

Mountains and Valleys

In the realms of mountains, one must go through the valleys to get to the next peak. Life on my mountain feels more akin to an emotional abyss. My heart is consumed with natural horsemanship, and this is causing an ever-growing divide between Frank and me. The friction in our marital machinery has seized all the moving parts. We are fast approaching the breaking point.

"We've been in California for a decade. You've been promoted to full professor. You can go anywhere now. It's time for us to leave," Frank says. He has already had a tall glass of bourbon. I see the anger building in his eyes.

"But we have our ranch now," I plead. I down my own glass of fiery liquid.

"You're never here. Why do we even need the ranch?" he counters.

"But my research is here at Berkeley, and I'm enjoying the natural horsemanship training."

"Why do we have to stay here? You can do your research somewhere else, and I don't know what you see in that stupid horse of yours. JJ is nothing but a money pit. You're deluded if you think that you two are anything special," Frank argues sharply.

My anger boils over, triggered by the comment about JJ. In an instant, I am out the door and in the woods behind our trailer home. It is a balmy August evening. I sit out in the darkness for hours, under the full moon, amongst the cry of the coyotes. Eventually, the cool mountain air washes over me, but my inner fire keeps my body warm. I have nowhere to go—I can't leave the horses. I feel like a caged animal.

I watch Frank driving the large ranch truck back and forth on the dirt road between our home and the barn. He is furiously screaming my name. I make myself invisible. I am part of the woods, breathing with the trees. I can't return until I find my calm. I have no alcohol or sugar at my disposal, only nature. I seek out the warmth of JJ across the road in the pasture. I feel his warm breath on my face. Then I feel Blaze. I soak in their strength. I can do anything as long as I have my horses. Finally, I return to the house. I pour a tall glass of bourbon and drink it down straight.

"Okay. I'll look for an opportunity to relocate elsewhere," I say in surrender. I can no longer sustain the commute from Twin Eagles Ranch. Something has to give, and I sense that it has to be me.

Perhaps it's serendipity—within a week, I have an invited research seminar at Notre Dame. My visit coincides with the peak of their autumn foliage, a time of year when I am most susceptible to the lure of the East. I am flooded with memories of Hawkswood Farm, growing up in the East, and time with cousins and Jackie. Perhaps I should consider moving back East?

The Notre Dame campus is splendid with its crimson red, sunset orange, and mustard yellow leaves waving in the trees. The crisp autumn air intoxicates me. At the end of my seminar, the dean asks if I would consider relocating to Notre Dame. I am relieved that Frank isn't here—he would have already accepted.

I am mindful of the beautiful farms near the campus and the fact that the leading orthopedics companies are a short drive away. I am also aware that the cost of living is a fraction of that in California. Could this be a place for me to achieve work-life balance? I try to shake the thought free from my mind. "I would be interested in exploring this possibility," I reply.

Over the span of a month, I am recruited in earnest by Notre Dame. They offer me an endowed professorship with an opportunity to build a strong biomaterials program at their prestigious institution.

I share this news with Frank once it seems like a possibility I would truly consider. Part of me wants to hold out for an opportunity to move back to New England. Indiana does not feel like home to me. But Frank is persistent.

"Lisa, you're a full professor. I have supported you through this process. Now it's time to live a *balanced* life," he proffers.

"I need more time to think this through," I stall.

"The solution is obvious," he stammers.

"It's a complex problem. There must be alternative solutions," I argue quietly. I can't bring myself to think about leaving Berkeley right now. Instead, I distract myself with my preparations for Vegas.

My mind and heart are at war. My heart is giving serious consideration to leaving academia altogether to pursue a life of working with horses. My mind wants to stay in academia, where it is safe—where I have tenure, respect, and accomplishment.

I have now been at Berkeley for a decade. The very fabric of my existence feels like it is about to be torn, and my residue of worthiness seems to be evaporating away. I am filled with dread and anxiety. My eating disorder and alcohol abuse, which I have never surrendered, keep me company during this time of duress.

Frank and I are invited back to the Notre Dame campus to look at real estate. We find a beautiful home in a pastoral setting, including a heated barn, an indoor arena, and pristine pastures for the horses. I try to imagine my life here. By all outward appearances, everything is perfect, yet something feels wrong.

Conflicting thoughts clutter my mind. On the one hand, I have a successful research lab and academic career at Berkeley, as well as a great horse mentor and the opportunity to expand my horsemanship in California. Alternatively, I have a highly lucrative offer from Notre Dame, where I could own a horse farm minutes from campus, and I would be in close proximity to orthopedic companies for research. The relocation seems so obvious, yet some inner part of my being feels it is wrong.

Guilt overtakes me. I accept the offer and agree to start at Notre Dame in the coming fall semester, effective September 2004. We sell Twin Eagles Ranch and put a down payment on the horse farm in Indiana. We will have a large mortgage, but we will be able to afford it on my new income. I should be thrilled, but misery engulfs me.

My saving grace is JJ. In December, I head to Las Vegas with my bright chestnut thoroughbred. I immerse myself in this opportunity to be at the Grand National Rodeo; it is an honor to be here with Dennis Reis and his entourage. Each day, we put on a display of natural horsemanship at the Excalibur. We demonstrate liberty work with our horses to the huge crowds. The grand finale is bridleless jumping over barrels. JJ and I are in our element.

On the day of our last demonstration, a man from the audience approaches me. "I will offer you $100,000 for your horse," he says.

"JJ is not for sale. Not now. Not ever," I respond. JJ stands by my side, peaceful, knowing he is my forever horse. I am grateful Frank isn't here, or my steed would be sold.

Early in the new year, Shirley and I are invited to continue working with Dennis and to come along to Denver with our horses for the Horse Expo. The dates of the exposition coincide with my spring break. I am nearly thirty-eight years old, and it is as though the universe keeps opening doors into the horse world for me.

Frank and I are practically estranged. I am now living in my horse trailer at the horseman's ranch and commuting each day to Berkeley. He is working as a technical salesperson. He has rented an apartment an hour away until we relocate to Notre Dame, and he is busying himself taking care of all the moving details. We have been married for nearly sixteen years, yet I feel we are as disconnected as ever. The divide between us is growing both metaphorically and physically. Frank believes that all of my horse craziness and workaholic tendencies will be relinquished when we move to Indiana at the end of the upcoming summer. He is clearly deluded.

My career at Berkeley will not be fully renounced when I move to Indiana. The dean of engineering at UC Berkeley has convinced me to take a one-year leave of absence instead of resigning. My one-year leave from Berkeley takes effect on July 1, 2004. I can't possibly see how I will be able to return to Berkeley with so much momentum built into this relocation. Deep in my heart, I feel that Berkeley is my academic home, but I push the emotions away. I sink into my coping mechanisms. Like a true addict in denial, I tell myself that I will relinquish my addictive behaviors after I relocate.

Marni has been at Stanford since completing her PhD, and she has seen little of me since I entrenched myself in horses. We meet up for lunch on the Berkeley campus, and she poignantly asks if my upcoming move will enable me to have a better life balance. Though I insist that my life will be much simpler, I am not at all convinced—and I sense that she sees that truth. "You need to take care of yourself," Marni offers. I nod, but I am not sure I know how to take care of myself.

I am eleven years out of my PhD, and I now fully understand why Subra told me that Berkeley is where I would do my best work. My career at Berkeley culminates when I receive the United States Presidential Award for Excellence in Science, Mathematics, and Engineering Mentoring. In May 2004, I am invited to the White House to receive the prestigious PAESMEM award.

"My academic success is owed in great part to my exceptional mentors and my extraordinary students at Berkeley," I say in my acceptance speech.

Frank is with me at the ceremony. My anxiety and anger fester. *How can he ask me to leave Berkeley?*

With the semester behind me, I am invited to stay at Dennis's ninety-day horseman's clinic during the summer before I start at Notre Dame.

A nagging thought lives under my academic façade: *Perhaps my true calling is not academia but instead a life working with horses?*

31

The Perfect Storm

The air is electric. My inner turmoil is tucked safely beneath a veneer of crisp cowgirl shirt, Wrangler jeans, custom chaps, boots, and hat. This cowgirl get-up feels surreal. Would any of my engineering students even recognize me in this attire? Would they be astonished by the mastery I have acquired in horsemanship?

The ninety-day horseman's clinic has arrived. It is mid-May, and I plan to soak up as much horsemanship as possible during my final three months in California. Shirley and I are excited about this opportunity to work together in the horseman's clinic, yet we both feel the sadness of my inevitable departure. More than thirty years separate us by age, but Shirley is a kindred spirit to me, and we share a deep connection centered upon horses. For the past several months, we have been taking JJ and Tristan out to Point Reyes and enjoying the coastal trails with our thoroughbreds.

We have JJ and Tristan tacked up and ready to give a liberty demonstration for the students in the clinic. It is a gusty day, and Tristan looks anxious; he's wide-eyed and won't stand still. I know how he feels—I can't shake my restlessness. Frank and I have been fighting constantly. He assumes this will all shift when we get to Indiana, while I only see the situation becoming untenable. We are completely bifurcated on this life decision.

The wind picks up, and in response, Tristan startles and pulls back. He should yield to his own pressure on the lead rope, but instead, he panics. Tristan rears up, and I am in the direct line of fire. I feel the awesome power of his front hoof impact the back of my skull. In an instant, I am dragged under Tristan. He is now in a full panic, and he has no place to go. He assaults me with his front hooves. Tristan has no idea who or what is underneath him. I might as well be a mountain lion meeting my demise.

I am thirty-eight years old, and my life is literally passing before me. In the process of being nearly trampled to death, something within me cracks open and reveals a truth that has been buried deep inside me. In this lucid moment, I receive a clear directive: I need to get divorced. I need to stay at Berkeley. The edict is etched into my armor as I am pulled free from Tristan's wrath.

I'm face down in a copious pool of blood, and time moves slowly and quickly all at once. I hear a siren in the background. I am imminently aware that I can't move. I can see JJ in my peripheral vision. I sense him letting me know that I will come through this. I must be hallucinating.

The paramedics place a brace around my neck. I hear them, but I am barely lucid. One of the paramedics indicates that he will need to cut me out of my chaps.

"Please don't cut off my chaps. They cost a fortune," I say in jest.

Morphine courses its way through my veins. As an addict, I greatly appreciate that someone has thought to numb my pain and emotions. *Do they sell this stuff in a to-go container?*

By the time I arrive at the hospital, I am well aware that I can't move and fear I may be paralyzed. I put all of my energy into wiggling my toes. With deep relief, I feel my pinky toe, then its neighbors, and then my big toe. My initial relief is replaced with dread as I realize I can't move anything else.

Soon a spine surgeon greets me. He introduces himself, but I don't catch his name. Fear consumes my brain.

"You are extremely fortunate to have survived this accident. You have a fractured skull and lumbar spine. Your kidneys, pancreas, and adrenals have been bruised. There is internal bleeding, and we will need to keep you in the hospital for a few days," he explains. "You are lucky to be alive."

I am in and out of consciousness, heavily sedated by the pain medication. I hear the jingle of spurs. It is Dennis. Then Shirley. Drunk on morphine, my speech is garbled. My parents arrive next. This panics me—if my parents have flown up from Los Angeles, then maybe things are quite serious.

"You didn't have to come. I'll be okay," I say.

My mom kisses my cheek. "We had to come."

I see the tears in her eyes. I see the distress on my father's face as he holds my hand. I feel the comfort of their presence.

Then I see Frank sitting in the corner. We had a huge argument when we saw each other last. I sense that we are both laden with guilt—his over what has transpired and mine over what will transpire. I have not lost my edict—I am well aware of the excruciating conversation we need to have.

I spend the next three days in the hospital. The surgeon assures me that my fitness probably saved my life. He feels that I have sufficient muscle strength in my back to avoid the need for any internal fracture fixation hardware. Instead, I will wear a brace until my spine is healed. "When can I ride my horse again?"

"I knew you would ask that. You had a major head injury, and your body can't sustain another trauma. You have multiple fractures in your lumbar spine; a fall could be catastrophic. Your best therapy will be walking. It will likely take ten to twelve weeks for you to heal."

Twelve weeks? Tears flood my face. That is my whole summer. There will be no ninety-day horseman's clinic. I either need more pain medicine or a stiff drink. I summon the nurse for more morphine.

Upon returning to the ranch, I make my way to see JJ and Blaze. JJ whinnies when he sees me—I sense his energy. He will be my therapy.

I still hold a great burden in my body. I have several difficult conversations ahead of me before the end of summer. I have not forgotten the clear directive I received during the trampling: I must get divorced. I must stay at Berkeley.

32

Dark Flowers

I stare at the dark flowers that sit in a vase in my horse trailer. They are dead, like our marriage. They carried beauty once, but in truth, they were dying all along. Like me. If I stay in this marriage, then I will surely die. *How did we end up here? Is it because we never communicated? Or because we never knew who we were or what we really wanted?*

This is the most difficult conversation of my life. My body, though numbed by pain medication, is surging with adrenaline as the words leave my lips.

"I want a divorce," I say simply.

My request is immediately assaulted by Frank's reactive feelings of anger. I feel his judgment. I wear the deep veil of shame, guilt, and sadness.

"You are not thinking clearly. You can't do this. I have stood by you for sixteen years. I have given up my life for you. We just bought this horse trailer with living quarters and a farm in Indiana. All for you!" he stammers.

"You can go to Indiana. You can have the farm," I reply.

"We need your salary to pay for all of these things. I can't afford that farm without you. A divorce will cause us financial devastation," he pleads.

This is an extremely difficult decision, yet I have never been more certain of anything. I have spent my whole life stuffing down how I truly feel and what I want to say. Now, I am raw and unbridled.

Frank will not agree to a divorce unless we go to marriage counseling. Within two weeks, we start the grueling process. My armoring is unyielding and brittle, like steel brought from a near-molten state and quenched into briny waters.

We sit in side-by-side chairs in the therapist's office. I note the pale green walls and the white-noise machine. If only I could drown out everything. The therapist is middle-aged, a bit cherubic-looking. Frank found her.

"I understand that you are considering divorce," she says soothingly.

"We want to see if we can reconcile," Frank offers in his pretend nice voice.

I want to stand up and punch them both. I don't want to be soothed. I think I am overdue for my pain medication. I feel the anxiety and anger pushing up against the inside of my armor. The air is thick with tension.

"I don't want to be married. I don't want this life," I say, my voice escalating.

"I have given sixteen years of life to this marriage. Everything has been about her," Frank rallies.

"You brought on all of our early financial devastation," I say, simmering.

"Perhaps for next time, you could each bring a list of things you love about each other," she says as our first session wraps up.

"That will be a short session. See you next week." I slam the door behind me. I manage to get myself back into my truck. Sugar and alcohol beckon to me.

My only solace is JJ. I am still living in my horse trailer on the horseman's ranch, just a few hundred yards from the horses. Each day, I walk with JJ as I regain my strength and mobility. We work on long lines, and he becomes my physical therapy. He provides me with an inner strength that enables me to go on with my life. He is giving me what I once offered him. We don't give up on each other.

By the end of the third therapy session, it is clear to the marriage counselor and me that divorce is the best solution. Frank is not yet convinced. We are standing outside the therapist's office.

"I am not going to sign the papers that will dissolve our marriage."

"What do you mean? I did the therapy as you asked. It is clear that this marriage can't be saved," I state.

"You had a major injury. You fractured your skull and spine. You had internal bleeding. It will take you all summer to heal. You are still struggling with memory issues. You are clearly not thinking rationally," he says.

"No, I am crystal clear in my thinking. I want a divorce."

"If you still want a divorce when we get to Indiana and we are settled in our home, then I will sign the divorce papers," he says.

"What are you talking about? We would then need to get a divorce in Indiana. No, we have to submit these papers in California." My head is reeling as he walks away to his truck.

Later, I share this conversation with Shirley at the ranch.

"Are you sure you want to get a divorce?" she asks.

"Yes! Why does everyone question this? He is not who everyone thinks he is, and we are not the couple we have been pretending to be," I plead.

"You stand to lose a lot of money," she says.

"I know. But I can't go to Indiana, and I can't stay in the marriage any longer."

I resort to an old tactic. In the past, when I needed to end one relationship, I simply swapped it for another. I set eyes on a cowboy. I know it is wrong—I have no business entering into any semblance of a relationship. I am not yet divorced, and he is not wholly available either. This affair is an emotional firestorm, but it is the only action I know how to take to end my marriage. It will be a repeating pattern of mine until I finally peel away from the strongholds of my addictions.

My father once said to me, "Desperate people do desperate things." I am now desperate. I have to get out of this marriage. I need to stay in Berkeley. I cannot let go of that directive. With my hurtful actions in play, I call Frank and break his heart.

"I will never love you in the future. I don't love you now. I have never loved you. I used you all of these years. I don't want you in my life anymore," I say. It is not entirely true, but it seals the fate of ending the marriage.

I hear his sobs over the phone. Tears spill down my face as I hang up. The signed papers arrive in the mail in the coming days.

Financial vulnerability accompanies my unyielding decision. Throughout my sixteen years of marriage, I had selfishly put all of my effort into my career and never honored the day-to-day operations of our finances. I quickly find myself without money or credit. My path is quickly transforming from a life of dreams into a living nightmare.

In the midst of all the emotional chaos, my spurned husband gives away Blaze. His action is justified. I can't afford to keep two horses. Moreover, the woman who receives Blaze will offer him an extraordinary home and the love he deserves.

I live in fear that Frank will take JJ. My beloved horse is the one treasure I can't lose at this juncture in my life. I am well aware that my loss of JJ would scale equivalently to the pain I have caused my husband. I have to relocate JJ before he is taken from me.

I sell all the jewelry in my possession to a pawn shop, including my diamond wedding band and engagement ring. I also sell my Red Sox baseball with Yaz's signature. I use these funds to move JJ to a private farm in Petaluma, where I know he will be safe. Selling JJ is not an option. He is my lifeblood.

As part of our financial agreement in our divorce, Frank takes the horse trailer. I absorb the farm in Indiana and its huge monthly debt. I immediately call an agent in Fort Bend and place it up for sale. It will take me nearly a year to sell the property.

Beth graciously lends me money and offers that I can live with her and Matt in San Francisco. I immediately reach out to patent attorneys with whom I have collaborated before—I need to bolster my income quickly. It doesn't matter that I still have to heal a fractured spine and internal organs or that I need rest to regain any semblance of health. I need to buckle down, work hard, and get myself out of this hole.

I am not expected back on the Berkeley campus. However, I am expected to be at Notre Dame by the start of September. I have many more challenging conversations ahead of me.

I speak with UC Berkeley's incoming chairman of mechanical engineering, Al Pisano. I let him know I want to stay at Berkeley. Al has been a good mentor to me throughout my career. In our conversation, he expresses his empathy for my personal struggles—my accident and my imminent divorce. He states that he will do everything in his power to put together a retention package to keep me at Berkeley. I can't tell my PhD students what is going on until I get these issues resolved.

I then speak with Berkeley's dean, Rich Newton, about how to best go about the situation with Notre Dame. Rich facilitates a conversation with the dean at Notre Dame, and I am freed from my need to fulfill my contract with them. I make personal apologies to the faculty at Notre Dame with whom I intended to collaborate.

Al Pisano and Rich Newton work tirelessly to negotiate a retention package for me. I am offered a matching salary to that of Notre Dame, and my lab will be fully renovated in the fall. Dean Newton asks me to take the role of associate dean for outreach education and lifelong learning. "I have long admired your commitment to K–12 outreach education," he says. I smile, accepting the new directive for the coming year. Inside, I weep, feeling like an impostor and not worthy of my academic recognition.

I email Dave and let him know that I will be staying at Berkeley after all. He is delighted. He and Barbara are away on sabbatical for the coming year. "I look forward to seeing you when I return. Will there be another ranch in your future?" he asks. "We shall see," I say through my fingertips. I feel a false bravado.

My PhD students are delighted when I tell them we are not moving the lab to Indiana. Some part of the universe shines on me during this incredibly challenging time. I won't see them until I return to campus at the end of summer, and for that, I am grateful. I am barely holding it all together.

33

Rock Bottom

The decision to get a divorce is not well-received. Frank's parents and family express their disappointment in me, and for that, I feel deep remorse. My deeper pain is that I compromise the relationship with my parents.

"How can you throw away a marriage?" they ask.

No words seem to justify my decision to end a sixteen-year marriage. My family loves Frank and thinks he is the perfect husband. This is the danger of a façade: no one ever witnessed anything but a happy couple and a doting husband. We kept our inner turmoil private. I am the one who openly asked for the divorce, and thus I am the villain.

Perhaps the bigger question for everyone, myself included, is why did he stay all of these years? I was clearly a workaholic. I was the one who put career and horses before family and marriage. I don't have the answers. I am filled with self-loathing, feeling nothing but hatred for myself. My inner flaw of unworthiness, nucleated when my sister passed away in childhood, is now racing toward a tipping point.

My Aunt Jackie is supportive of my decision to get divorced. She never married. Realizing how I've missed her, I tell her, "I will come visit you the next time I have a conference on the East Coast." I speak with her several times a week, yet she repeats the same story of going to Rockport to have fried clams with friends. She can't possibly be going to Rockport every day while working as a principal of a public school, can she? I am in denial, yet I know something is going on with her mental faculties.

Marni is busy in her role as the outreach education director at Stanford. The physical distance between her work and my home has shielded me from seeing her—she would call me out in a second if she saw me now. I am thin, and my eyes are sunken. I have been dishonest with her when she pointedly asked if I am taking care of myself. "I'm fine," I dodged. She has reached out to me several times to get together, but I always have some excuse. I am too ashamed for her to see me.

When I return to campus in the fall, my academic life resumes at full capacity, but my "full capacity" is a façade. I put on makeup to cover the circles under my eyes. I wear layered dress clothes that hide my thinness. I only stop by the lab to see my students when I have the most energy. I am working long hours to keep up with consulting, research, and teaching.

I am thirty-eight years old and at the peak of my academic career, but my body is in a deep state of fatigue. My adrenals never fully recovered after the horse accident. My energy levels wax and wane at inappropriate times. I am wide awake at night and depleted in the morning. Exhaustion courses through my veins. For decades, I have pushed myself to the brink of physical limitations, but my body is no longer willing to submit to the ongoing demands I place on it.

I consume extreme quantities of caffeine and sugar throughout the day, yet my energy debt is too high and my body struggles to keep pace.

I sink more deeply into my eating disorder, alcohol abuse, and now the added cocktail of pain medication.

I have received a salary increase as part of my retention at Berkeley, and I have taken on additional consulting to help offset the debt of my accident and the divorce. With some financial solvency in place, I move from my sister's home into an apartment in Petaluma.

JJ is fifteen minutes away at Hawkwood Hill Farm, a beautiful facility with a name ironically close to my beloved Hawkswood Farm. It is nestled in the rolling hills of Sonoma County and is complete with a covered arena, jumping fields, a cross-country course, and trails. This is horse heaven, but I no longer have the energy to ride. Without the passion provided by horses, I have no true reason for living.

At the university, I am a highly decorated professor, but at home, I am a grief-stricken addict looming toward a total physical breakdown. Each night, I find myself alone in my apartment with its stark white walls and the impermanence of its rented furniture. Loneliness might settle into my bones if it were not for the persistent company of shame, anxiety, and sorrow. These demons haunt my mind and escalate their antics at night. Sleep eludes me. No amount of alcohol or food takes away my pain. I find myself on the floor, sobbing and begging the ethers for forgiveness for terminating my marriage, subsisting as an addict, and remaining unworthy. *God took the wrong daughter.*

As the spring semester begins, I continue my charade of academic excellence. How is it that no one notices I am crumbling beneath my successful professor act? Are people just giving me space, knowing that I have had a life-threatening accident and have ended a long-term marriage in this past year?

In my office, I secretly indulge in dozens of donuts washed down with coffee. I follow with bags of candy as I tackle my work. My energy remains drained. I purge in a trash bag that I will later dispose of carefully. I lie on the floor of my office, my heart pounding and tears streaming down my face, staring up at a wall of engineering degrees and prestigious awards. A great irony, given that I thought academic achievement would make me worthy.

My body is on the verge of failure. I am wearied and riddled with chronic anxiety. My body has not been the same since I was trampled by Tristan—it can no longer keep up with my academic expectations. Each day feels like an eternity—I can no longer create the energy reserves I am accustomed to, no matter how I try to utilize my addictive toolbox.

I can barely keep up with my PhD students. My research lab has ballooned into an enterprise too big for me to contain. In engineering parlance, I feel like a flawed, thin-walled pressure vessel about to rupture. I need to consolidate my research before I burst. My students don't see my inner flaws; they only see the exterior shell. They have no sense of how embrittled or fragile I have become. *I am the ultimate academic impostor.*

In early May, nearly a year after my horse accident, I drag my weary body across the finish line marking the end of the semester. It has been twelve years since I started as a professor at Berkeley. I have pushed my body to its limits many times over, but this past year has depleted me. I have nothing left to give. My armoring is collapsing. Catastrophic failure feels imminent. *I am unworthy of this world.*

I stop at the grocery store and fill my cart. Cake, cereal, cookies, donuts, pasta, ice cream, candy, soda, milk, wine, bourbon. I am going to make my pain go away. Forever.

Once home in my stark apartment, I binge until I am ready to explode. I repeatedly vomit until I am empty, metaphorically reflecting the emptiness I feel in my soul. I lie on the bathroom floor and sob, my heart pounding violently.

I have long known that bulimia can be fatal. It is possible to rupture an esophagus, stomach, or intestine. It is possible to cause heart failure. I desperately want this to be the bulimic episode that finally takes me away. I don't want to go on anymore.

I call out to the ethers of the universe. "Please take me," I beg. "Please let this be over."

PART
THREE

*An Arduous
Path to
Recovery*

34
Awakening

Puffs of pink fill the fading blue sky as the sun yields to another day. My leggy thoroughbred eats his evening hay across the field among his equine companions. His crimson coat glows as if to beckon the sun to stay a little longer before dropping behind the expansive rolling hills.

I had been ready for total darkness, but then I felt JJ tug on my soul. Heavy with gloom, I am cemented outside his pasture gate. Visceral guilt, shame, and remorse shake free from my body and pour down my cheeks. I have failed my family, myself, and my life. Preparing for eternal judgment, I unlatch the heavy chain binding the metal gate and step into the unknown ... toward JJ.

I hear his soft nicker and then his thunderous hooves. The sweet nectar of horse assaults my senses. The life force of his presence pulses through my veins; his breath becomes my oxygen.

I am enraptured by his stature in a proverbial horse hug; his warm muzzle envelops my heart. His divine wisdom permeates through all the cracks in my armor. JJ serves as the rivets that hold my fractured vessel together—without his bolstering, I would shatter. I feel a glimmer of hope.

My reflection mirrors back through his large, knowing eyes. *Is he looking into my soul?* The air stirs. There is no judgment. My spirit fills with his unconditional love. I do not know how long we stand together—minutes? Hours? Days? Time is still for me. He offers me light when I had been prepared for total darkness.

I feel him in my mind, my body, my soul. JJ communicates to me through some shared consciousness. We are one; we are the acorn and the tree, the leaves and the flowers. Many grains of sand have passed between us in this hourglass of life, and many more will follow. It is not my time to leave. I have much more to offer. He is my earth angel, animal medicine, and spirit guide. When my time comes, we will fly together past the moon and deep into the stars. He is my forever horse.

I weep with gratitude, flooding the ground beneath my feet. A lightness fills my body, lifting the heavy gloom away. I feel mercy and forgiveness. In my heart, I know that JJ will carry me forward until I am ready to stand on my own.

35

Affirmations

The bright morning sunshine barges through the narrow slots of the blinds, beckoning me to wake up. I roll over to see what time it is, but a beautiful card sprayed with color blocks the clock's face. The affirmation reads: "When I wake in the morning, I plan for a great day. My anticipation attracts good experiences to me." *Is this a dream?* I pull the memories through the tangled web of my brain.

A day after receiving my directive from JJ, I stopped at our local bookstore. I was drawn to the self-help section, as if a book were calling me by name. *You Can Heal Your Life* by Louise Hay practically jumped off the shelf into my hands along with a deck of her affirmation cards. As soon as I returned to my bleak apartment, I read her inspirational teachings from cover to cover. My apartment is now spackled with her affirmation cards.

I assess my current condition. Decades of vomiting have taken their toll on my body. My throat is chronically sore and scratchy. My gums are raw. I have ongoing stomach pain. My eyes are bloodshot. My body continually craves sugar and caffeine. I am thirty-nine years old, and I will need professional support to rewire the neurological signaling in my brain. It is time to seek help.

I find a psychologist who specializes in eating disorders. I pay cash, not wanting the therapy to show up on my medical records. Dr. Blythe is tall, lean, young, and blond. I feel her judgment before I even find my place on her sofa.

"What do you want to talk about today?" she asks.

What do you think I want to talk about?

"I want to break free of my eating disorder," I say.

"Tell me about your eating disorder. What is its nature? When did it begin?" she asks, writing tablet in hand.

I'm not sure I can relive all of this openly. *Where do I start?*

"I have been bulimic since I was eight years old …" I begin.

"Tell me about your relationship with your mother," she says.

Why is it always the mother? I'm not sure I can subject myself to her psychological theories. She reminds me of Paula, the therapist who informed my parents that I had attempted suicide, back when I was sixteen.

The session is emotionally exhausting as we dig up old wounds from my past: What was it like as a child to lose a sibling? To lose a dog? To be bullied at school? To never feel worthy?

I am fully triggered when I leave her office. Without thinking, I find myself at the grocery store, binging before I even reach the checkout stand. I sit in the car and eat everything I just purchased. Then I seek out a restroom and purge it away.

It only takes me three sessions of therapy to deduce that she is fueling my bulimic behavior. I cancel the rest of my sessions. Perhaps it would get better if I stayed in therapy, but I am only hanging on by a thread. I need a different path forward.

I brush my teeth, spitting out blood seeping from my raw gums. I have neglected this problem for years. The beautiful affirmation card taped to my bathroom mirror catches my eye. I say the words aloud: "I lovingly do everything I can do to assist my body in maintaining perfect health."

I call my dentist, and within a week, I have a referral to see a specialist. It is not surprising when I am diagnosed with periodontal disease. I require a procedure in which tissue is harvested from the roof of my mouth and stitched into my gums. Decades of corrosive bulimia have caught up with me. *Perfect health feels a long way off.*

The periodontist performs the surgical procedure and sends me home with a heavy dose of pain medication. The healing process is agonizing. My pain meds are keeping my other coping tools at bay. What will happen when I run out of pain medication and I begin to eat solid foods again? Freshly transplanted gum tissue will not survive the daily ravage of bulimia. I focus on my affirmations.

"I deeply love and approve of myself. I am willing to change," I say to my reflection. It feels awkward as the words roll off my tongue. I have never looked in the mirror and reflected back a kind thought to myself.

In the past, I have called myself stupid, fat, ugly, or unworthy. I have slapped my face repeatedly in front of the mirror to conjure up deep self-hatred. I have done this often in the past year.

I need to find someone to help me anchor myself in recovery. I search the internet for a local outpatient program. I have no intention of committing myself anywhere, nor do I intend to use my medical insurance. I don't want anyone in my academic world to know I am an addict. I have had a long lineage of secrecy in my life—starting with the loss of my sister, then the drinking with Auntie and binging. I have kept my abusive relationships hidden. I have become a master of keeping secrets, and unburdening myself of them in my academic world does not feel wise or safe.

I find Julia Ross, a nutritionist who specializes in recovery. Her practice is ideally located in Mill Valley, halfway between Berkeley and Petaluma. Her center specializes in outpatient treatment for addiction. I call her office. Julia requires a private one-hour interview before any treatment can happen. She can see me the following day.

Drenched in sweat, I walk into Julia's office, my anxiety fueled by the memory of the recent battery of questions posed by the therapist in Petaluma. Julia wears the look of wisdom. Her office is filled with books and research papers—not a white-noise machine and a pillow-laden therapy sofa. I immediately feel at ease in her presence. She pointedly asks about my addictions. I share my history with her willingly. I need help.

Julia doesn't drag up emotional wounds; instead, she wants to know specifically what my addictive cocktail looks like so she knows how to best help me. Perhaps it is her academic presence that makes me feel safe. For the first time in my life, I disclose everything about my addictions. I share with her that I have been bulimic for more than three decades and an alcoholic for nearly as long.

"I use bulimia to stuff down my emotions and pain. I use alcohol to provide social ease and relaxation. I use sugar and caffeine to bolster my energy for work. I limit myself to four hours of sleep a night. At least that was how much sleep I had when I was actually sleeping," I say.

I share with her the fallout of my horse accident and the mayhem of my life for the past year. She can barely believe that I have survived this long.

"Will you consider taking a medical leave from the university to focus on recovery?" Julia asks.

"I can't afford to not be working. More importantly, I don't want to let anyone at Berkeley down. I just want to get better," I reply. I then share my spiritual incident with JJ.

"You need to be spending more time with your horse," she says.

"I see JJ a few days a week. I have no physical energy to ride him," I explain.

"I suspect you have worked yourself into adrenal exhaustion. You need rest, and you need to commit to recovery," she advises. She orders a series of tests.

Julia has the results on her desk at our next appointment. "In all of my years of treating addicts, I have never seen such poor adrenal function. This is why you have such deep cravings for sugar and caffeine: your body is desperately seeking alternative sources of energy," she explains.

"What exactly are the adrenals?" I ask.

"Adrenals are the glands that make adrenaline and steroid hormones. They help control heart rate, blood pressure, and other important hormone functions. They are located on top of your kidneys. You likely injured them in your horse accident. Though I suspect they were already compromised with your addictive toolbox. Adrenal depletion is associated with low energy, depression, and sweet cravings. You have exhausted yours."

"Can I recover?" I ask. *What have I done to my body?*

Julia is convinced she can get my adrenals functioning. She puts me on adrenal support and a protocol to achieve more sleep. She is firm with me.

"You need more sleep and less work. Your life depends on it."

I am immersed in a full outpatient treatment plan with Julia. Her protocol is complex. I have a strict mandate to remove caffeine from my diet. Within a few weeks, I start to feel an improvement in my energy.

Addiction is an entirely different beast. I have made a lifelong friendship with my eating disorder, and she has no intention of leaving me. My anxiety mounts as I realize the financial cost of my outpatient program. I continually ask Julia how long it will take until I am cured.

"Why would you think recovery would be swift and easy?" Julia asks.

"I just always thought that once I no longer wanted the addictive coping tools, I could just stop," I say. It sounds ridiculous as I hear the words roll off my tongue.

"Lisa, you have abused your body for three decades. Your brain chemistry is altered, your adrenal system is exhausted, and your liver function is compromised. You are on the road to recovery, but it will be arduous. You should also consider a twelve-step program."

"You mean a twelve-step program for alcohol?" I ask sheepishly.

"Yes. They also have twelve-step programs for eating disorders."

"I have a friend I know from my horse work; she's been in Alcoholics Anonymous for quite some time. I will reach out to her."

"Lisa, your academic work is also an addiction. You need to limit yourself to forty hours of work each week," Julia says.

Is there such a thing as Academics Anonymous?

"I don't think that's possible. Can I limit my work to fifty hours?" I plead.

I know this is a promise I can't keep. In addition to my usual academics, I need to do consulting work to offset the cost of recovery. It is quite a conundrum.

"When's the last time you took a true vacation?" Julia asks.

"I travel all over the world for conferences."

"If you're working, then it's not a real vacation." She nullifies every trip I mention. She is unyielding.

"Lisa, you need to delegate your business travel. Can your PhD students go to these meetings instead of you? You're a full professor. Why do you need to be the one who does all the travel?" she persists.

I have trips coming up to New Zealand, Italy, and the Netherlands. It is difficult for me to consider relinquishing my travel until I begin to envision the joy it will bring my students and how they will flourish with these opportunities. My graduate students will love this, I realize—it is a perfect solution!

Julia stresses that I need to take a true vacation. Perhaps I can find a vacation involving horses, but that will require money and more consulting work—it's a circular problem.

36

Twelve Steps

I read the affirmation card on my wall. "I am grateful for my healthy body. I love life." It is time for the next step in my journey. I call Margaret; she has been in Alcoholics Anonymous (AA) for over twenty years. I met her through natural horsemanship.

"Hi, Margaret. How are you?" I ask. This feels stiff and cold.

"Lisa, it's wonderful to hear from you. How is JJ?"

"JJ is great. But the reason I'm calling is that I need your help. I think I need to go to AA."

"I have seen the change in you when you drink. I think AA would be good for you," she says. *What is that supposed to mean?*

"Can I go to an AA meeting with you sometime?" I ask.

"I can pick you up early. There is a 7:00 a.m. meeting in Petaluma."

"Thank you. I will see you in the morning."

Margaret arrives first thing in the morning. She is cheerful and gifts me a copy of the "Big Book." It is the bible of the twelve-step program. The dark blue book feels heavy in my hands, and its contents feel heavy in my heart.

Bubbly with enthusiasm, she is confident this will be the start of my new life. Tired and cynical, I'm more interested in how long it will take to get through the twelve steps so I can get on with my life. I am ignorant about the work that recovery requires and the realm of sobriety.

We walk into the large, unadorned hall. Anxiety rises in my throat; I won't have any coherent words to share. My heart pounds so loudly I wonder if others can hear it. We take our seats, and the cold metal chair assaults my body. My mind races as a sweet aroma seduces my senses. My eyes sweep the room, and I see my antagonist—a mountain of delectable donuts in the back taunts me.

I imagine how good the crullers and chocolate-covered donuts would taste with the hot coffee brewing by their side. The mere thought of it triggers olfactory overload in my brain. My mouth waters. I can barely focus because my mind won't relinquish my obsession with the plates of donuts and the cups of coffee that start to surround me. This is torture. Panic consumes me.

How can I possibly give up drinking? What will happen when I go to a technical conference? What will I tell my academic friends who are often impressed with my prowess with alcoholic beverages? The donuts seem to be calling my name. *Maybe just one? It's never just one. If I have one, then I'll eat a dozen, or two. Focus on this one AA meeting. Focus, Lisa. Focus.*

People begin to introduce themselves. The voices get closer, and then it's my turn. "My name is Lisa, and I'm an alcoholic," I say. I am ice cold and shaking. *Do I really believe my words? Or do I just think they are magic words that will release me from the grips of alcohol?* I feel like Dorothy in *The Wizard of Oz*—I just want to click my ruby red slippers and be home.

Margaret introduces me to some of her friends when the meeting closes. I want to get out of this room as quickly as possible so I don't succumb to the temptation of the remaining donuts. I suggest breakfast at Halley's restaurant. Starving, I order herbal tea and a veggie omelet. I inhale my food as I listen to Margaret describe the twelve-step process.

"The first step is that we admit we are powerless over alcohol—that our lives have become unmanageable," she explains.

"I am ready to admit this," I reply. At least I think I am.

"The second step is that we come to believe that a power greater than ourselves can restore us to sanity," she continues. I am less certain here.

I can't seem to get past the third step, which states: "We make a decision to turn our will and our lives over to the care of God as we understood Him."

I start playing my inside tape of unworthiness. *Karen wouldn't need a twelve-step program.* I don't know how to give my life over to God. I am filled with deep shame. I have lived my life as an agnostic because my limited exposure to religious beliefs has instilled in me that I won't have a place in heaven.

"Will you be my AA sponsor?" I ask, hoping she can help me find a path to the celestial skies.

With her affirmative answer, I raise the obvious question. "How long will it take to work the twelve steps?"

Margaret has an answer like Julia's response: "Recovery is an arduous journey; it might take years."

I don't want to hear this. I want my adrenals healed and the twelve steps behind me so I can live an energized life with my horse.

A week passes, and I haven't had a single drink and have been to three AA meetings. I believe I am cured.

Of course, I haven't gone to any conferences or socialized with any of my "drinking buddies." More importantly, I have not relinquished my eating disorder. I have simply channeled all my inner turmoil into bulimic behavior.

After a few weeks of sobriety and AA meetings, I am convinced I am on the fast track to recovery. I am trying to abridge the Big Book into a fast-paced redemption scheme. I am convinced I am already at step 4 and that step 12 will be just a bit longer. This isn't so bad. Then I will tackle bulimia.

"Lisa, the fourth step can be quite difficult. You are asked to make a searching and fearless moral inventory of yourself," Margaret tells me. "You can write these down. Eventually, you will be making amends to people whom you have hurt with your alcoholic behavior."

I begin to take a moral inventory of my behavior over the past three decades. My journal fills quickly, and I find myself in a spiral of self-hatred. I had no idea that sobriety would involve such a rigorous, introspective examination of my life. This step feels as though judgment day has come.

Self-loathing erupts, overpowering my repentance. I find myself overwhelmed with emotion. This is just the tip of the recovery iceberg—I can't imagine the moral inventory for three decades of bulimia. My pain is palpable. I feel like I have fallen through a trap door into a deeper rock bottom. *How will I ever find my way to recovery?*

How many people have I hurt? How much anguish have I caused my family and ex-husband? I have let no one into my life in any meaningful way—I have been so fearful that anyone who truly knew me could not possibly like me or love me. *Karen would not have ruined her life—God took the wrong daughter.*

There is only one way through this process. I must walk through my personal fire. I find myself on my knees with hands in the prayer position, begging forgiveness from the universe. I ask forgiveness from those whom I have hurt both knowingly and unknowingly. I apologize to God, over and over again. Ultimately, I will have to forgive myself, but that is too far off to see at this juncture in time.

I have moved from taking my moral inventory to the need to ask for redemption. My sponsor does not know that I jumped over the God parts (steps 5–8) and I am now trying to work step 9. If I were an engineer in training trying to build a bridge, the same methodology would ensure imminent failure of the load-bearing structure. My emotional spiral does not have me thinking straight.

Drenched in sweat, I call my parents. My dad answers. I breathe a sigh of relief, and then I panic as I realize that I may offend him. Before I lose my courage, I spurt out the heavy weight of my burden.

"Dad, I'm an alcoholic. I'm going to AA meetings. I'm sorry for all of the pain that I have caused you and Mom," I blurt. I quickly sideline him with my emotional burden and then burst into tears.

He responds with compassion. He is not surprised. I learn that we have a history of alcoholism in our extended family. I try to imagine what I can possibly say to Mom to heal our relationship.

"Mom, I am sorry for my behavior and the hurt I have caused you."

I don't know how to truly apologize for nearly three decades of poor behavior. It will take time for my mom to understand why I had to end my marriage. Later, she will offer, "I think I understand why you needed to get divorced. You had to save yourself." This starts a path to healing between us.

I then ask forgiveness from Beth for my cruelty when we were growing up. I have isolated my life from her so I don't have to feel the weight of her academic excellence beside my inner sense of unworthiness. I feel like an impostor while she is the real deal.

Beth is compassionate and understanding. She can't believe that I am still carrying the burden of my childhood antics. *Is she just being nice?* I was a dreadful sister, not only as a child but as an adolescent and adult.

I call Frank and share with him that I am in AA. I apologize for the hurt I caused him. For sixteen years, I held him accountable for all of our problems, yet I had never owned up to my contribution to our marital woes. I failed to show up for the marriage. My apology can't possibly capture the depths of forgiveness I am seeking.

"I'm not surprised," he says.

There is no true forgiveness being offered. I hadn't really expected that he could forgive me—I am still trying to forgive myself. I have a long journey ahead.

37

Healing with Horses

I have been seeing Julia for months, and my energy is improving. I am making good progress with my adrenal treatment. Julia is pleased with my sobriety. I wish I were making progress with my eating disorder as well, but Julia is confident I will recover from bulimia. "It will just take more time as that is your more deeply-rooted addiction," she observes.

Each day, I work with JJ on my natural horsemanship skills. I feel that I have evolved to the realm of being unconsciously competent with my aids. JJ offers incredible softness to me in both our groundwork and in the saddle. We seem to be of one mind. There is an old adage that the outside of a horse is good for the inside of a man—horses hold something magical and healing for me. I still have a deep inner desire to do more with horses, but for now, I am pleased to have the energy to enjoy JJ. My life feels as though it is finally on the right path.

An enticing opportunity presents itself. Dr. Eleanor Criswell, an equine somatics expert whom I met at Reis Ranch, will be giving a series of workshops. She asks if I would like to do a demonstration with JJ. I jump at the opportunity. I work with Eleanor to learn the somatic releases for the various muscles in the horse's body. JJ loves this work. With her tutelage, I demonstrate the equine somatic work to her students, using JJ as the model horse. I also demonstrate natural horsemanship, liberty work, and bridleless jumping.

After a few of these successful events, Eleanor invites me to do the same at the Marin County Fair over the Fourth of July weekend celebration. JJ is a huge success with the crowds—he eats up this attention, especially from the children.

I meld my engineering and horse worlds, inviting my research group up to Marin to watch the demonstration. My students see me in full cowgirl gear: chaps, boots, and hat. They see me wield my elegant steed around the expansive arena with my energy and our finale of bridleless jumping. Horses are no longer a separate part of my life; they now permeate into my academic world.

A woman approaches me after our last demonstration. "That was a spectacular demonstration," she enthuses.

"Thank you. It's really JJ. He makes me look good!" I reply with a laugh.

"I wonder if you know Ariana Strozzi?" she asks.

"No, I don't think so. Should I?"

"Ariana is an expert in equine-guided education and leadership with horses; I think you would enjoy working with her."

Intrigued, when I get home, I log onto my computer and find that Ariana has an upcoming workshop. I immediately enroll.

The finale of my first sober summer is a trip to Portugal to learn classical dressage on schoolmasters. I have lured Shirley to join me. We will be riding Lusitano stallions at the Alcainca dressage school just outside Lisbon. Portugal is incredibly restorative to my psyche. My body is fueled by the exhilaration of classical dressage, truly feeling the magical movements of these resplendent horses that readily offer passage, piaffe, and tempi changes. I know that I will be coming back to Portugal. In fact, I will return several more times over the coming decade and beyond to enjoy the school masters.

I find myself enraptured by classical dressage. I think about Juan, the Andalusian from the horseman's clinic two years earlier. I ask Shirley if she will reach out to his owner. My inquiry is timely because his owner is now interested in another horse more suited to trail riding. We negotiate a deal that we are both happy with, and I purchase Juan.

My first canter with Juan in the arena is nothing like the collected canter offered by the Lusitanos. He will require more work than I had anticipated. I pony Juan from atop JJ. I keep Juan on the inside track of JJ while we are using the arena and behind him on the trails. Juan learns to canter in a balanced way and masters how to balance himself on the hills. Juan becomes light on the aids as I retrain his liberty work. He is a remarkable horse, yet I know I will never have the same relationship with him that I have with JJ. I sense that Juan is seeking his forever person—but it's not me.

38

Leadership with Horses

The coastal ranch has me mesmerized. I drive through the main gate, cross the first cattle grating, and gaze across the majestic rolling hills dotted with oak trees, sheep, and horses. When I step out of my truck, the sweet scent of grass takes my breath away. I inhale the salty ocean breeze and absorb the leathery aroma of horse, my body swept into the refreshing energy of this place.

Ariana comes out of the barn to greet me, and I am struck by her strong presence. The ringlets of her long dark hair gently bounce beneath her cowgirl hat as she strides with confidence. Her bright eyes and smile exude wisdom. Her ornate cowgirl shirt is crisp yet well-worn. She has a spiritual lightness mirrored by the resplendent eagles that soar above her land. She leads me to the classroom that abuts her indoor arena. The artistry on the walls tells Ariana's story—cowgirl, rancher, artist, leader, and modern-day medicine woman.

"Horses are prey animals; their ability to sense energy has facilitated their evolutionary survival. These intuitive beings sense our energy and can reflect behaviors for which we lack conscious awareness," Ariana says to the group in her classroom. I quickly scribe into my journal all of her words of wisdom—so much of it is in full alignment with my learnings of natural horsemanship. I am forty years old, and I am as excited about this topic as I was when I was nineteen and in my first metallurgy class.

All of us are eager to learn leadership through horses. I seek to lead my own life. I am in my infancy of sobriety and still actively working to overcome a long-term eating disorder. I no longer want to rely on bulimia. I want a clean and authentic life, one that is aligned with integrity.

We learn that horses thrive in the realm of leadership. In a herd setting, horses always have a leader. Their safety relies on this knowledge because without it, they would likely fall victim to a mountain lion or other predator. Their intuitive ability enables horses to serve as guides in leadership training.

Ariana brings us to her arena, filled with the wisdom of her herd of mares. They need to know who leads whom at all times; they sense what we know well before we get close to them. With a clear directive and authentic energy, we can align with these equine guides to find direction in our own lives. We work in small groups and as individuals to see if we can align our energy with her horses. There are no tools, no ropes, no whips. As we ground ourselves and work with our body language, her mares begin to follow. I want to align with my own life—I want to be free of compulsive cravings for sugar. I no longer want to work like a machine, driven by a hunger for worthiness.

Ariana doesn't *just* educate us on the way of the horse. She introduces us to animal medicine and spirit totems, nature and poetry, as well as creative outlets for personal growth. I absorb her philosophy of equine-guided leadership. Her teachings are fully aligned with everything I have learned in natural horsemanship. I soak in her wisdom and enroll in her equine-guided education (EGE) coaching program.

"Ariana, may I bring JJ with me for the coaching program? I think he would thrive in this type of work," I ask.

I share my background in natural horsemanship with her and express that I would like to use JJ as an equine guide. She encourages me to bring him along.

In her EGE program, I am lured further into the inner kingdom of horse consciousness. I learn that horses are not only our partners but also our greatest teachers. These magnificent beings can empower us to create declarations that are aligned with our personal life purpose.

Horses are keen to our body language and can sense incongruencies in our energy. I learn to interpret the horse's body language to coach people. We practice energy exercises in the arena with the herd of horses and one-on-one sessions in the round pen. I embody the wisdom offered through horses. I now see how horses can help us find our own authentic spirit. These sentient beings offer me knowledge that I have never been able to access through engineering.

As I complete my course with Ariana, I meld my passion for horses with engineering education. I offer equine-guided coaching to engineering students, starting this work through one-on-one sessions with my doctoral students. Ultimately, I evolve my offerings to include workshops for engineering students, staff, and colleagues. The engineering students who work with my horses in the workshops are transformed. My horses start to appear in the acknowledgment sections of doctoral theses. Equine-guided coaching provides personal growth for all who participate—many find life balance for the first time. Dave Dornfeld jokes with me, "All of the faculty should spend time in the round pen with JJ."

The equine-guided leadership work nourishes my spirit and facilitates a mechanism to dissolve the boundary between my love of horses and academics. I feel a semblance of worthiness rising beneath my academic armor. I feel another inner voice starting to whisper, "I have a calling in this world."

39

Recovery Takes a Detour

The road to recovery is like driving along a backcountry road at dusk—such roads are often winding and not well-signed. It's easy to take the wrong turn. What starts as an adventurous drive can easily become a white-knuckled ride in which we get desperately lost. This has certainly been true for me.

At forty years of age and a year into sobriety, I decide to buy a town-home in Petaluma. The price is outrageous, but I am able to utilize a university loan. It doesn't take long for the mortgage payments, home-owner fees, and property taxes to catch up with me. I soon realize I can't afford this home unless I have an ongoing consulting income.

I take on two large patent infringement cases, one in orthopedics and the other in cardiovascular devices. It pays well, but the workload is overwhelming. I am confident I can manage the work, but I am wrong. I find myself binging and purging more often to offset my stress. This is not good for my recovery.

In my role as associate dean, I manage our webcast programs, work with our new director to create international exchange programs for undergraduate students, serve as the faculty liaison for the National Leadership Conference, and mentor our undergraduate K–12 outreach clubs. Julia would not be pleased to know how much work is on my plate. I don't disclose the scope of my work endeavors to her, nor how many hours they entail.

The real estate bubble bursts shortly after I make my purchase. People begin to abandon their townhomes. My neighbors move out in the middle of the night, taking all of their appliances with them. Bank foreclosures surround me. My townhome is now worth a fraction of its initial value. My stress level quickly escalates when I realize I will not be able to sell or refinance my townhome in the foreseeable future. I maintain my sobriety from alcohol, but my bulimic episodes escalate.

I attend only one scientific conference during the semester. It's in Boston and gives me the chance to see my Aunt Jackie. We have plans to meet for dinner on Thursday night after my technical sessions wrap up.

On the first day of the meeting, I hear my name paged over the hotel intercom. "Lisa Pruitt, please come to the concierge desk." I panic. *Has something happened to one of my horses?* I rush to the lobby. *Why is Aunt Jackie here? Has something happened to my mom?*

The hold on my heart loosens when I see my aunt's big smile beneath her coral lipstick. Her bright blue eyes meet mine. I see that her blond hair is meticulous, the way she likes it to look when she doesn't want the world to think she's a day older than thirty-eight. I am now officially older than she is. She strangles me in a big hug, and her strong perfume assaults me. In this moment, I realize how much I have missed my beloved fairy godmother.

"I thought I would surprise you," Jackie says.

"It's almost lunch. Let's grab something to eat," I reply. I order a heaping salad—a far cry from our days of ice cream, chips, candy, and wine coolers.

"Lisa Anne Prune-Pit, guess what? I have been recalled from retirement to serve as acting principal," she announces, beaming.

"But I thought you retired because you didn't enjoy it anymore?"

She dodges my question. We finish our lunch with small talk about extended family. Her stories start to repeat.

"Jackie, I have to get back to my technical session. I'll see you at five on Thursday, and then we can go out for a nice dinner."

"Let's go to the Top of the Hub, my treat."

My aunt returns the next day and summons me from my meeting.

"Don't you have school?" I ask.

She shrugs. "I had to do an errand in the area. I just thought I'd stop by and say hello."

"Thank you, but I have to go give my talk. I look forward to seeing you Thursday night." I give her a hug and kiss. Something stirs in the back of my mind. *What is going on with my aunt?*

On Wednesday, I get a call in my room from the woman at the front desk. "Dr. Pruitt, you have a visitor. She claims to be your fairy godmother."

"Please tell her I'll be right down." My pulse quickens. I greet my aunt and question whether she has confused our dates, reminding her we're having dinner the following night.

Jackie laughs. "Oh. I know that. There's just a lot of construction in Boston, so I thought I would do a practice run." Then she gives me a hug and heads off in her whimsical way.

Does she not remember that she's already had two practice runs? I have an ominous feeling about my aunt. My nana succumbed to dementia in the later stages of her life. I try to push this thought away. My aunt is far too young for Alzheimer's—she is only sixty-three. Some part of me knows that something is wrong with Jackie, but I can't bring myself to face it.

On Thursday night, I find myself standing in the lobby with growing trepidation. My aunt is now an hour late for our dinner date. I pace the floor, studying the pattern on the marble floors, its veins intricately weaving their way in a beautiful puzzle. She never answers her cell phone, so I don't fret when it goes to voicemail. I call her home phone—no answer.

Throughout her life, Aunt Jackie has been notoriously late for many events, too focused on getting her skin moisturized or her hair perfect to keep an eye on the clock. I return to my room and busy myself with work.

After an hour, I call her home again. No answer. I continue working for another hour. I am starving and decide to go get something to eat by myself. Walking through the hotel lobby, I spot the blue-and-red lights of a police car outside the entrance. Just behind the patrol car is my aunt's vehicle. Was she speeding? Is she drunk?

I walk over to the police officer. He explains that my aunt was lost and she had asked him to lead her to the hotel. *Something isn't right.* She has had no trouble finding the hotel for the past three days.

My aunt seems to find the whole situation entertaining. She thanks the officer in her usual eccentric way. *Is she flirting?* I try to put the pieces of this puzzle together, but my mind can't make sense of it.

I suggest we eat at the hotel so we don't have to drive anywhere. We order our food, but neither of us orders alcohol. This seems strange—Aunt Jackie has been my longtime "drinking buddy." I had been prepared to explain why I don't drink anymore. Now I wonder why she isn't drinking anymore. I listen to her stories—the exact same ones I have heard before. I nod politely. She feels like an impostor posing as my aunt.

Some inner part of me weeps. We have had a deep kinship throughout my life. Jackie has been some strange cocktail of aunt, fairy godmother, big sister, and friend. She has always been a light in my life. I have lived my life behind my façade, yet she has permeated more deeply than anyone else. The thought of her slipping away fills me with fear. In a moment of weakness, I suggest we order dessert. We indulge ourselves with two hot-fudge sundaes. I feel the sugar rush immediately, hitting me like a drug.

After dinner, we say our farewells. I am filled with anxiety about the idea of her trying to navigate her way home, but alas, my neurological wiring receives its dopamine hit from the ice cream, and I now am only worried about where I will get more of this sweet creamy stuff. I return to my room and head straight to the bathroom. I purge my dinner. Then I head across the street to indulge myself in more sugary foods. I spend the next two hours binging and purging.

Shortly after I return from the trip to Boston, I get a distressing phone call from one of the teachers at Jackie's school. "Jackie has been showing up at school and disrupting the classrooms," she informs me.

"But she has been recalled as the acting principal. Maybe she's just checking on the classes?" I suggest.

"Lisa, she is not the acting principal. This has been going on for months, and we are worried about Jackie. She seems to have some form of dementia. I called you because she always talked about you. I found your office phone number on the Berkeley website," she explains.

"I will let my family know. Thank you for calling."

My heart pounds with anxiety as I process her words. I call my mom and then my sister. We each make plans to go back to Boston at different times so we can get a sense of what is going on with Jackie. Getting my aunt the help she needs will turn out to be far more difficult and heart-wrenching than any of us can possibly imagine.

My stress intensifies when I return to Boston a few months later. I have asked my cousin Laura to come with me. We knock on Jackie's door.

Moments pass, and I wonder if she is not home.

Her door creaks open, and I am confronted by someone who has hijacked my aunt. This woman barely resembles my beloved auntie. Her hair is wild, gray, and straggly. Her clothes are unkempt and soiled. There is a horrifying smell emanating from within her home.

With some convincing, she invites us into her home. Her front room is tidy, and it is hard to determine the extent of the problem. The pungency of the air is stifling. I nudge Laura, and her look tells me she is aware that something is very wrong.

Laura distracts Jackie while I investigate. The kitchen is filthy. Her fridge is filled with containers from Dunkin' Donuts; trash is piled in the corner. I open the dishwasher and find it filled with bathroom supplies. I walk into her bedroom, and the smell in nauseating. Her toilet is filled with waste. She seemingly has no flushing capability in her bathroom.

I am trying not to wretch or sob. I quickly take out my phone and take as many documenting pictures as I can muster. We will need these to get her the help she needs. We take my aunt out to dinner, and we all pretend that everything is fine. I am the master of pretend. I eat a bingeable quantity of food. My stress is off the charts.

Back at my hotel, I call my parents and Beth to let them know what I have just seen. Then I purge my dinner, but the act is insufficient to offload my stress. I need sugar—lots of it.

When I return home, we embark on a lengthy process to get my aunt committed to an Alzheimer's facility. It is heartbreaking for me. Beth takes on the brunt of the work. I am burdened by shame and guilt for not being able to do more.

I can't forget the promise I made to my fairy godmother when I was a child—that I would always take care of her and never put her in a nursing home. But there is no alternative. I can barely take care of myself.

I feel my inner flaws expanding yet again.

40

Food Addiction 101

Bulimia has served as my primary mechanism for coping with stress for the past three decades, and it will not go without a fight. My lifetime friend is now a mortal enemy. She constantly summons me to the grocery stores, bakeries, and cafés. She seduces me into thinking it will make me feel better. But I never feel better; I only feel more guilt and shame. Is bulimia raging because my life is out of order? Or is my life out of order because I have abandoned my recovery? I have been remiss about seeing Julia. I left her thinking I was well on my way to recovery—she knows nothing of my relapse. Another lie.

I finally confess my ongoing challenges with bulimic behavior to my AA sponsor. I expect her typical compassion, but instead, Margaret suggests I'm in the wrong twelve-step program.

"I think your real addiction is food. It would be better for you to work the twelve steps in Food Addicts (FA) Anonymous. There's a large group that meets near you in Petaluma; my sister attends that meeting."

"Will you still be my sponsor?" I ask sheepishly.

"No. You should have a sponsor who knows how to work with food addicts." *Have I just been kicked out of AA?*

I arrive at my first Food Addicts meeting. I have to muster the courage to get out of my truck. This forum is held in a much larger building than the AA meetings I have attended, and it is surrounded by a park-like setting. I take note of the large swans elegantly skimming the water. I feel like a swan struggling to find her place on rocky terrain, desperately seeking the water that will be my peaceful refuge.

I work up my courage to open the large glass doors leading into the meeting hall. Hundreds of people pack the room. There are no donut plates calling my name here—not a morsel of food in sight. Most of the audience seems to be middle-aged, perhaps more women than men, but not significantly so. I note all body types—some look like anorexics, others appear to be of "normal build" like me, and the balance openly struggle with their weight. I sit in the back and listen to people share their personal stories of food addiction.

The shared stories captivate me. There are binge eaters who struggle with obesity and anorexics who can't bring themselves to eat. Their bodies tell some portion of their stories. Others are like me, bulimics who hide their eating disorder under a healthy-looking body.

I learn of variations of bulimia that include not only purging via vomiting but also purging via exercise, drugs, or laxatives. There are also "spitters" who taste food and then spit it out.

Every storyteller uses food to numb away their underlying pain. All of us in this room have some inner hole in our psyche that we try to fill with some unhealthy relationship with food.

I am glued to my seat. It never occurs to me to leave—I seem to belong here. We are reminded that, unlike other addictions, we can't simply "abstain from food." I hadn't fully processed the implications until I hear it spoken aloud. Sobriety in this twelve-step program requires abstaining from sugar, alcohol, and flour. I will soon learn it also requires following the strict eating rules of one's sponsor.

At the end of my first week of Food Addicts meetings, a tall, lean woman approaches me. Her dark curls have hints of gray, and her smile reveals fine wrinkles at her eyes. She has a confident air about her. The little girl inside me is begging to run away. I should have listened.

"Hi, my name is Pamela. I've noticed you sitting in the back over the past week. You must be a food addict?"

"My name is Lisa. I'm bulimic," I reply. My body is cold. My heart is racing.

"Do you have a sponsor?"

"No. Would you be my sponsor?" I ask.

"Possibly. I have ten years of experience in the Food Addicts program. You will need to follow my rules, or I will not agree to sponsor you," she warns.

"Okay. Thank you," I say naïvely.

"I'll set the limits on the quantity of food you eat each day. You will have two scales at your home: one for weighing your food and the other to weigh yourself. You will weigh yourself on Friday mornings before you eat. You will give me this number. You will not lie, and you will not step on the scale at any other time. These are my conditions to serve as your sponsor. Do you agree to the terms?" Pamela says.

I nod in agreement, too afraid to speak. She reminds me of the Scared Straight tactics used to keep people out of prison.

"You will call me each morning at 5:00 a.m. We will discuss your eating plan for that day," she instructs as she hands me a Post-it with her number. "I also expect you to attend at least three meetings per week." I meekly nod.

I am 126 pounds at my first weigh-in. Because I have been bulimic for more than thirty years, I have no idea how many calories my body needs for my level of activity. I cycle nearly twenty miles per day and ride two horses several times a week. I teach and am on my feet much of the day on campus. It is remarkable that my body still works after three decades of abuse. An engineer might say that I am a nature-inspired material with exceptional resilience.

My sponsor allows me one ounce of oatmeal and two ounces of protein for breakfast, along with a piece of fruit. My lunch is six ounces of vegetables, four ounces of protein, and a piece of fruit. My dinner is four ounces of protein, nine ounces of salad, six ounces of vegetables, and a piece of fruit. She sets the window of time for when I can eat each meal. Absolutely no snacking is permitted. Any deviation from her eating plan is deemed "a loss of sobriety." It is an easy system to fail in, which does not bode well for a perfectionist such as myself.

The days pass by, and I remain "sober." I am painfully hungry—the eating plan is brutal. At my second weigh-in, I am 121 pounds. I haven't binged all week. I have a visceral fear of failure in this program and a fear of my sponsor.

"Lisa, you shouldn't be losing weight. Are you throwing up? Are you not eating all of your food?" Pamela asks accusingly.

"I have eaten everything in my eating plan. I haven't purged," I answer honestly.

By week three, I am at 118 pounds.

"Lisa, you must be purging," Pamela insists.

"I am not. I don't think this is enough calories for me. May I have more food to eat at one of my meals?" I plead, tears brimming in my eyes.

"Lisa, there will be no more food for you," she says sternly.

The following week, I am down three more pounds. I dread sharing the number. I think it's only my tenacity and work ethic that give me the discipline to stay with the program. Yet, there is something even deeper—my sense of unworthiness and fear of failure. I am convinced I will succumb to bulimia and die an awful death if I fail out of this program. My mental judgment is being compromised.

It is early summer. I am at the Horse Expo in Sacramento with Ariana to do a demonstration on equine-guided education work using JJ and Juan. Shirley shares a room with me. She may be my elder by thirty-one years, but she is also a wise friend with eagle eyes.

"Lisa. You are getting far too thin. You can't live on this amount of food. Why can't you just go back to Julia?" Shirley asks, concerned.

"I could never break free of my bulimic behaviors with Julia. This is the first time in my life when I've had any respite from bulimia. It's been almost a month since my last binge-purge episode."

"Don't forget that we return to Portugal at the end of summer. Will you have the energy to ride the stallions? I think this twelve-step program is wrong for you. Your sponsor sounds abusive. You went in as a bulimic, but you may end up being an anorexic. I am deeply concerned about your health," Shirley proffers.

"I can't talk about this anymore. I'm going to work Juan and JJ so they're ready for the seminar tomorrow. I'll be back in an hour." I sulk all the way to the stables. I don't think I can live this way, and yet I can't go on living as a bulimic. The latter is a slow form of suicide. I must overcome bulimia, but I am so hungry and undernourished that food consumes my thoughts.

I ask my sponsor for more food, and my request is blatantly denied.

"You need to work your steps. Maybe you're thinking too much, and this is eating up too many calories," she says.

Is she for real? I'm a professor. I think for a living. Why am I staying in this program? Am I paying penance for my food addiction? Maybe so.

Working the steps in FA has caused an emotional spiral. I must ask forgiveness from those whom I have hurt because of my bulimia. My list seems endless—this is an order of magnitude more difficult than working the steps in AA.

I descend into self-hatred. My energy level falls; my mind is consumed with thoughts of sugar-laden foods. My body seems to be eating itself. I keep growing thinner with each passing week. I dread giving the real numbers to my sponsor.

Pamela cuts me down daily when I do my check-ins. *Perhaps I deserve her emotional abuse for all the pain I have caused others?* I can barely look at myself in the mirror anymore. I rip the affirmation cards from my wall. I can't endure the positive words.

I limit my visits to JJ and Juan. I can't work with them in this state. Perhaps Portugal will be my healing balm, as it was in the past.

By the time Shirley and I arrive in Lisbon, I have lost almost twenty pounds. I have never been so hungry or food-centric in my life. I carry extreme shame as I try to work my steps around bulimia. I hope that the majestic Lusitano stallions can pull me up from the abyss of self-hatred and suicidal ideations.

When we arrive at the Alcainca dressage school, the instructor immediately sees the change in my body over the past year. Paulo asks if I have an illness. I try to explain that I am having adrenal issues after my horse accident—this has been my story to everyone in my academic circles. I can only imagine the actual state of my adrenals now that I am this thin. I have been avoiding Julia and everyone else in my life who might lay stake to my recovery.

Portugal does not provide its usual solace. I am exhausted and hungry. I am required to call my sponsor every day, and each day I plead for more food.

"Lisa, let me be crystal clear with you. There will not be any more food in your daily allotment. You need to cut back on your activities," Pamela says.

I hang up the phone and sob. If I don't have the energy to ride horses, then what is the point of living?

My flight home is the breaking point. I have sixteen hours of travel. My request for a second meal is denied. By the time the flight lands, I am filled with raw anger. I am angry at Pamela for her abuse and with myself for allowing myself to be treated this way. I get home in the middle of the night and send Pamela a farewell email. I decide against the use of *auntie language*, though I am spewing it out under my breath.

I am raw with emotion, filled with anger, shame, remorse, and guilt. My self-hatred fuels a hunger deep within me—hatred for the abuse I sustained from Pamela and anger at myself for being an addict and all the unworthiness that accompanies it. I spend the next month in a full-on sugar-laden, caffeine-rich bulimic relapse. My body resumes a "healthy body weight," but I have also steered myself back into adrenal exhaustion.

I feel JJ beckoning me to the farm, and I find myself standing at the gate of his pasture. Yet again, my spirit horse comes to me—no judgment for being away or for falling through the trap door into another rock bottom. I only feel the warm breath on his velvety muzzle and his unfathomable knowing eyes. His love augments my fractured vessel.

I receive his directive loud and clear. *We need to go to Ariana. We need to follow the road to recovery together.*

41

Fire Horse

My bright chestnut equine companion by my side softens the anxiety pulling on me. JJ's presence grounds me in this moment. The sweet fragrance of his muzzle awakens my senses. I feel the sand supporting me beneath my cowgirl boots.

I soak in the vast rolling hills of this beautiful coastal ranch and gaze at the horses in the distance, listening to the faraway screech of red-tailed hawks. A butterfly flickers on my floral cowgirl shirt. We are in the same round pen where I have observed Ariana coach people aside her horses. Normally, this is a peaceful refuge, but the serenity is lost on me because I am facing a number of agonizing questions.

Ariana sits outside the round pen. "Take a deep breath and give a long exhale. Feel your feet, open your arms, and soften your gaze. Soak in the healing energy of JJ and the ranch," she instructs.

"For much of my academic life, I have felt like the ultimate impostor," I admit. "I worked myself to exhaustion, working like a machine, hoping to find some semblance of worthiness in this world." JJ remains anchored by my side.

"Where do your feelings of unworthiness come from?" Ariana asks. "Why do you work yourself like a machine?"

Remorse pours down my face. I describe to her the loss of my sister and my feelings of darkness. I share with her my path into bulimia and alcohol addiction.

"You need to be compassionate to yourself. You don't see JJ as a problem that needs to be fixed, do you?" she offers.

"I used to think JJ was the problem, but then I decided it was me."

"Let's change your narrative," Ariana suggests. "JJ absorbed energies from his upbringing at the track. You helped him find his path. Now he's here to do the same for you. You embodied the emotions that permeated your childhood home when your sister died. You may need to do somatic work to fully release these."

I nod gently as tears cascade down my cheeks. I feel the softness of JJ at my side as the sand shifts beneath my feet.

"You are not a problem that needs to be fixed. Deep within, there is still a scared little girl struggling with feelings of guilt, shame, and unworthiness. She needs to find her sense of belonging in this world."

I walk alongside JJ, stating, "I am not a problem that needs to be fixed." He strides with me. Mother hawk screeches in the distance. An eagle soars above, and a butterfly flickers at my side.

Ariana continues to reframe my story. I finally see that my addictive behaviors were merely coping mechanisms and survival tools. I am left with the feeling that everything happens for a reason. All of the challenges I have faced in these forty years of life have been leading me to this very moment. *What if I am exactly where I need to be? What if everything has unfolded perfectly in my life?*

"I've seen you do liberty work with JJ," Ariana says. "Who is this powerful woman within you? You need to find her because she's the part of you who has the strength to heal your life."

JJ and I move together in the round pen. As I raise my energy, he offers a soft, collected canter around me. We are synchronized, moving together as one. I feel a powerful presence within myself. I have found her.

"I see her in your energy," Ariana says. "What is her name?"

It is a name that is deep within me. She is one with JJ and all of nature. It then comes to me from the ethers of the universe. *Fire Horse.* I feel her viscerally in my body. "I am Fire Horse."

I feel fully empowered. I enter into stillness with JJ. A butterfly passes between us. I hear the call of the eagle. I soak in this moment.

Ariana encourages me to journal on this experience. When I return home, I take out a sketch pad and create a beautiful female horse, my equine alter ego. Then I write my first poem.

HORSE OF FIRE

Today the air was thick
Nature was preparing a gift from the spirit world
A young eagle and her vulture companions soared through the sky
A butterfly flickered through the air
Something was transforming on the horizon
And from the earth a horse of fire was born
The filly expressed her exuberance as she came to life

This fiery chestnut is a spirited creature
of internal beauty and strength
Her long mane flows as she runs through the wind
She is like no other horse
She has the heart of a thoroughbred
the courage of a war horse
and the stamina of a draught

The eagle and butterfly stay near her
She is guided by the spirit world and will be a healing horse
She will always run wild
sharing her spirit with others but never to be contained

She deserves a name
For now she is known as Fire Horse

42

The Universe Is Listening

Ariana coaches me through the use of horses, art, and poetry. I paint, write, and journal. The little girl within me is finding her way. With Ariana's guidance, I use animal medicine to find my power totems. I start a daily gratitude practice. It has taken me four decades to get to this juncture of my life, and finally, I feel some semblance of authenticity.

I recognize the significance of my namesake. Fire Horse matches my zodiac sign—I was born in the year of the horse with fire as her element.

I continue to meet with Ariana throughout the fall semester. I am better able to focus my energy on mentoring and pedagogy. The patent infringement cases I have been consulting on are going to trial in the coming year; this provides me with the added income I need for my home, my horses, and my work with Ariana. I am also looking for another vacation with horses.

I find my dream vacation: an equestrian safari in Africa. The first part of the safari is in South Africa, where riders stay at a private preserve, and the second portion of the safari is in Botswana with point-to-point riding to various campsites. The trip promises advanced riders the opportunity to gallop among the giraffes, zebras, and wildebeests.

I'm making good progress on my recovery. I have been free of a bulimic episode for more than three months—the longest stretch in thirty-two years and done through self-love rather than external punishment. I am riding JJ and Juan daily. My sessions with Ariana have been spaced further apart to reflect my progress. As we come to our completing session, she asks a thought-provoking question: "What do you want to accomplish with your life?"

"I want to blend my passion for horses, mentoring, and engineering education," I respond.

There is certainly great truth in this answer, but JJ is circling around me with exuberant energy. He won't settle for this answer. There must be some deep desire still lurking within me.

"Is anything missing in your life?" Ariana asks.

She hits the bullseye with her insightful question. Something stirs within me. Unexpected words come forth from deep within.

"I want a family of my own. I want to find a man who will love me as I am, and I want to have a child." *Has that been hiding deep within, beneath my armor?*

As the words hit the air, I know they are capturing the inner truth nestled tightly in my heart. JJ immediately becomes still and comes to my side. He places his muzzle on my heart. I feel his spiritual guidance. This horse has a direct connection to my soul.

I feel the little girl within me who has been waiting for self-love and compassion. She is my inner knowing and intuition. She has been waiting to feel safe so she can speak her truth. We want a family. We want a chance to love a child. I try to stay with these feelings, yet fleeting thoughts of fear bubble up. "I have never shown up in any meaningful way in a relationship," I confess. "I am forty years old. It seems the odds are stacked against me."

Ariana is not concerned with my worries. "Speak aloud the attributes of this man whom you want to call into your life. Use the embodied power of Fire Horse."

I listen to the soft voice within, the voice who has been imprisoned in armor for all these years. My heart flutters lightly. A sticky residue of shame lifts away.

"I am seeking a man who is loving," I venture. "He loves nature and horses. He loves children. He believes in divine possibilities. He will love me as I am."

I sense that the universe is listening.

43

Winter Solstice

Winter solstice marks the day when darkness prevails. It feels symbolic in my life. I organize a celebration with the horses and a group of metaphysically minded women. The workshop progresses in strange ways; women in long flowing scarves dance among the horses. The little girl within me finally feels safe, and she wants to come out and play—today, she dances. The day is filled with chants and drums, not equations and problem-solving. Sometimes, I forget that I am a professor of engineering.

That evening, there is a winter solstice dinner in the city. After my enlightening session with Ariana, I joined a club that brings single people together for weekly dinner conversations. These dinners have been uneventful. I am tempted to put on my pajamas. Instead, I dress in a crisp cowgirl shirt, Wrangler jeans, and cowboy boots. I must be in the persona of Fire Horse—not Professor Pruitt. Any prospective soulmate needs to know that I am a cowgirl at heart.

At dinner, I find myself seated across from a tall, handsome man by the name of Ric. He is a park ranger.

"Ranger Ric!" I say with a laugh. It's met with a friendly retort. I am immediately at ease in his presence. He is witty and lighthearted with our conversation. The evening quickly passes as he engages me with games, riddles, and playful antics. I don't want the evening to end.

I can't bring myself to be present for the awkward separation from the dinner table. I excuse myself and purposely linger in the restroom until I am almost certain the restaurant has emptied. Then, I quickly make my way to my truck and head home. I berate myself on the long drive home for not saying goodbye and for not giving him my phone number.

I log into the dinner-club website when I get home. There is a portal for making requests to see a dinner member again. I make my request, but it's nearly Christmas. I will have to wait until the new year to see if the organizers can work their magic.

In early winter, Dean Newton loses his battle with pancreatic cancer. Rich was pivotal in my retention at Berkeley, and I have served as his associate dean for the past eighteen months. He supported my professional growth and was an advocate for all my K–12 initiatives. The loss is hard, not only for me but also the campus at large.

Weeks later, Marni Goldman passes away while on vacation with her parents. It is unexpected. I am filled with grief and remorse. I have spent much of the past two years avoiding get-togethers with Marni—I didn't want her to see me at my rock bottom. While I have mastered the art of my academic façade for most, I would never have been able to hide the depth of my turmoil from her. She had a sixth sense about such things, much like the horses. My heart breaks as I realize I have lost a true friend. Marni was my academic daughter, mother, and mentor rolled into one amazing being.

Her parents ask me to speak at her memorial. There, I truly see the remarkable impact this woman has had on so many. We all share our stories, and it's clear that Marni had an enormous sphere of influence. Each of us adds some levity as we share our experiences with Marni.

"Marni was a force," I say. "She was a beacon of light in my life. I'm not sure if I was her mentor or if she was mine. One thing is certain: she was a gift to me, and she will forever have a place in my heart." Tears stream down my face.

I am overcome with sorrow for this immense loss. Her parents offer me a small elephant figurine that rekindles my fond memories of watching the elephants with her at the zoo.

In parallel to these losses, I find love. Ric and I arrange our "first date," deciding to have dinner at Point Reyes Station. Ric lives in Pacifica, and I live in Petaluma. He generously offers to make the journey north.

We stop at Hawkwood Farm on our way to dinner and walk up the hill to the pasture. I watch the response from my horses. I immediately see the shift in JJ's body language, as if he were to say, "Who is this guy with my Fire Horse?" My bold thoroughbred positions himself strategically between Ric and me. Juan greets Ric and immediately welcomes him into his herd. Ric has found himself a friend.

We bring the horses down to the outdoor arena so I can demonstrate the liberty work. I ride JJ bridleless. I am showing off my horse skills, and JJ senses this immediately. I receive a stern warning from him in the form of a buck as I ask for the canter departure. I just hope my thoroughbred doesn't decide to buck me off. I look over to see whether Ric is watching and am relieved to see that he is not. His full attention is on Juan.

"Can I get on Juan?" Ric asks.

"Really, without a saddle?" I ask. I tie up the halter around Juan's neck, and Ric rides bareback. They saunter around the arena as though they have known each other forever. They appear to be kindred spirits. JJ relaxes as he, too, observes the change that comes over Juan in this man's presence.

Perhaps this is the man I called in from the depths of the universe? Did Juan have a stake in this calling as well?

A few weeks later, over dinner, I describe the African equine safari that I plan to do in June. I sense Ric's interest. "Do you want to go?" I ask.

With his affirmative response, we start making the travel arrangements. Ric and I take the horses out on weekends. We need to build up his riding stamina. The coastal trails of Point Reyes offer many suitable training options. The rides in Africa will not only be long but also fast-paced, and riders will need to be comfortable galloping. We use Bodega Bay to do our gallop work on the beach. Juan and JJ love our training rides—I have never seen Juan look so happy.

As we plan our trip, we decide to spend time in Cape Town before embarking on a two-week equine safari. This adventure soon evolves into the planning of an exchange of vows on Boulders Beach just outside Cape Town. Something that has hastened us toward marriage: we both would like to have a family. The universe was listening—now I am listening to her. I feel a deep calling to take care of my health. Another residue layer of shame, guilt, and unworthiness lift away.

I reach out to Julia and make an appointment to check on my adrenal system. I have not been in touch with her since before my time in Food Addicts. She is angry when I share with her what happened in the twelve-step program. It takes me a moment to realize she is not angry with me.

"Lisa, you're not my only client to get abused in that program," she informs me. "I don't know if this is limited to a few sponsors or if this is a systematic problem, but I intend to take professional action. They have no nutritional or psychological training. They could have starved you to death! This foray and your relapse probably set your adrenals back."

"Actually, I feel pretty good now," I say. "My path to recovery was with horses—maybe you can send some of your clients to Ariana? Actually, the reason I've come to see you is that I am getting married in June. We would like to have a family. Will my adrenals pose a problem for pregnancy?"

Her eyes are as wide as saucers. "I'm thrilled that you have found this man, but you may not have the adrenal health requisite to support a pregnancy and the hormonal onslaught that will accompany it."

She asks about my workload, and I provide a full disclosure.

"Are you getting seven to eight hours of sleep each night, as we discussed when you were in recovery treatment with me?" Julia asks.

"No. But I've always slept about four hours a night," I admit.

"Lisa, you *limit* yourself to four hours a night. There is a reason you accomplish so much in your life, and it's because you rob yourself of sleep. I'm pleased with your sobriety, but you remain in denial when it comes to work. Something has to go—your body can't sustain the life you seek to lead," she says.

"But I feel good. I am energized and riding my horses," I protest. Then I share my experience in the round pen. "I feel that having a child is part of my destiny."

"I recommend a medical leave so we can truly focus on your health. You have been unwilling to do this in the past, but it is essential if you are to consider having a successful pregnancy, especially now that you are over forty," she says.

For the first time in my life, I truly commit to my health. I opt to take the medical leave for the balance of the spring semester. One of my doctoral students offers to teach the remaining weeks of my medical device course. My other doctoral students assist with the discussion and lab elements of the course. The success of my research and teaching while going through such enormous personal challenges is owed in great part to my extraordinary students.

I have accrued sabbatical credits and request to take a sabbatical in the coming year to focus on my health. I resign from my post as associate dean and recuse myself from the upcoming patent trial. I try to push down my anxiety as I cut back on consulting.

Julia tells me the answer is obvious. "Sell your townhome, take the financial loss, and live with your husband-to-be at his home in Pacifica," she suggests. Inwardly, I groan. My financial misfortune feels like a personal failure. It will take me a number of years to accept my financial blunders and move on. For now, I keep my life centered in Petaluma.

As we prepare for our upcoming trip to Africa, I focus on restoring my health. I take up yoga, utilize acupuncture, and work on creative outlets with Ariana. I stay regimented in my adrenal treatments.

More layers of shame and guilt lift away. I am starting to sense that there may be worthiness deep within. An irony, as I spent my life chasing worthiness through academic achievement—not self-love.

We vest time in the saddle to prepare for the fast-paced safari that will soon be upon us. I feel the African savanna calling.

44

African Savanna

Cape Town is a majestic waterfront city with immense beauty. The iconic Table Mountain sits as her backdrop, and a penguin colony takes up residence at Boulders Beach. Cape Town offers long blond beaches, curvaceous hills, colorful people, and diverse culture. I soak in its sheer magnificence.

Ric and I have traveled nearly thirty hours to get here. We filled our luggage primarily with gear for two weeks of safari on horseback—leather chaps, riding pants, cowboy boots, helmets, and gloves. Our wedding attire is merely an adornment. I have brought no laptop or cell phone. I have three weeks unplugged. This is my first "true" vacation. It feels like pure freedom—and it is well-deserved.

We stay at the Lezard Bleu Inn next to Table Mountain. We are in the treehouse room with an expansive view of the garden. Our plan is to exchange vows on Boulders Beach, but African law requires that the marriage take place under a roof. Our gracious hosts, Chris and Niki, serve as witnesses and offer us their inn.

After the formalities are complete, we make our way to the beach for our spiritual ceremony. The day is gray, and drizzle is upon us; we share an enormous black umbrella. Our cowboy boots follow a path onto the expansive boulders. The mist gives way to gentle winds that bring the essence of the sea to our senses. Our wedding party waddles in from the colony of African penguins that take refuge at the beach. We are donning simple wedding attire, but our penguin companions make our ceremony feel like a black-tie affair.

Out upon the massive collage of granite rocks, we read the vows we composed for each other. With the blessing of our minister, we exchange the wedding rings we designed ourselves. Our wedding bands are engraved with feathers from an eagle, owl, and hummingbird to represent integrity, wisdom, and joy.

After spending a few days exploring Cape Town and its beautiful surrounds, the true adventure begins. Our equine safari starts at an exquisite game preserve in the northern portion of South Africa. Our abode is a hunting lodge with a thatched roof and capacious windows offering a glimpse of the vast African savanna. Hunting pictures grace the walls while hand-carved wooden statues of elephants, zebras, and giraffes tickle the eyes.

The trail guide matches us with our mounts. Each day, we gallop among giraffes, zebras, or gazelles. The feel of our horses' hoofbeats resonates with the herds surrounding us. The horses are not predators. We are welcomed into the magical dance of the African savanna. My heart skips a beat as I process my surroundings. The expanse of the land, with its abundant acacia trees that serve as shelter to the spotted creatures, takes my breath away.

We spot warthogs, rhinos, and antelope. Daily, we are surprised with a meal somewhere within the picturesque preserve or sundowners amidst the tall grass. The finale is a night safari culminating in a dinner set under the lighted acacia trees. The experience is surreal.

Each night, I sketch the animals we have seen into my gratitude journal. On our last night in South Africa, we sit outside looking up at the bright stars of the southern sky. We make a wish that neither of us dares to speak aloud. *The stars are listening.*

After completing our safari in South Africa, we head north to Botswana. A kindhearted couple by the names of Kor and Louise greet us. We are each paired with a horse based on our riding ability. This is an important match, as our horse will be our equine partner for a week of point-to-point riding. I am given a young African cross-breed named Albany. Ric receives Bantu.

Each day at dawn, we head out into the open range. The air is crisp. It takes until mid-morning for the sun to warm my bones. Kor carries both a rifle and a bull-whip, in the event we are attacked by lions or charged by a bull elephant. We have received specific instructions for all possible scenarios. Safety is paramount.

We spend several hours a day on our horses. The pace is fast, and the views are stunning. The meadows serve as home to termite mounds, while crocodiles and rhinos take up residence in the rivers and watering holes. Tall grasses can be home to lions. Here we are prey—we must all be alert. My body is viscerally awakened.

All pictures must be taken with our eyes. The gallop of the horse is synchronized with surrounding herds, as though we are one living being. The scent of the air is a mix of horse, grasses, dirt, and beast. It is sensory overload.

Each day, we arrive at a new campground and find that Kor's team has set up our handsome platform tents. After we complete our ride, we must rid ourselves of the dirt thrown into our faces by the horses' hooves. We eat dinner by the campfire, but for the sake of safety, we may not leave the group unless escorted by a guide. Our guides sleep with fires lit around the campsite to safeguard the horses against lions. One night, I hear the primitive roar of a lion. His call reverberates through every cell in my body.

I have never before experienced the depths of beauty, adventure, or restoration that this trip has offered me. I wish I could take a piece of the African savanna home with me.

45

The Expanding Herd

Africa nourished my soul. My spirit stirs as I unpack our hand-carved elephants, giraffes, and zebras. It was a trip of a lifetime forever burnished into my heart. I have the fall semester ahead of me to focus on my health. I am confident that I am in the realm of full recovery. I wish I could have packed up the African savanna itself, with its beauty beyond mortal words.

I have been feeling queasy since we returned from Africa. Initially, I presumed that my tiredness was owed to the long journey, but after a week at home, my exhaustion hasn't waned. Inwardly, I hope this is not some relapse into adrenal fatigue.

Juan and JJ need exercise. When I get to the farm, I drag myself up the hill to their pasture. I am sweating profusely from the exertion. I manage my way through the pasture gate, but there is no way I can ride or get the horses down to the arena to do groundwork.

JJ soon greets me, his warm muzzle whispering in my ear. I manage my way up and wrap my hands around his neck. I soak in his sweet essence.

"What is wrong with me, JJ? Why don't I feel well enough to ride you?" I ask.

His knowing eyes stare deep into my soul. He gently rubs his nose up and down across my belly. I am getting a clear message. *I am pregnant. How can he possibly know this?* I don't know how he manages to communicate with me. I just know that we have a clear line of telepathy if I keep my heart space open to him.

On the way home from the farm, I stop at the drugstore to pick up a pregnancy test. It confirms what JJ already told me. I then book an appointment with my physician.

Ric and I are ecstatic. We share the news with our families. My mom is over the moon with excitement. I am forty-one years old, elevating the likelihood of complications. We won't tell anyone else until we safely make it through the first trimester, but there is no keeping my news from Shirley. She is keen to observe that JJ, Juan, and Tristan are taking turns greeting my ever-expanding girth.

Ric spends part of his week in the North Bay and the balance of his week in Pacifica to mitigate his commute to the San Mateo County Parks. I am already dreading my commute to Berkeley when I resume teaching. Then it hits me—*how will all of this work once we have a child?*

We find an obstetrician in Petaluma. I am honest with her about my full medical history. Dr. Jones jots down some notes, but she doesn't seem bothered by my long-standing challenges with an eating disorder, adrenal fatigue, and alcohol addiction. I have been sober from alcohol for nearly two years, and I have been free of a bulimic episode for several months. I'm wondering if she has fully appreciated my past history since she seems more concerned with my age. I will be almost forty-two when our child is born. Dr. Jones prescribes genetic counseling for us.

The session with the genetic specialist has me riddled with anxiety. We are provided with all the statistics of what can go wrong because of my age.

Why not my husband's age? He is eleven years older than me—it doesn't seem fair that my age solely contributes to the burden. I feel scrutinized for waiting this long to have a child.

Ric and I are trying to process all of this information. High-resolution ultrasound imaging is scheduled, and amniocentesis is advised. From the high-resolution imaging, we learn that we are having a baby girl. We decline the recommended amniocentesis procedure. We will love this child no matter the circumstances.

She will be named Savanna after her conception in Africa. We decide on two middle names: Aissa, a South African name that means grateful, and Albany after the horse I rode in Botswana.

Throughout my pregnancy, I feel a deep need for creative outlets. I paint the walls of Savanna's room with a full African Safari theme. The little girl within me has been awakened. I embark on writing a story that chronicles JJ's life from his perspective, *Horse of Fire*. Telepathically, he provides me with his words for the first four years of his life, before I knew him.

Throughout my pregnancy, I continue to ride JJ. He has chosen himself to be the guardian of Savanna. He always greets me at the gate and gently noses my belly, as if to send an internal greeting. Juan and Tristan follow in the same ritual. Shirley and I continue to ride on the trails, as JJ leads and walks at a snail's pace. He has a baby to protect.

The obstetrician decides to induce me on Savanna's due date. Dr. Jones has monitored me closely since Christmas when I inadvertently ate soup with poisonous bulbs. It was a bit of a comical story in hindsight. Ariana gave me a bag of unmarked bulbs as a holiday gift, meant to be planted. But I thought they were onions and used them in a squash soup. I managed to give myself, Ric, and my parents food poisoning. What does one expect from a girl who rarely cooks?

On my delivery date, I'm riddled with fear. Ric and my mom are excited at the prospect of greeting their new family member. It feels surreal as we enter the lobby of the Petaluma Hospital. I hear the wail of new life as we walk toward the delivery room. My anxiety mounts: *Will I be a good mother?*

My self-care has kept my inner critic at bay, but she still lurks within and awakens in fear or anxiety.

A scowling nurse greets me. Nurse Lucy is either having a bad day or has decided that I remind her of someone she doesn't like very much. She takes me to the scale for my intake weight.

"I don't want to know my weight," I say. I have avoided the scale throughout my pregnancy. She seems to take pleasure in reading the number aloud. *How can I have possibly gained more than fifty pounds? Am I delivering a butterball turkey?*

By mid-morning, Dr. Jones administers the drug that will summon my daughter. I have no idea what's in the cocktail coursing through my veins, but I hope it contains something for pain and anxiety. I hope my bundle of joy will be in my arms by lunchtime.

Hours pass. There are no changes. Except my boredom. *Why didn't I bring a book to read?*

"No baby today, maybe tomorrow," Dr. Jones says as she examines me. Then she disappears. I swallow down my disappointment.

Within a few hours, I feel pain well up in my spine and deep in my abdomen. I press the call button for the nurse.

"Can I get something for pain?" I ask.

"You should just focus on your breathing. I have women who are in actual labor in the other rooms," Nurse Lucy says dismissively. She rolls her eyes as she disappears from the room. She is friendly to everyone in the room but me.

Within the hour, I summon the nurse back. "I think my water has broken."

Her eyes roll again. With an exhale of exasperation, she grudgingly examines me. *Does she think I am one of those difficult patients who has no threshold for pain?*

I wait for my lecture. Nurse Lucy is silent, but her eyes are wide open. Without a word, she quickly leaves the room. Within minutes, another nurse is in the room. The new nurse is quick to assess the situation.

"We need to get Dr. Jones back to the hospital immediately," she says. "Your baby is on her way."

Ric and Mom try to comfort me in the delivery room as we anxiously await the doctor. Mom squeezes my hand.

"Just breathe," Mom says.

I ask Nurse Lucy for pain medication. "You're too close to delivery now," she says. *Is she kidding me?* I want to reach out and strangle her.

By the time Dr. Jones is back in the room, Savanna is ready to make her debut in the world. In less than an hour, we welcome our baby girl into our lives.

Ric cuts the umbilical cord. In a short time, Savanna is placed in my arms. Compared to what many women go through, my delivery is relatively easy and uncomplicated. My challenges are yet to come.

Holding my daughter for the first time is magical. I look into her big, bright eyes. She takes my breath away—it's as though I can see the whole universe in her eyes. *She is an old soul.* I immediately realize the immensity of the gift I am receiving in this beautiful child.

Then fear overwhelms me. *Am I worthy of her?* I feel that deep inner flaw of unworthiness that has yet to be fully annihilated, awaiting an opportunity to grow in size.

46

Baby Blues

Savanna lights up the room. Ric shines as a new father, his happiness sparkling in his eyes. My mom blossoms in her role as loving Nana. She has offered to stay for a few weeks as we settle in with our new baby. My dad arrives shortly after we bring Savanna home. He radiates cheerfulness and coins himself "Gramps." Savanna is fortunate to have such loving grandparents.

Beth and Matt—who have decided not to have children—come up to meet their niece. It's clear they will be an extraordinary aunt and uncle to Savanna. They, too, pick out their new personas. "Auntie Beth and Uncle Matt." Everyone seems to be stepping into their roles with our new baby with ease. Everyone except me.

I had expected some physical transformation to take place in my body once Savanna was placed in my arms. Oxytocin and dopamine were supposed to surge through my body and flood me with happiness. Instead, fretfulness, anxiety, and gloom have taken up residence in my being. Nursing Savanna proves arduous. Sleep eludes me. I feel as though someone has hijacked my body.

Does anything ever truly prepare us for life with a newborn? For all of my academic rigor and decades of pushing myself to the brink of exhaustion, I am vastly underprepared for the physical demands of motherhood. Hormones surge through my body, heightening my anxiety and perceived unworthiness. Is this what Julia had been worried about? That my adrenals would be ravaged by motherhood?

We are soon back in the hospital. Savanna has turned a yellowish color because her liver is not processing the bilirubin in her blood. She is not nursing well and is losing weight. The same can be said for me. I am up every two hours trying to nurse her and have been relegated to pumping between feedings. My thoughts drift back to Karen. The thought of losing Savanna is untenable. The nurse is constantly checking on Savanna and my progress with pumping. It feels futile and exhausting.

"Is there a possibility of using formula?" I ask.

The cold, dark eyes of the nurse cut right through me. I feel her wrath of judgment. "Why would you not use breast milk? Don't you know the facts?" she says. Brochures soon appear on my night table. She is sending a clear message—children never reach their highest potential without breast milk. I am too tired to question the premise.

The silver lining of our hospital stay is the pediatrician who cares for Savanna. Dr. Faye Lundergaand is lighthearted and compassionate. I wish she were my doctor. It seems the world is set up to take care of the babies. Who takes care of the struggling mommies?

I am exhausted. Weight is pouring off me because I'm expending so many calories trying to generate milk for my daughter. I am turning into a blubbering mess, crying at the slightest provocation. I am grateful for the extended maternity leave I am afforded through the university. I would not want any colleague or student to see me in this state.

I wonder who I am. I seem to have fallen through some trap door dropping back into darkness. *Where is Fire Horse? Perhaps she is at the farm, riding JJ while I am held hostage in this ravaged body. Is this what people mean when they refer to the "post-baby blues"?*

Weeks later, when I take Savanna in for her checkup, Dr. Lundergaand affirms that Savanna is thriving. She then observes my appearance.

"Lisa, are you getting enough rest?" she asks. "When did you last sleep for any block of time?"

Words tumble out of my mouth as I fight back tears. "I'm not sleeping for any blocks of time. Savanna is not nursing well … when I'm not trying to nurse her, then I'm pumping … Ric has been incredibly helpful in night feedings … but I am exhausted …" I sob. Snot runs down my face. I am having a full breakdown in her office.

Dr. Lundergaand looks at me with kindhearted eyes. "Lisa, more than anything, Savanna needs a healthy mother," she says. "I want you to go home and get rid of that blasted pump. Savanna will do just fine on formula."

With baby formula in the house, I find some respite from my physical exhaustion, but the weeks of sleep deprivation have already taken their toll. I am riddled with anxiety. At night, I check on Savanna constantly to make sure she is breathing. I have a compulsive fear of losing Savanna, rooted in the loss of Karen. I am exhausting myself with worry.

My mom has returned home, and Ric's paternity leave has come to an end. Full-blown, relentless fear consumes me. Ric has a long commute, often leaving before Savanna wakes and not returning until after she is asleep. I know how hard it is for him to leave Savanna. He treasures his days off to spend time with her. I would welcome a day on the campus with my students without the worries that come with being a new mother.

Nothing in my life up to this point has prepared me for this. My academics and the work I have put into my career for the past two decades seem like a walk in the park compared to the challenges I now face as a mother. *How do people make this look so easy?* I see young women gathered at the park with their babies in strollers, part of some mothers club. I hear their idle laughter. I see the joy on their faces; they don't look like they have been tortured with sleep deprivation.

My energy reserves are depleted. I have bags under my eyes. I am back to my pre-pregnancy weight, yet it seems that my body will never find its pre-baby shape. In engineering parlance, I have been plastically deformed and fatigued. A structural life calculation would predict that failure is unavoidable.

Home alone with a new baby, I find my sense of worth fading. Each afternoon, I put Savanna in her stroller and take her for a long walk. As long as the carriage keeps moving, she sleeps. We live just around the corner from a park, a grocery store, and a Starbucks. I don't yet appreciate that these are landmines for me.

The grocery store seems to be calling me. Some magnetic force has pulled me to the bakery section—I feel an overwhelming urge for sugar and caffeine. I don't think about the consequences of my actions as I fill up a large coffee cup and then stuff my bag with donuts and cookies. *My old friend is back.* She has been idle for the past year but was still lurking within. She knows how to take my pain away. She guides me to her favorite aisles.

Quickly, she finds all of her favorite foods. This binge must be done on the move; the stroller can't stop. I push the stroller around the blocks of our extended neighborhood as I indulge in cookies, donuts, ice cream sandwiches, and caffeinated beverages that I know will give me a surge of serotonin. As soon as we get home, I change Savanna and put on a *Baby Einstein* video to distract her while she sits in her little bouncy chair. I step into the adjacent bathroom and purge violently, releasing the torrents of my stored emotion.

The binge brings a false high, and the purge offers a short respite from my emotional prison. I am soon filled with shame for my relapse into bulimia and promise myself I won't do it again. But my foe has been fed, and she knows this is a hollow promise that only she knows how to fill. I am back under her spell.

The next day, on our afternoon walk, I feel the store beckoning again. I repeat my actions. This goes on for weeks. I don't tell anyone that I have relapsed into my eating disorder. Shame and darkness consume me.

At my next checkup with the obstetrician, Dr. Jones notes that my weight has dropped below my pre-pregnancy weight. I weigh in at 122 pounds. "You've lost too much weight and far too quickly," she notes. "Is everything okay?"

"I think I'm struggling with postpartum depression," I say.

"You likely just have the post-baby blues; let's see you next week and see how you feel."

At my follow-up, I confess to my obstetrician that I have relapsed into my eating disorder. She looks angry, like the nurses who judged me at the hospital.

"You never told me you had an eating disorder," Dr. Jones chastises.

Anger wells up in me. Through tears, I find my words. "I told you at our first meeting," I say. "Ric was here too. Check your notes."

She finds the information in my medical folder. "Women with a history of eating disorders are more prone to postpartum depression," she states. *Is that supposed to make me feel better?* Without acknowledging her oversight, she writes a prescription for antidepressants.

Within a few days, I am near certain that the medications are not working. I am crawling in my skin, plagued by self-damaging thoughts.

I will ruin Savanna's life if I stay in this destructive trajectory. Ariana's words, "Children absorb the energy around them," overwhelm my thoughts.

I cannot lay my negative energy on my daughter's life. I am deeply ashamed. I am forty-two years old, and I can't believe I have fallen down the rabbit hole again. My old haunting voice is back—*God took the wrong daughter.*

I am hiding the relapse from my husband, but he sees the distress on my face. "Why don't you go see JJ?" he suggests.

I quickly make my way to the truck. I feel the leather seat beneath me. I try to line up the key to the ignition portal, but my hand shakes violently. I feel a compulsive urge to drive off a bridge, plummeting my body into a rocky riverbed. Some force urges me to go back into the house.

Ric is surprised to see me. I break down in sobs. He has no sense of my despair. "I have relapsed into my eating disorder," I blurt through tears.

"Let's go see the horses and set up appointments with Julia and Ariana," he soothes. We strap Savanna in her baby seat, and Ric drives me to the farm.

When we get to the pasture, JJ chases Juan and Tristan away. JJ greets me with his large fluid eyes. I feel the rekindling of Fire Horse.

Has Fire Horse been here with JJ this whole time? Or has she been held captive in my body by the strong force of my inner darkness? I stand with him for minutes and let him breathe life back into my soul. Tears pour down my face. I feel him beckoning to me. He will be my guide—we will come through this together.

47

Life Balance

Is the pendulum of life ever idle? My pendulum swings to its extremes and evades equilibrium. My life constantly pulls and pushes on my psyche. I desperately need a mechanism to dampen the arc of the swing, to find a gentle rhythm.

I have received my directive from Julia: life balance is essential for me to survive. She sets me on a corrective course of action by safely taking me off the antidepressants and rebuilding my adrenal system.

Julia is firm with me. "Lisa, you will always be susceptible to adrenal exhaustion. You must be extraordinarily careful in balancing your life."

I am finally realizing the seriousness of the matter. She reiterates to me that when I return to academia, I will have to limit my hours. I will have to work hard at not working so hard.

I have come to understand that my inner sense of unworthiness gets triggered by anxiety and fear. Exhaustion amplifies these effects. I am learning to monitor my energy reserves, noticing what activities feed my energy and what activities drain it. I need more of the former over the latter to keep my life positively balanced.

Ariana coaches me on creating more balance in my life. "You need to carve out time for yourself each day," she says. She encourages me to utilize day care so I have time to rejuvenate my spirit and get daily exercise.

"You'll also need to find someone who can help you with somatic release," Ariana says. "You are still carrying enormous reserves of shame, guilt, and sorrow in your body."

I will never truly be free of my inner darkness until I can release these emotions. I need elements in my life that nurture my spirit, and the obvious place to start is horses. Ariana suggests that I tap into my work with horses and the power of my creative outlets. I leave inspired.

I publish my first book, *Horse of Fire: The Story of an Extraordinary and Knowing Horse as told by JJ Luck*, and it is well-received by the local community. Our local bookstore hosts a book reading. The local feedstore carries the book. The Petaluma newspaper gives it a full-page writeup. I am writing a textbook with one of my academic daughters and also embarking on a children's book. I am finding my flow in art and poetry, healing my inner child.

On the weekends, Savanna comes to the farm with me. She rides with me when I take JJ out for trail rides, his rhythmic footfall lulling her to sleep. Savanna's large brown eyes light up when she sits on Juan. Savanna essentially rides horses before she can sit up or walk on her own. It is clear that Juan and Savanna are kindred spirits.

As a surprise birthday gift, Ric enrolls me in a Buck Brannaman horsemanship clinic. Savanna, merely a toddler, watches the magic of natural horsemanship unfold as I work Juan under Buck's tutelage. The spell of horses has been cast on her too.

The pendulum of life is always in motion. The pull now comes from home. Ric has injured himself at work and requires two hip surgeries. Shortly after, he is diagnosed with Lyme disease and succumbs to a double case of pneumonia. For the sake of his health and the welfare of our family, we decide it is best if Ric takes an early retirement. This difficult decision enables him to spend more time with Savanna and lets me put more of myself back into my academic mission. It is the silver lining to his health challenges and a godsend for our family.

48

The Tangled Web

It is a crisp autumn day in New England. The foliage delights the eyes. The leaves appear to be painted in hues of mustard, crimson, and persimmon. A technical conference in Boston gives me the opportunity to bring Ric and Savanna along to meet my extended family. I am forty-five years old, and Savanna is now three. We have made our visits to see relatives and enjoyed the freedom trail, the swan boats, and the aquarium. There's only one person left to visit before we return to California: my Aunt Jackie, held hostage by the ravages of Alzheimer's disease.

As we drive along a backcountry road, I soak in the colonial architecture. Ric is at the wheel, and Savanna happily chatters in the back seat. We have made our way from the frantic roads of Boston. I see the sign for the Alzheimer's facility. Guilt rises as I consider what awaits me. *Why did she ask her godchild to promise to never put her in a nursing home?*

My heart beats faster as we pull into the driveway. I see a family sitting with their elder on a large wooden bench. My heart aches—my aunt no longer goes outside. She no longer smiles or engages in conversation. I don't know if Jackie will even recognize me.

We make our way to the front lobby. "Mommy, this house smells funny," Savanna says. She still carries the spirit of an old soul. My little earth angel looks up with her big brown eyes and blond curls, melting me with her smile.

I take her hand and give a gentle squeeze. We pass silver-haired folks sitting in their chairs playing quiet games. We won't find my aunt on this floor. We take the elevator to the second floor—there is no laughter on this corridor. Savanna squeezes my hand a little tighter.

I walk slowly, preparing myself, dreading what I will find when we reach her room. The door is open, and we step in as a family. The room feels dark and cold. Jackie sits in a well-worn armchair, the sun casting a shadow over her drawn face. She stares off into nothingness. My heart breaks, the inner child within me reeling in pain. *Where is my beloved auntie? Where is my fairy godmother?*

I sit next to my aunt and hold her hand. I feel her warmth.

"Jackie, I've brought my family to meet you," I say gently. "I told you about them in the cards I sent. This is my husband, Ric." He steps up and smiles at her. She gives a slight nod.

Savanna sits on my lap. "Jackie, this is my daughter, your grandniece. Her name is Savanna." I choke back tears. I don't expect any words—she hasn't spoken to anyone in the past year.

"Savanna," she says.

A flood of tears pours down my face. I squeeze her hand. We sit for some time, and I tell her about our life. Savanna grows restless, and Ric takes her for a walk. "I'll meet you at the car in a few minutes," I tell him.

I sit with my aunt, staring into her blue eyes.

"Jackie, are you in there?" I ask. "I miss you. Please forgive me for placing you in a nursing home. I love you." She never speaks another word. My veil of guilt feels heavy.

"This disease is harder on the families than the patients," says the Alzheimer's specialist when she sees me leave the room in tears.

My thoughts drift back to the past few years as I think of how this disease slowly robbed me of my beloved auntie. At first, her quirkiness served to mask the earliest stages of her dementia. She had me fooled for quite some time. She would forget words. "You know what I mean, the whatchamacallit that keeps food cold," she would say.

I started calling more often only to hear her repeat the same stories over and over. Maybe I didn't want to see the earliest stages of her demise—I had already seen dementia steal my nana away.

Then, there was no denying that my aunt could no longer take care of herself. Yet, it was difficult to get her the help she needed. She was a sly fox, with years of elementary school knowledge, and she masqueraded normalcy in front of officials tasked with assessing her mental capabilities. Like me, she was a master at creating façades.

It was not my sister or me finding her in squalor that resulted in her getting the help she needed. It was the distressing call from my cousin who alerted us that Jackie had been found in her car in a store parking lot just around the corner from her condo. It was the middle of the night, and she didn't know how to get home.

Beth navigated the legal system to make Jackie eligible for healthcare in an Alzheimer's facility. At that time, I was too helpless to help, too deep in the realm of adrenal exhaustion, pulling myself out of the depths of addiction. Aunt Jackie had been my fairy godmother, and to face the truth had been too painful.

I leave the Alzheimer's facility with my mind reeling. Ric and Savanna are playing in the fallen leaves. Savanna runs to me and offers a much-needed hug.

As we make our way back home, my thoughts teeter between memories of joyful times with my aunt and the pain I feel. I will never see my auntie again.

Two years later, in 2013, I receive the dreaded phone call. "Jackie choked on her lunch. She lost consciousness and was taken by ambulance to Mount Auburn Hospital."

My hands tremble as I call the hospital. I am ultimately faced with the decision of whether to keep her on life support. My parents are traveling out of the country, and I can't reach my sister. I have my aunt's health directive, but the verbal decision to stop life support is my burden to bear.

Perhaps it is bittersweet that it is me who has to make this choice for my beloved fairy godmother. The guilt of this decision weighs heavily on my spirit for years to come.

PART
FOUR

A Semblance
of Balance

49
Teaching as Leadership

I am teaching our first-year course, Introduction to Engineering Design. This is my first freshmen class, with two hundred eager engineering minds. The students attend common lectures and participate in five-week modules in order to get an immersive exposure to the professional field of engineering.

I create a module entitled "Teaching as Leadership." A collaborative venture with the Lawrence Hall of Science built on my previous outreach activities, this module provides the framework for the development of the core competencies necessary for leadership in the context of teaching and design ingenuity. The first-year engineering students work on interactive exhibits that teach the K–12 sector and the public at large about the engineering design process.

The students are teaching concepts of "lift and drag" with varying parachute designs that can be tested in a wind column. They work on an exhibit where children can test small vehicles with varying gear ratios across different terrains, and they tailor bridge designs that can be tested against mimicked seismic loads. The undergraduates wear pins that read "Ask me—I am a Cal engineer."

I create a five-week module that provides the framework for the development of personal leadership and teamwork, mission statements and plans of action, as well as opportunities for strategic thinking, problem-solving, and brainstorming. I have a team of extraordinary graduate student instructors who help me make this course a huge success. Through surveys, we find that the professional skill sets and confidence levels are greatly enhanced for the students who participated in the leadership module as compared to those who did not, and we find that the effects are even greater for the female students. For this work, we receive a best paper award through the American Society of Engineering Education meeting.

I am also honored to receive the A. Richard Newton Educator Award from the Anita Borg Institute for my work in broadening engineering participation of women through the use of undergraduate engineering education and K–12 engineering outreach. This award is incredibly special for me because my sister Beth compiled the nominating package, and the award carries the namesake of my former dean.

Over the summer, I offer an equine-guided leadership course to a group of graduate students. For the workshops, we set up obstacle courses in the large arena, and the doctoral students work on a series of team-building exercises. The horses enable the students to build their self-awareness of body language and create an authentic realm of trust for themselves. I am finally blending my wisdom from horses with my academic passions, just as I had stated five years ago in the round pen with JJ.

My life finally has some semblance of balance, yet I know the pendulum will never be idle.

50

Academic Façade

I have been in active recovery from my eating disorder for nearly five years. Yet, there is not a single day when I don't pause to consider the foods I eat. I write down everything I put in my mouth—not because I count calories but because I no longer have any sense of satiety. As a result of thirty-five years as a bulimic, my body no longer has a signal to know that it is full or empty.

My toolkit at forty-eight years of age is very different than it was just five years earlier. I am vegetarian and gluten-free. I limit the sugar I eat and abstain from alcohol. I exercise every day—I liken it to brushing my teeth; I don't question it—I just do it. I write in my gratitude journal every night. I spend time each day with my horses. I savor time with Savanna and Ric. I work one day a week at home and never spend nights or week-ends working in my office. These are my anchors for sobriety. No one in my academic circles knows of my personal challenges beyond my horse accident and divorce. My prior struggles with alcohol, food, and work addiction live safely behind my academic façade.

Dave Dornfeld is our new chairman. He remains highly supportive of my pedagogical creativity, even when my colleagues express concern about me using horses with our students or when I do K–12 outreach projects instead of written final exams. Dave has been not only a good mentor but also a good friend. Early in his chairmanship, he calls and says to me, "Just say yes."

"What exactly would I be saying yes to?" I say.

"Would you serve as my vice-chair and oversee the graduate program for our department?" Dave asks.

Inwardly, I groan. I have been asked to serve in this role in the past, and I have declined. My concern is the workload—I can't afford another relapse.

"I would value your insight on how we can improve our program and mentorship of our students," Dave adds.

"Dave, I don't know. Savanna's still young. I have my horses and a big commute, and Ric is still not well."

"I'll give you full creative freedom with our program," Dave offers. "You still have flexibility in your schedule. Savanna can come to work anytime; she's welcome to hang out in my office."

I feel the academic pull. "Okay," I agree.

"We'll have fun together!" he exclaims, then he whinnies.

Savanna will be starting kindergarten in the coming year. Ric and I need to decide whether our permanent home should be in Pacifica or Petaluma. The travel time to Berkeley is nearly the same, but Pacifica affords me the opportunity to take the train for forty-five minutes of my commute. We settle on Pacifica.

Julia has been advocating for me to sell the Petaluma townhome so I can relinquish my need for consulting work. I finally agree to a short sale—the home sells for half of what I paid for it. My financial portfolio was annihilated by the horse accident, my divorce, and the housing market crash. But it's time to forgive my financial blunders and make peace with myself.

With my life in full swing, I find someone closer to Pacifica who can step into the roles previously filled by Julia and Ariana. Robert Rudelic is a body guru and an integrative life coach with somatic expertise. He begins working with me to release the emotional pain that has been held beneath my academic façade. His somatic work is likely the very thing that Ariana advocated for me to begin years ago.

After we move to Pacifica, I relocate the horses to Moss Beach. The trails are spectacular. Juan and JJ live out in a large pasture with several horses and seem fully settled in this coastal oasis. At the ranch, I have access to a round pen and a large enclosed arena. I reinstate my equine-guided life-coaching practice, offering workshops to doctoral students, staff, and some of my colleagues in mechanical engineering. The horse work nourishes my soul and recharges my energy.

I enjoy my role as vice-chair. I find myself enlightened to the challenges that many of the doctoral students face and feel drawn into the realm of being an advocate and life coach for many of them. The work is challenging but rewarding. Dave continues to support my creative work, including the use of equine-guided leadership workshops.

We have launched a new design institute on the campus. I have mixed emotions when I learn that Dave will be its inaugural director. The chairmanship of mechanical engineering will be transitioned to Professor Roberto Horowitz. I enjoy working with Roberto, but I miss the daily interactions with Dave.

I am nearly fifty years old when I am informed that I have been selected for Stage II consideration of the UC Berkeley Distinguished Teaching Award. This the highest teaching honor for our campus. I literally jump for joy, like a child in a candy shop. I quickly send a reply of gratitude to the Committee on Teaching and then to Dave when I learn that he had nominated me.

As part of this process, I must submit an extensive teaching portfolio along with evaluations for my courses offered in the last three years. I am asked to solicit letters of endorsement from former students, graduate student instructors, and colleagues who have observed my teaching. My final submission package looks as extensive as the one I submitted for my promotion to full professor.

Members of the Committee on Teaching will be making surprise visits to my classroom in the spring semester. I feel nearly as nervous as I did when I taught my first course at Brown University as a graduate student.

Just before spring break, I receive the news that I have been selected as a recipient of the teaching award. It is one of the greatest honors in my academic career as a Berkeley professor.

My life is finally coming together. I feel safe in my realm of recovery.

51

You Can Run, but You Can't Hide

How do you celebrate a half-century birthday? I want to do something challenging, fun, and memorable. In honor of this milestone, I register for the Disneyland half-marathon. My birthday is in April, and the race is in September, so I will have plenty of time to train.

I am completely ignorant about the actual demands of running, but the idea of a half-marathon in Disneyland sounds incredibly fun. I entice Ric and Savanna to join me so we can also have a family adventure to celebrate my fiftieth birthday. I download a half-marathon training program. It seems simple enough: two short runs on weekdays and a longer run on the weekends.

Serendipitously, I then see an advertisement for the Half Moon Bay half-marathon, which happens to fall on my Aunt Jackie's birthday. I'm excited to mark my birthday with two half-marathons.

"Since the races are less than two weeks apart, it's almost like running a marathon," I remark with a smirk to Ric. *Is the skeptical look on his face because I am not a runner?* I've always been an equestrian and a cyclist and have completed several century bike rides. *How hard can it be to run thirteen miles?*

When my neighbor hears that I am training for a half-marathon, he invites me to run the Milagra Ridge with him. I have often observed the hawks that circle above the crest line and am easily convinced to do the run with Tom. I assume we'll hike up the dirt trail and then run along the paths atop the ridge. We meet outside my home at 6:30 a.m. Tom quickly stretches.

"Are you ready?" he asks.

I offer my nod of approval. I hear the beep of his running watch. Tom sprints down the road. I feel like I'm tracking a gazelle on the plains of Africa. We hit the dirt fire trail, and he shows no signs of slowing down. There is a short respite before we reach the steep incline. My lungs are on fire—I am convinced I am going to die of heart failure. The only good thing is that once we run atop the ridgeline, it's all downhill to my home.

"Want to run again tomorrow?" Tom asks.

"No. Tomorrow is a teaching day," I say. *Is he crazy?* My body is on the verge of seizing up. I'll be lucky if I can even move tomorrow.

I use the trails along the coast for my weekly training runs. Within the month, I'm passing Tom on the hill that links us to the ridge. I assume the hills will give me an added advantage of strength and cardio for the half-marathons. But I don't factor in that trail running is not necessarily good preparation for a flat pavement race, nor do I account for the amount of damage one can do to one's feet or joints when running downhill.

"You better be careful. Running can be addictive," Ric jokes.

"Ha! No worries here. I'm retiring my running shoes right after the Half Moon Bay half-marathon."

It's Monday morning after my fiftieth birthday celebration weekend with family. I am feeling good about my life. I am sitting on the train heading to Berkeley, scrolling through my phone, reading my email. A cryptic message from our new chairman catches my eye—we have an emergency meeting this morning for mechanical engineering faculty and staff. My commute is ninety minutes door-to-door without any delays. I won't make it in time to attend the meeting.

It's unusually quiet when I step through the doors of Etcheverry Hall. *Maybe the meeting is still going on?* I anxiously wait for the elevator. I hear the hum of its approach. The doors open slowly. I expect it to be empty, but instead, I see one of our beloved staff members in tears.

With trepidation, I ask her, "Is everything okay?"

"You haven't heard the news?" She softly spills the words through her sobs, "Dave passed away."

"Which Dave?" I ask. We have four faculty with the first name of Dave or David. My mind scrambles, but I already know the answer before she whispers his name.

It is David Dornfeld, my mentor of twenty-three years. My friend who offered me levity, guidance, and camaraderie throughout my academic life. My colleague who made working in Etcheverry so enjoyable. Gone from a sudden heart attack. He was only sixty-eight years old. I had just exchanged a lighthearted email with him over the weekend. *How can this possibly be?* Sorrow overwhelms me. I have never openly cried at the university, but there is no stopping the floodwaters now.

Etcheverry feels hollow, as though some great spirit of kindness has evaporated from its bones. I head down the stairwell to Dave's lab. I know all of his students, and I know their despair. As I step onto the first-floor hall, I see the poster highlighting the green manufacturing research group. Dave's big smile throws a stabbing pain into my heart. I reach the glass doors of the Dornfeld research lab, where pained faces greet me. His students are gathered around a long conference table. The normal uplifted energy of this room is absent as we sit together in silence. We are raw. I fumble for reassuring words, yet grief stifles me. I give each of his students a hug.

I then head to the student services suite on the sixth floor. The staff meet me with sadness in their eyes. My heart tightens. We cry together before we agree that the best thing we can do at this moment is to think of ways we can support Dave's students. We make arrangements for a grief counselor to come meet with his students.

As one of the most beloved faculty members of our department, Dave's loss reverberates throughout the building and across the campus. As vice-chair of graduate studies, I scramble to make sure Dave's students get the support and mentorship they need to complete their doctoral degrees. Faculty rally to absorb his students into their labs. It is a devastating loss. I think back to the mentorship I received as a student—I would have been shattered to lose a mentor.

The loss of Dave Dornfeld is challenging for me. He recruited me to this campus. As my mentor, he listened to my ideas and encouraged me in the realms of academic growth. He and Barbara brought me into their home. They traveled to my ranch. Dave supported my horse work with students. He was my advocate for creating life balance—he saw me as a whole person. Dave was not just a colleague, but he was also my true friend. In the past few years, I have lost Marni, Rich, Jackie, and now Dave. The accumulated loss feels visceral.

Robert Rudelic continues to work with me on releasing emotional pain from my body. It is hard to relinquish the emotional burden of grief I still carry in my body. I have no true coping tools for grief, and I have never learned how to sit with loss. I remain in active recovery. I do not numb myself with alcohol or sugar or lock myself up in my office. Instead, I run more, seduced by the notion that I am coping with grief through my training program. I convince myself that running is a healthy habit.

In actuality, I am running away from my emotional pain. I stop following the training program and no longer take the rest days. As I get closer to the Disneyland marathon, my feet get sore. I load up on ibuprofen and keep pushing myself. My weekend runs are now ten to twelve miles. Only a week out from the Disneyland half-marathon, I notice that I have faint bruising under my toes.

On the eve of my race, I try to get to bed early. I should be exhausted from a day in Disney's California Adventure Park with Ric and Savanna, but I'm too restless to sleep. I get up at 3:30 a.m. I am in my starting bin before 5:00 a.m. The race begins at 5:30 a.m. Each corral offers a pacing runner who carries balloons. If I follow the man with the white balloons, then I will make my two-hour time goal. The air is electric. The excitement quells the pain in my body. I hear the countdown: ten, nine, eight, seven ...

The crush of runners is enormous. I weave my way around people in front of me. I must stay with the man with the white balloons. My gaze drifts beyond the balloons to Sleeping Beauty's castle, lit up in all its splendor. I feel the magic. Every imaginable Disney character cheers us on.

We run through California Adventure Park. I have the man with the balloons in my sight as we pass the illuminated Ferris wheel. All too soon, we're on the streets of Anaheim. Every mile marker comes complete with a band or cheering squad. The next milestone is the infield of Angels stadium, and we see ourselves on the big screen as we run through the baseball field. My feet hurt, but I keep pushing. I cross the finish line behind the man with the balloons. I make my time goal and collect my finisher's medal before heading off to find my family and share the excitement of my run. I down another 600 milligrams of ibuprofen. My feet are done for the day. I suggest a movie and the pool.

I have a week before the next half-marathon. I think about withdrawing, but I have chosen this run to honor my Aunt Jackie. The Half Moon Bay Half-Marathon feels like the exact opposite of the Disneyland run—there are only a few hundred people, not tens of thousands. There is no entertainment, no man with white balloons, and no Mickey or Minnie to cheer me on. Just me, my pain, and the memories of Aunt Jackie.

I spend the first five miles in gratitude for all that my aunt did for me in my life. By mile six, my sore feet begin to share the pain, the tightness building in my calves. At mile marker eight, I feel a looming tightness in my back, hips, and hamstrings. I let myself feel the pain. On the verge of collapse by mile twelve, I continue to run anyway, reminding myself this is Jackie's birthday, and I'm running for her. I feel the pain in both my body and soul. This last mile is for Jackie—I ask her forgiveness. My finish time is the same as the Disneyland half-marathon, but my body is reeling.

Robert is able to work out the soreness in my body, but my feet are a different matter altogether. I have bruises under my big toes and my metatarsals.

"You need to rest your body," he advises.

I assure him I will. This is a false promise—a telltale sign of addiction.

It's been three days since my second half-marathon. This would be a normal running day for me if I were still in training, but I remind myself that my half-marathons are behind me. I go to the gym and work out on the elliptical machine. My need to drink, to binge and purge, has been replaced by a need for endorphins. The endorphins are not found on this machine. I soon find myself on the treadmill, chasing out a quick mile.

It has been a week since my second half-marathon. *Surely, that's enough recovery time?* I never needed recovery after my long bike rides. I lace up my shoes and head out for a run down the coast. I plan for four miles, but this stretches into nine miles. My feet are sore. I stand in the cold Pacific Ocean until my feet are numb.

I go for my run when Tuesday arrives, then again on Thursday. On the weekend, I put in another long run. My feet are sore and bruised. *Why am I doing this? Aren't marathons behind me?*

Week after week, I continue to do the same. I am no longer riding my horses because my body is too tired and sore to ride after my runs. *Why do I keep running? I can barely walk.*

I find myself at the UCSF Orthopedics Institute when the pain becomes unbearable. I have earned a full set of X-rays on my feet. Fortunately, I have not fractured any bones, but I have deep bruising that needs to heal. The orthopedist prescribes a high dose of anti-inflammatories for the next two months.

"If you continue to run before healing your feet, then you may do irrecoverable damage," Dr. Tamara warns. "Absolutely no high-impact activities for at least eight weeks."

I feel severe withdrawal from the endorphins released by running. I add a new layer of positive affirmations into my gratitude journal for healthy feet and perfect healing. Part of my personal growth is self-reflection and acceptance without falling into a spiral of self-hatred. I had let running take over my life because I had no tools for coping with grief.

Yet again, my spirit horse gives me the "nudge" I need. JJ is always able to see deep into my soul—he reminds me that I need to stay committed to horses as part of my ongoing self-care. As I forgo the running, I have the energy to ride Juan and JJ.

I feel at peace when I ride JJ, fully present, my body completely supported by the sentient being beneath me. I am ever grateful to this bright chestnut horse who always serves as my beacon of light.

PART
FIVE

The Gift of Worthiness

52
A Crack in the Façade

The universe is literally knocking on my academic façade. Gentle knocks on my office door are often followed by a request for sage advice. "Professor Pruitt, may I speak with you confidentially about a personal matter?" students ask.

I find myself having soul-stirring conversations with undergraduates and graduate students. These students bravely share their personal challenges with me. Many plights resonate deeply for me—eating disorders, addiction, depression, anxiety, impostor syndrome, illness, loss of loved ones, or feelings of unworthiness. It is easy for me to empathize because I know their despair.

I am fifty-one years old, yet I sense a piece of myself within each student. I commend them for their bravery in coming to see me, and I guide them to resources where they can seek support. They are grateful for my advice. However, I feel an escalating sense of incongruency. The depths of my personal challenges remain hidden in my academic realm.

Students only see my outward-facing persona and academic accomplishments—not the depths of anguish I have overcome.

My academic façade is beginning to crack. Some deep inner voice is asking to be heard. She does not want to hide anymore. She is threatening to fracture the façade I have spent a lifetime creating. I feel my inner sense of unworthiness, shame, and guilt coalescing, gaining the traction they need to break free of this stifling academic armor. Everything that has been stuffed down wants to be free.

One afternoon, I meet with a group of prospective graduate students. These young, eager minds ask the question I have heard so many times before: "What is your secret for success?"

I give my usual carefree response. "I just followed my passions, and I was fortunate to have terrific mentors." The little girl within me is reeling as the truth ricochets around in my mind:

I have been successful in academia because it was the perfect place to hide from my fears. I created layers of addictions that served to protect my scared inner self, who didn't know how to be worthy in this world. I found solace in the rigor of engineering, and I hid behind my work. Academia was a place to seek out some semblance of worthiness.

My inner voice haunts me in my sleep. Memories from my life pop up in my dreams and continually wake me. *How can this be happening?* I have a highly successful and respected career. I am happily married with a beautiful daughter. I have two magnificent horses in my life, live in a beautiful home, and remain steadfast on my path of recovery. To all outward appearances, my life seems perfect, but something is deeply wrong. *What am I missing?*

I know the answer: I have never been fully authentic in my academic or professional world. Until I reconcile this inauthenticity, I will forever carry my inner restlessness.

I reflect on this incongruent energy that has been awoken in me. I finally realize that my skills in teaching, mentoring, and leadership were honed through my personal journey. Nevertheless, I have never openly shared my life story in a professional setting.

I have a knack for offering wisdom, sage advice, and life coaching. Many people feel at ease seeking my guidance for their personal challenges. But no one ever asks me how I gained such knowledge. It was certainly not covered in the engineering curriculum.

My vibrational frequency hums. The words may not yet be able to leave my mouth, but they flow readily through my fingertips. I am up well before dawn each day and start pouring my personal odyssey onto the keyboard. Shortly after I begin my reflective journey, I attend a writing workshop. I am captivated by one particular speaker when he says: "If you can heal even one person with your words, then you are a literary healer—even if that one person is you."

I feel a stirring in my soul. Could I possibly share what I've written with at least one other person?

53

Unbreakable Bonds

The truest relationship I have forged in my life is with my bright chestnut thoroughbred. JJ plucked me from the depths of my darkness and inspired me to step into realms of my life I might never have found without his guidance. He has offered light to numerous people. He has sparkled in front of crowds in Vegas, Denver, and Sacramento and delighted crowds at county fairs. He has served as a guide to executives, life coaches, faculty, staff, and students.

JJ is my earth angel. I tried to walk away the first time I met him, but he was inescapable. He navigated me through tumultuous storms that placed me on my path with equine-guided education and natural horsemanship. He taught me strength, resilience, and tenacity. He gave me spirituality. The thought of not having him in my life is nearly overwhelming, although I know we share a bond that can never be severed.

I tried to forge a similar bond with Juan, but it was unattainable for me. I watched Juan light up when Ric came into my life, but it was Savanna who brought this beautiful horse to life. Juan raised Savanna up from infancy. He has offered her gentleness and friendship for the past ten years. They, too, share the unbreakable bond.

Savanna is merely ten years old, yet she innately resonates with natural horsemanship. She already has a knack for the liberty work with Juan. She and I ride the trails together on the weekends. Savanna rides Juan with a simple bareback pad and a rope halter. They follow behind me atop JJ on our extensive coastal trails. I have watched her grow up on this horse from her days of princess dresses and fairy wings to her contemporary cowgirl attire.

It is autumn. The horses are hot after we finish a hilly ride on the coastal trail. Savanna hoses Juan down then shampoos his tail and mane. His beautiful coat glistens by the time she finishes; his soft expression never changes.

"Why does Juan have tears running down his face?" Savanna asks.

I take a closer look. His right eye seems inflamed. We clean his eyes gently and then put on a fly mask.

"I'll ask the vet to look at his eye," I say. "We get a lot of coastal wind and sand; maybe it's just a blocked tear duct."

The veterinary prognosis is that the occlusion near the tear duct is a melanoma. The vet finds more melanomas under Juan's tail. I feel my concern building—Juan is the family horse, and we love him immensely. Juan is the love of my daughter's life, her kindred spirit. He is also the cornerstone of my life-coaching practice, his kind temperament and loving disposition beckoning to many in need of guidance or comfort. I can't imagine not having Juan in my life. I schedule the surgery to remove the melanomas, but my reprieve is short-lived.

A few weeks later, I receive a distressing call from Auntie Di, a highly competent horsewoman who helps me care for Juan and JJ. "Juan is colicking," she lets me know. "I saw him thrashing in the mud; it took four of us to get him up. We are hand-walking him now. He can barely stand; he is in severe pain."

"I'll be there within twenty minutes. I'll call the vet," I reply.

Dr. Adams arrives within the hour. Juan is covered in mud, and his legs barely support his massive body. She gives him an injection for pain, inserting a long, flexible tube up through his nostrils and down into his belly. Then, she surges him with liquid in hopes that any blockage can pass without requiring emergency surgery. "You will need to hand-walk him through the night," she instructs.

By morning, Juan is out of imminent danger, but the scare reminds me to appreciate my precious time with these sentient beings.

The need to cherish life resonates with me on many levels. My parents are heading toward their eighth decade; I'm acutely aware my cherished time with them is limited. I want Savanna to have as much time as possible with my parents. Her paternal grandparents passed away when she was an infant, and she has no memories of them. I want my parents to live on in her heart, as they will in mine.

We always spend Christmas holidays with my parents. Beth, Matt, and their dog Sierra will join us this year. It has been a few years since we have all been together at Christmas. My parents' home is filled with Christmas cheer—gifts overshadow a little holiday tree, and a makeshift Dickens village sets the stage with its flickering holiday lights—it feels magical.

The day before Christmas is a beautiful sunny day, and we head to San Pedro port to play bocce. Beth and I team up with Mom while Savanna joins forces with Gramps and Uncle Matt. Ric has stayed back at my parents' home to rest.

We are enjoying the game when my pocket buzzes—I assume it's Ric and take the phone from my pocket. I have just missed a call from Katie. Her horse resides in a paddock just across the pasture where I keep my horses. I step away from the bocce court, my pulse quickening as I call Katie.

"Lisa, I was getting ready to leave the ranch, but Badger kept nudging me until I finally looked up at your pasture," Katie tells me. "Juan was flaying in the mud by the trees. I was able to get him up, but I can barely keep him walking. It's Christmas Eve; no one is here. What do you want me to do?"

"I'm in Southern California. Let me call the vet and Berto," I say. "I have Banamine in my tack room. Can you medicate him?"

I immediately call Ric. We divide our efforts. Ric calls Berto, who is the ranch manager, our farrier, and a highly competent horseman. I call Katie back and let her know that Dr. Adams and Berto are on their way to the ranch.

Beth sees my distress. "I have lots of frequent flier miles. I can get you home within a couple of hours," she offers after hearing about Juan. She lost her beloved dog Moxie not long ago, and the recent pain wells up in her eyes.

"Thank you. Let me speak with the vet first so I have a better idea of what needs to happen," I say.

Savanna comes over and sees the tears in my eyes. "Mommy, what's wrong?"

I explain as best I can. Savanna knows that Dr. Adams saved Juan the last time she treated him. Savanna is confident it will be the same outcome. We decide it would be best to get back to my parents' home.

Within the hour, we hear from Dr. Adams. Ric and I listen to the prognosis in the guest room while Savanna helps with Christmas Eve festivities in the kitchen.

"Juan is in extreme distress," Dr. Adam reports. "I'm sedating him so I can do a full examination and make a more informed prognosis. This appears more serious than the last time I treated him. Katie has offered to trailer him to the hospital if we decide surgery is needed. I will call when I have more information."

Savanna comes to the back bedroom and sees the tears in our eyes. As she approaches, I instinctively say to her, "Savanna, why don't you give us a few minutes?" She starts to walk away. I look at Ric and adjust my thoughts. *No, this is all wrong—Juan is her kindred spirit horse. Savanna needs to be in the room with us. It doesn't matter that she's only ten or that it's Christmas Eve—Savanna needs to know what is going on with her beloved horse.*

"Savanna, come back, honey." I explain what's going on with Juan.

Dr. Adams calls. "Juan has a mass in his colon, most likely a tumor that has grown from the last time I treated him," she says. "His only chance of survival is immediate surgery."

"Can you tell us what that entails and his prognosis for survival?" I ask.

"The surgery is complex and costly, on the order of ten thousand dollars," Dr. Adams informs me. "If we get in and the tumor is too extensive, then we will need to euthanize. I must add that since he is an older horse, he may not make a full recovery. There's also the possibility that he may not survive the trailer ride to the hospital. His best-case scenario involves a number of weeks at the hospital with confinement to a stall. If all of that is successful, then when Juan returns to the ranch, he would continue his recovery in a small paddock."

We are all in tears and ask if we can have a few minutes as a family to make our decision. We hold hands and talk it through. Juan is twenty-four years old—this would be a challenging surgery and recovery. He would not understand why he was separated from his herd, and Juan has only ever known a life out in pasture with his equine friends. If he survives everything else, he might die of a broken heart. We all know what needs to be done, but no one says it aloud. We create a prayer circle, each expressing our gratitude for the blessings Juan has bestowed upon us.

Sorrow filling our hearts, we call Dr. Adams and ask if we can FaceTime with Juan to say our goodbyes. Barely recognizable, Juan's magnificence masks his pain. He is covered in mud, his eyes drawn. We each say our farewell. It is Savanna's farewell that catches his spirit.

"Goodbye, Juaners. I love you. You are the best horse ever," Savanna says through tears. Then JJ and Juan nicker their farewells to each other before day yields to night.

My heart and soul literally break wide open. All the flaws of my life coalesce and rupture the façade that has held me together for five decades. All the grief I have ever held now has a conduit for escape.

54

Grief

The dusty road masks the mist, fogging my eyes. I have been down this dirt ranch road many times, knowing my two beautiful horses would greet me at its end. Sorrow wrings my heart. The wild bushes scratch the windows of our truck as it follows along with the twists of the road. The final turn has always been my light—the sight of my beloved steeds, always together.

On this day, I hear only one gentle nicker. My other sentient being, the one who caused me to fall in love with my husband, who beckoned my daughter into the world, and who healed the hearts of so many, is no longer here. My grief swells when I see JJ standing, alone, his longtime friend gone.

As I walk to the pasture gate, I see the red cowboy halter that belonged to Juan, hanging by itself, just like my bright chestnut horse standing alone with his head hung low. Anyone who thinks animals don't feel emotions has never observed the grief these beings express when they lose a member of their herd.

The sorrow in the air is palpable, and I can barely see JJ through the blur of my tears. I hear his small whinny, and he meets me at the gate. I bring JJ down to the round pen. With hardly a shift in my energy, he offers a beautiful canter around me in a tight enveloping circle and comes to rest by my side. I scratch his forehead as he gently drops his head into me. I gaze into his soft, knowing eyes. He, too, feels the loss of Juan. Our love flows into each other.

This crucible has broken me open. I weep for the loss of Juan. My sorrow becomes a portal as I cry for the loss of family and friends. Then I find my deeper sorrow that has viscerally adhered to every cell in my body. I weep for Karen and Jackie. I weep for Marni and Dave. I weep for my childhood dog, King. I feel the grief as it rolls through me. I cry for everyone I have lost in my life until I run out of tears. Finally, my grief flows free.

55

Horses in the Otherworld

Early in the new year, just a few weeks after Juan's passing, Shirley takes our family to see *Shen-Yun*. It is her Christmas gift to us. We are enjoying our time with her and remembering our time with Juan.

"You should ask Nikki Cuthbertson to reach out to Juan. You know I used her to communicate to Tristan when I had to euthanize him. I still use her," Shirley says with tears in her eyes.

"Okay. I will look into it," I reply.

When I get home, I go to Nikki's website. She is an established animal communicator. Without thinking, I find myself making an appointment for a "communication" with Juan. She asks for a picture. Nothing more.

On the appointed day of our "communication," I go to the ranch and take a long walk on the trail surrounding our pasture. I am of two minds—one analytical and the other spiritual. I try to stay in the realm of curiosity. I sit on a fallen tree in the pasture, well above where JJ and the other horses are grazing. I have my journal and pen—I intend to write down everything she tells me.

Nikki calls. I purposely remain circumspect, though I do wonder what information Shirley has already provided her about Juan. Nikki asks me to breathe deeply so that I am grounded for the experience.

"Are you ready?" she asks.

"I think so." My heart pounds wildly.

She starts the process. I wait with bated breath.

"Lisa, there is someone else here with Juan, and he would like to communicate with you. Is this okay?" Nikki asks.

"I guess so," I say, a bit unnerved.

"Does the name Dave mean anything to you?" she asks.

I am completely unprepared for this. Could this possibly be my mentor Dave? I try to process this information. I have goosebumps.

"He worked with you. He wants you to know that he has been watching over you. It's time for you to spread your wings and soar."

"Nikki, on my wall at home, I have an image of a hawk with a quote that reads, 'Spread your wings and soar,'" I say.

This feels surreal. I quickly write this down in my journal so I won't later think I'm crazy. I am speechless and drenched in nervous sweat. *How is it that she has access to the spirit world?*

Nikki then informs me that Juan is ready to communicate.

"Juan wants you to know that he was not in pain until the very end. He always looked forward to seeing you and the family. He is showing me a little girl, is that someone he knows?" Nikki asks.

"Yes, that is my daughter, Savanna."

"Juan wants you to know that he is your daughter's guardian angel. He will always watch over her."

I am raw with emotion, tears streaming down my face.

Nikki continues, "Juan is showing me a hawk. When you see a hawk, then you know he is watching over you."

I see a large red-tailed hawk circling above me in the pasture. *Am I dreaming?*

I ask her to convey to Juan that we are filled with heartfelt gratitude for the joy he brought into our lives. I thank Nikki for her reading and quickly write down everything in my journal.

I walk down through the pasture to see JJ. He nuzzles into my heart space. I feel his peace flow into me, dissolving my inner sense of unworthiness. He is the crucible that serves to annihilate my flaws. I hear the screech of the nearby hawk.

I am fifty-two years old, and I finally feel worthy of this world.

56

Spread Your Wings and Soar

Red-tailed hawks have become a mainstay in my life since Juan's passing. A large red-tailed hawk built her nest in the cypress tree just outside our yard, and another built her nest in the eucalyptus tree next to JJ's pasture. I continuously see hawks on the Berkeley campus as I pass through the redwoods.

Back when I worked closely with Ariana, I was drawn to animal medicine and spiritual symbolism. Hawks are thought to represent the messenger between this world and that which is beyond the veil. The sighting of many hawks is a message from the universe to stay the course and focus on the parts of your life where leadership is needed.

Perhaps the hawks have always been there and I had never noticed them before, but they are undeniable now. I feel their calling. I sense their messages. I feel a beckoning to share my story.

In this highly reflective time, I embark on the creation of a personal leadership course for our engineering undergraduates and graduate students, Engineering Your Life, and Introspective Leadership, respectively. The College of Engineering is now under the leadership helm of a remarkable woman, Dean Tsu-Jae King Liu. She seeks to change the culture of engineering. She has asked me to serve as the Associate Dean for Students, and I will have the privilege of working closely with her for eighteen months.

I have the dean's full endorsement to create personal leadership courses for our engineering students. My aim is to provide a framework for emotional intelligence, introspective awareness, time management, conflict resolution, teamwork, and societal service. Engineering Your Life is the course I wish I could have taken when I was a freshman.

I understand that I cannot embark on the path of teaching personal leadership in the engineering curriculum until I am ready to share my personal story in the academic community. In this introspective process, I finally recognize that my earliest crucible—the passing of my sister—set the stage for the development of resilience. Early struggles in school later served as the seed for my outreach teaching. My deepest crucible was hitting my rock bottom. In my journey to recovery alongside my equine guide, I found my true sweet spot, which is my ability to empower others through the lens of compassion. I could not be where I am today if I had not been shaped by the crucibles of my life. My life is finally coming full circle.

JJ has been my guiding light through this journey. I often work out my pedagogical challenges while riding him on the coastal trails just south of my home in Pacifica. He will forever be my guide, enabling me to use my horse wisdom to empower myself and others.

One of my first steps in these leadership courses is to examine our personal stories and crucibles. I will set the stage with my personal story. My courses will be safe spaces. We will not share each other's personal stories outside of the classroom. We will see that we all come through some form of adversity—this is often where we hone our skills and talents. Through this course, I will invite students to find their authentic selves—a discovery that took me more than five decades to accomplish.

In early 2020, the notorious semester when the world will be soon sidelined by the global pandemic, I launch Engineering Your Life to fifty undergraduates in engineering. In parallel, I launch a graduate equivalent to this course, Introspective Leadership. On the first day of class, I hear the screech of a hawk as I cross the road from Etcheverry Hall onto the main campus. He beckons me to have courage.

I welcome the students into the classroom, alongside my co-facilitators, Marvin Lopez and Tiffany Reardon, who spearhead our special programs for the College of Engineering. I have had the great fortitude to meet them in my role as associate dean for students. Later in the week, I will do the same for the graduate course with my co-facilitator, Keith Gatto, whom I first met in an ethics workshop and now work with through the Fung Institute for Leadership.

I introduce myself, "Good afternoon, everyone. Welcome to our inaugural personal leadership class. First, let me tell you about how I got here." I start with my academic accolades.

I feel an electric current through my body. A hum. Not fear. Not trepidation. A calling. A summoning. Then I step out into the middle of the room, and I take off my armor. I share my life story. Time stands still. Everyone is fully present. I see myself in each of them, and now they can see me within themselves. When I finish my story, I tell them that if they prefer, they can call me Fire Horse.

Students come up after class, thanking me for my courage. The students never imagined that an esteemed faculty member might have struggled so deeply in her life. Some share their personal stories quickly, and others will peel their protective layers with time. We will grow together on this journey.

57

The Long Goodbye

It is winter solstice, nearly two years to the date of losing our beloved Juan. My scientific mind watches the images appear on the screen. The bright colors ebb and flow with each heartbeat. A surge of jet-flow reverses through the heart chamber. My emotional ears listen to the veterinary team: heart failure, backflow, murmurs, comets, quality-of-life decisions.

Numb, I stand by JJ, my fingers sinking into his soft chestnut coat, glistening in the winter sun. His nostrils are flaring as though he has been out for a gallop. The peacefulness of his eyes invites the realization that JJ may be coming to the end of his days. I push the thought away.

His health challenges revealed themselves just before Thanksgiving. He developed a cough and seemed to be breathing hard with no physical exertion. Sometimes, JJ would eat for me; sometimes, he wouldn't. JJ remained happy to go on long, slow trail rides or work in the arena. He always felt light in my hands, yet I knew he lacked his usual energy.

As the veterinary team completes the imaging of his heart, Dr. Nora asks if I can put JJ back in the paddock so we can discuss his prognosis. I take the lead of his cowboy halter and gently coax him into a paddock. I leave him with a bucket full of his favorite grain, hoping he will miraculously find his appetite.

I walk toward the three young women comprising the veterinary team. There is a solemnness in their posture—I can almost predict the words about to be spoken.

"JJ is a lovely horse and clearly a very special soul," Dr. Nora begins. "I'm so sorry to be the bearer of such sad news, especially in this year of 2020, and especially over the holiday season. JJ is in heart failure. I believe this will continue to progress. Within days or maybe weeks, it will be clear that a difficult decision will have to be made about the quality of life for JJ. He should not be ridden, and his caregivers should be cautious around him, especially your daughter, as there is a chance that he will have an acute fatal cardiac episode."

I have brought the veterinary team copies of JJ's memoir. "He has quite a fan club here at the ranch," I say. I don't know how I will muster the strength to tell his human village that his days are numbered. *How will I possibly cope in this world without him?*

JJ and I slowly make it up the hill to his pasture. His herd—Badger, Billy, Cash, and Echo—greet him at the gate. I feel their pull on my giant thoroughbred. He is happy to return to his equine family. The red-tailed hawk sits in the tree above us and makes his call. *Is he beckoning JJ to the spirit world?*

"Please don't take him before Christmas," I plead.

Winter solstice is special in 2020 because Jupiter and Saturn align in the night sky in their closest encounter to our planet in four hundred years. Ric has taken Savanna to the beach so they can see the "Christmas Star" with his telescope. I opt to stay behind to be alone with my thoughts.

I sit out in the cold winter air with our young husky—like many families, we adopted a dog during the pandemic. I am grateful that Goose found her way into our home. I am convinced that JJ played a part in finding this dog for our family and for me. I soak in the night sky and the bright stars above as I run my fingers through her thick coat.

It is ironic that the universe would summon my earth angel in this phenomenal year, but JJ is such a spiritual being that I can barely imagine it being any other way. A large great-horned owl swoops overhead to his perch in the tall cypress tree next to our home. I feel his hoots reverberate in my body—another spiritual being in my life letting me know that JJ has his guardians in place.

I lie in bed, consumed by the veterinary team's news. JJ has been my beacon of light for much of my adult life, journeying beside me through my highest of highs and lowest of lows. He made me who I am today. He has been my life force. My anxiety grows as I think of how his departure from this world may tear the fabric of my life. "How can I possibly go on without you?" I say through my sobs. I hear the hoots from outside, inviting me to listen.

Through our shared frequency, I receive my message from JJ. "I did not bring you out of darkness for you to retreat into the shadows. I will always be your light."

The next day, I feel JJ calling me to the ranch. I have no idea how imminent his departure will be from this earth body. I intend to spend every last day of his life with him.

"Can I go with you to the ranch?" asks Ric.

"Of course. He would love to see you."

"I never had a chance to say goodbye to Juan before we lost him," he says.

The memory of losing Juan two years ago still pains my heart.

"You need to tell Savanna," Ric says.

"I know. It's been such a hard year with this pandemic. She's been feeling so isolated. Today she has an opportunity to spend time with her friend. I don't want to ruin Christmas for her," I say.

"JJ might not make it to Christmas," my husband adds.

I feel tears welling up. I have no words—the thought of losing JJ before Christmas is too painful to process. *I need time with him. I need a long goodbye.*

As we drive up the dirt road to the pasture, I soak in the landscape. The hills are thirsty for rain, and the horses await the arrival of the seasonal grass that will soon follow. The cold air assaults me as I step out of the car. I hear JJ's soft whinny and see him peering down at us through his knowing eyes. I feel his grand presence.

I share the news with his longtime caregiver, Auntie Di. She sobs just as I had. Diane offers to share the news with others. "It takes a village to raise an aging thoroughbred," I joke through tears.

Over the past few weeks, as JJ's appetite dwindled, loving women at the ranch—Lisa, Katie, Louise, Cindy, Cathy—have offered up various types of hay, alfalfa cubes, oats, and other grains to coax him into eating.

Ric and I are greeted with the kind words of Cindy and Cathy. They had been planning a book reading with JJ to celebrate his story. They offer to help with any care he needs and declare themselves to be a part of his prayer circle. His human herd rallies for him.

I feel a healing energy in the pasture, as though the horses are offering a shared life force for their wise elder.

JJ must feel the healing energy of the ranch. His eyes hold a peacefulness. For the first time in weeks, he eats a small bucket of grain and inhales a pound of carrots. *Maybe the vet is wrong?*

Two days before Christmas, a happy whinny greets me as I walk up to the pasture gate to find JJ standing with his herd-mates under the grove of eucalyptus trees. The winter winds whip through the branches above them, yet there is a serenity to this equine community. JJ saunters to the gate with grace as his companions make way for him to pass through. *If only humans could support each other this way.*

The hawk above me screeches.

Not before Christmas, please.

I offer JJ a bucket of Katie's alfalfa cubes and oats along with his long-time favorite grain. I let him eat outside his pasture gate, enjoying the presence of his herd. Cash and Echo stand underneath the trees facing JJ while Billy and Badger take up their posts by the gate.

There is a stillness to their energy, like a forcefield protecting my sentient being. I run my hands through JJ's thick winter coat. His mane is coated with mud, but beneath, his fur is as soft as a spring rabbit. I soak in the sweet scent of his muzzle and breathe in the life of my horse.

I stand with him for thirty minutes. He has eaten a pound of carrots and half of his grain. The new sprouts of grass lure him away. I let him graze on the path running across the front of his pasture. His herd follows. When I bring him back through his gate, he is absorbed into this equine community with ease. I feel the peacefulness in the air. "I will see you tomorrow, JJ Luck."

In the evening, as I read in bed, Savanna asks the inevitable question. "How did JJ's vet appointment go?"

Hot tears spill down my cheeks. I struggle for composure as I share the news with her. I feel her body convulse as the sobbing takes over. I know her pain. I know her fears. I hold her tight.

"We won't have any horses left after JJ passes," she says through tears.

"We will still have horses in our life," I soothe her. "We have been blessed to have two spirit horses in our lives. They can't be replaced. JJ has given us a gift—a long goodbye. We get to savor every day that we have with him. He is giving us a life lesson. We never know when we will lose a loved one. We should be this way with everyone we love."

I feel gratitude swelling in my heart. JJ's wisdom is spilling forth as though it were my own—or is it my own?

It is Christmas Eve. Savanna has accompanied me to the ranch, and we have brought JJ a pound of baby carrots. I let Savvy go up on her own. JJ offers his sweet nicker and greets her by the gate. His pasture-mates circle round as if offering their own prayer circle. *Is this our last Christmas Eve with this gentle giant?*

I soak in the crisp winter air and the colorless sky. The trees have shed their autumn leaves, the hawk peering at me from the branch above.

Not yet, please.

We bring JJ down and coax him into eating some alfalfa cubes and oats. Savvy hides baby carrots in his grain, hoping we can entice him to eat more. He's on to us. He picks off his oats and carrots and leaves us with a bucket of soaked cubes. We let him graze on the grass. We brush the mud from his coat and try to detangle his mane. He swishes his tail as I try to uncoil its tight tendrils weaved with its strands of black and chestnut hair. I let their tight strands fall, and he softens his gaze as his whiskers gently probe the ground for stray pieces of grass.

I am grateful when the evening comes to an end without an emergency text or phone call from the ranch. My heart swells with gratitude for the village of people who care for this beloved horse.

It is Christmas morning. The lights on our tree sparkle; presents overflow its skirts. *How long will it take to open gifts?* I am anxious to see JJ. I rally the family to the ranch. The winds whip through the eucalyptus grove, and rain is imminent. JJ is not interested in grain today. The winter storm stirs his soul. I feel the anxiety in the air—is it his or mine?

"I think he would like to have a blanket on," Ric suggests.

"I have one. Let's see if he will tolerate wearing it," I say.

I run down the hill to my tack room. The wind is biting cold; my hands are numb. I find his blanket and hope he will accept wearing it. When I return to the pasture, JJ is working fiercely at the small strands of grass making their way through Mother Earth.

I unfold the blanket and toss it over the mountain of my seventeen-hand horse. JJ doesn't flinch, and within moments, I have all the buckles fastened. He seems content when we return him to his herd. We latch the gate just as the sky opens up and releases her rain upon us.

Our guardian hawk observes us carefully.

Not yet, please.

The next morning, the sky is bright blue, the air scrubbed clean by the previous night's storm. The crispness opens my lungs. When I arrive at the ranch, JJ probes down at me through his perceptive eyes. He seems bright today—I sense a shift in his energy. He offers an exuberant whinny. My heart flutters.

I have brought a pound of organic carrots and fill a bucket with only his favorite grain. I will not try to lure him to eat soaked cubes of alfalfa or pellets. I break the carrots into the bucket and place it under the tall trees by his pasture gate. His herd clears a path for him as I open the gate, and he heads straight to his bucket. For the first time in weeks, JJ eats with enthusiasm. *Could this be my Christmas gift from the other side?*

I grab his rope halter from the post by the gate, slip it gingerly over his muzzle, and catch it behind his ears. His eyes are awake today. I soak in their wisdom as he looks into my soul.

"Let's go for a walk," I say.

We have no agenda. There is no specific plan—I am simply here to cherish each and every day I have left with my spirit horse. This is my time to give back to him. We slowly make our way along the path in front of his pasture.

He eats grass at his leisure until we reach the intersection of the fire road. For many years, these hilly trail systems were part of his fitness. Now, we just meander the gentle rolling paths. I have no intention of wasting any of his precious heartbeats. *How many heartbeats has he given to racing? Or three-day eventing?*

We make our way down by Auntie Di's paddock. He looks for her, but she is away for the holidays. As we loop through back to his pasture, he finds nibbles of grass and strands of hay. I coax a little more grain into him. There is a luminosity to him today that I haven't seen in nearly a month.

Is it too unrealistic to hope the grim prognosis might have been off, and maybe he will be with me for years to come? I hear the screech of the hawk as he circles above. In my heart, I know that the spirit world is already preparing my sentient being for transition.

It has been a week since I received the veterinary prognosis. I reach out to Nikki Cuthbertson, the animal communicator who connected with Juan two years ago. I have so many questions for her. She is reaching out to JJ from afar.

"How is JJ feeling?" I ask.

"JJ is aware that he doesn't feel *that solid* in his body, but he is not wispy," Nikki replies. "He is not imminently ready to release his earth body."

I breathe a sigh of relief.

"Is Juan with him?" I ask. "There is a hawk who is always near the pasture."

"Juan is helping him with his transition," Nikki says. "JJ is processing the emotion of the herd. No one wants him to leave; they are giving to him right now. He is borrowing a life force from them. The receiving is helping him to come to completion with this earth life. A depth of love is being revealed to him," Nikki adds.

I think of how connected he has been to his pasture-mates over the past few weeks. I feel the visceral truth of Nikki's words.

"Is there anything special that he wants from me?" I ask.

"He likes his blanket. He is enjoying his slow walks with you. He is showing me a grove of trees," says Nikki.

"I've been taking him for daily walks on the path by his pasture."

"He is enjoying this time with you."

"Will he still be my spirit guide after he passes?" I ask through misty eyes.

"He is moving from life into life, not life into death," Nikki says on behalf of JJ. "He will be right here—in the light—in the interconnection of the web. He will be your light. You will sense him in rainbows, sunsets, or prisms of light on your windows. He will be the sunlight kissing dew. You will always sense his presence."

"Wow, he sent a similar message to me last week," I tell her.

"JJ will continue to share connection and insight with you. There isn't anywhere he will be where you are not," Nikki adds.

"He has made me who I am today. I am filled with immense gratitude."

"You enabled each other to be who you are today. Gratitude is on both sides."

Tears flow down my cheeks as I try to process the ebb and flow of my emotions.

It is New Year's Day, and my daughter is with me. We are optimistic that 2021 will be better than 2020. She and I still hold hope that we will have JJ for the foreseeable future.

The morning air is crisp. The hawk sits on the fence post by the pasture—his eyes pierce my soul, and I feel the power of his spirit. JJ nickers and the hawk follows, landing on the post closer to him. My heart stutters. *Don't take him yet.*

"Savanna, look at the hawk," I say. She tucks through the opening in the gate, stealthy in her movement. The hawk doesn't take his eyes off her. JJ stands still. The hawk swoops to the post behind the water trough. Then, he lands several feet in front of Savanna and JJ in the pasture. *Time is still.*

The hawk takes flight; we hear his screech. JJ ambles to the gate, his eyes cheerful, with purpose in his step. I open the latch, and JJ quickly finds his grain bucket. The hawk lands in the branch above us. He stares down at us with awareness. We are on borrowed time.

"It's Juan," says Savanna. "He's here watching over JJ."

I think back to my recent conversation with Nikki. I hope Juan is only here to look over our beloved horse. I am not ready to relinquish my spirit horse yet.

JJ seems to have found his appetite, finishing off his grain bucket and two pounds of carrots with gusto. The green grass beckons to him. We let him have forty minutes of grass as we stroll along the trail. I notice the swelling under his belly. *Was that there before?* I'm sure it wasn't. I recall the words of the vet—this is a sign of the progression of heart failure.

Auntie Di comes over and gives JJ a big pat. "He sure loves his hot bran mashes in the mornings," she comments.

Katie walks up and offers JJ a bucket of soaked alfalfa cubes with oats. "I don't think he eats those anymore," I say.

"He eats them for me," Katie says with a smile. JJ quickly makes a liar of me.

Moments later, Cathy walks up and offers him a few carrots. "I need to come up to the pasture and tell you the parts of your story that I like best," she says. JJ becomes a total ham and leans into her gently. We decide to have a formal book reading for JJ.

"You are one loved horse," I say.

It is mid-January when we have JJ's book reading. JJ is in his element, and his eyes are peaceful. His fan club has shown up with copies of *Horse of Fire*. I notice that Cathy and Cindy have their books tabbed and highlighted. I am moved beyond belief—I had no idea that JJ's life story and our journey would touch so many. One excerpt they've chosen causes a flood of emotions to wash over me.

"One day a young woman came to see him. Like the others, she noted his gangly experience and imbalance but she also saw a spark in his eyes and a grace in his movement. She left that day without him and JJ was heartbroken. *Wouldn't anyone take him home and let him blossom into the horse he was meant to be?* He was discouraged—he had thought there was a connection with that woman. She too was a fiery chestnut and born in the sign of Aries—*didn't she know that they were destined to be together?* He was sure of it. Weeks went by and he remained in his pasture with no one to love him. One day his owner placed JJ in the horse trailer. He wondered—*where am I going now?* When he arrived at the new farm he was disoriented. *Where was he?* Then JJ saw her— the woman who had ridden him just a few weeks ago. JJ decided to call her Fire Horse. JJ was certain that he and Fire Horse would be together through all of time. She was his destiny and he would blossom in her care—he knew it. He had come home finally."

As we conclude the book reading, everyone takes snapshots of JJ and collects his hoof prints in their books. I swear JJ is smiling—what an amazing journey he has had. He seems to be glowing.

I can almost convince myself that the veterinary diagnosis is wrong, except for the swellings that are appearing under his chest and abdomen.

His spirit is luminous, but his earth body is waning.

It is January 29. When I arrive at the ranch, JJ stands stock still in his favorite place on a sandy knoll in his pasture, overlooking the large arena. Echo sleeps beside him. JJ looks at me as I get out of my car. I feel his eyes beckoning me. He offers me a soft whinny but doesn't move.

I walk over to Auntie Di sitting on her bench by her paddock. She has the perfect vantage point to watch over JJ's pasture.

"Is he taking a sun nap?" I ask.

"He's been standing still for hours; he wouldn't eat for me."

"Oh. I wonder if he'll eat for me."

We both have that dreaded feeling that neither of us wants to openly express. *Is this the end?*

I prepare his bucket with his senior blend containing molasses and sunflower seeds, sprinkling some of Katie's magic oats on top. I also have a bag of his favorite baby carrots in my jacket pocket. I make my way to the gate, but JJ doesn't move. He always meets me at the gate. My heart pauses.

I open the gate and call out to him, "JJ." He doesn't move. I walk over to him with his cowboy halter in my hand. Echo doesn't leave his side. This feels a bit surreal. When I approach, JJ looks at me, but his body is as still as a statue. I take note of the swellings that have been steadily increasing in his underbelly.

I rub his forelock. He rubs his head softly into me. It is clear he won't be walking back to the gate with me today.

"Let me get your bucket of grain for you."

I return with the grain. He acknowledges the gesture, but nothing more. Echo frees her body from her napping spot and offers to help her friend with the bucket. JJ doesn't care that she eats his grain—this is not a good sign. I offer him the baby carrots, but he is not interested.

The hawk swoops to the post across from us.

Not yet. I need to say a proper goodbye.

"JJ, I love you so much," I say aloud. "I don't want you to suffer. I am listening to you. Let me know if I need to call the vet. I won't fall into another deep hole when it's time for you to leave. I promise." My tears flow. "I am so grateful to have you in my life. Thank you."

I stand with JJ for the next hour, looking deep into his sleepy eyes. They hold so much love and wisdom. I stroke his forelock and breathe in his sweet breath. I let my hands sink into his soft rabbit fur over his magnificent body.

Finally, it is time to say goodbye. *Is this our last goodbye?* I have been here every day, always wondering if this would be my last day to spend with him.

I spend the rest of the afternoon and night with my cell phone nearby in case someone from the ranch calls. I check it one last time before bed.

At 4:00 a.m., I wake with a start. I have been getting messages from JJ in the wee hours of the night for the past several weeks.

I think he is preparing me, assuring me I will be okay. But this message is different: *Savanna needs to come to the ranch tomorrow.*

Savvy comes with me to the ranch. It's a beautiful, crisp Saturday, and the ranch is abuzz with people. We are both prepared for this to possibly be our last chance to say goodbye to JJ. We are armed with carrots and horse cookies. Savanna is determined that she will coax JJ into eating.

When JJ sees Savanna, he offers a boisterous whinny and strolls purposefully toward the gate. She looks at me as if the previous day had been some fluke. *Was it just a bad day?* This emotional roller coaster is exhausting.

"Why don't you bring him down, and we'll offer him some grain," I yell up to the pasture.

He meanders down the hill with ease. I have a bucket full of grain. He makes haste and polishes it off along with the horse cookies and carrots.

"He seems to have an appetite today!" Savanna says playfully.

JJ walks across to Katie's area and nibbles on some of her goodies before visiting Auntie Di and Auntie Lisa. He has become a bit of an icon around the ranch, like a mascot, and many offer him free rein over their hay, grains, and pellets.

JJ spends hours grazing among us while Savanna grooms him to show-quality polish. I am left perplexed about the day before. *Maybe it was just an off day? Or is he just making sure to say farewell to all of his human herd?* I push the thought away.

Louise drives up with her fifty-pound bags of horse feed. As she pours them into her large barrels, JJ appears beside her in his prankster mode. Within minutes, his head is stuffed in her large gray barrel, eating her horse's feed with gusto. JJ is now gorging on the same pellets he has refused to eat for the past six weeks. Then, he starts throwing his head and grain with it as if playing the comedian. We all belly laugh.

We let JJ graze on the green grass for hours in the winter sunshine. Savanna has brushed him to a high gloss and washed and detangled his tail and mane—he looks luminous. He seems in his element today.

"Do you want to bring him up, Savvy?" I ask.

"Let's bring him up together," she says.

"See you tomorrow, JJ. We love you," we say together.

The hawk circles above us in silence.

I drop Savanna off at the western end of the ranch for her Sunday morning riding lesson and slowly drive down to the end of the ranch, where I will find my beloved steed. He greets me with an exuberant whinny as I step out of the car.

"JJ jumping beans!" I say with glee.

He looks bright, with a spring in his step. I open the gate, and JJ quickly finds his way to the patch of grass outside of his pasture.

I gently take his lead rope in hand, and we walk on the long path leading down to the ranch road. I feel his warm breath on my neck. We walk at length with a purpose, as though we have somewhere important to go. There is a lightness between us. *Is JJ going to walk straight to heaven and take me with him?*

When we get back to his pasture, JJ stands solemnly at the gate, refusing to move. I lure him in, and his pasture-mates greet him, forming a semicircle around us. I look into his eyes. They are peaceful, yet the light is leaving. I feel it in my soul.

I see the jugular pulsations on his neck. His nostrils are flaring. I stand by his side with my hands on his forelock and neck until the pulses calm.

"I love you, JJ. I will see you tomorrow," I say. He beckons me with his eyes to stay. I stand with him a little longer. The hawk screeches in the sky above us.

At 4:00 a.m., I awake with a start. *Is that you, JJ?* I feel his love in my heart.

I see the tears in Ric's eyes as he comes running to the back of the house.

"I am so sorry," he says simply.

"What's happened?" I ask with trepidation. *Has something happened to one of my parents?*

"Didn't you see your text yet?" he asks.

The text must have come in just after I left to go out for a short run with Goose. I hadn't taken my phone. All at once, it hits me: *How could I possibly forget that this day was coming?*

"JJ passed away in the night," Ric tells me. Savvy comes running when she hears the news.

"No!" I cry. The sobs become torrents in my body. I am so prepared and so dreadfully unprepared all at once.

Ric and Savvy hug me. I drop to the floor. Poor little Goose—she doesn't know why I am crying. She licks the tears from my face, wagging her youthful husky tail.

"I'll take you to the ranch," Ric offers.

The drive to the ranch is fast and slow all at once. A lifetime of memories floods my mind. *How can I possibly fill the void left by this magnificent being?* I know the answer. It is the binding contract I have with JJ and what finally enabled him to transition to the other side. *His spirit will fill me. The hole in my soul and the crack in my heart are his conduits—he can now take root—we are one.*

Potholes from the winter rains dot the road leading from JJ's end of the ranch. Ric tries to get there quickly, but the dirt road will not cooperate. We pass by the pastures. I see the horses frolicking, taking advantage of the luxury of warm sunshine between winter rains. The grasses are lush. This has been JJ's favorite thing to do over the past several weeks—graze on the rich grass.

I step out of the car and see the immense body of my equine companion. He lies in his favorite nap spot, soaking up the morning rays. Echo stands by him as if standing guard.

As Ric and I walk through the gate, Echo greets us with her large moon eyes, as if she could say, "I am so sorry for your loss. We all loved JJ."

Crying, I approach JJ's body, stretched out as though in the midst of a glorious nap. His eyes are soft and half-closed. Still beautiful, but the light is gone.

"JJ. My sweet baby boy!" I sob.

I am on the ground in an instant. My hand is on his face, caressing his forelock. It was always my favorite place to touch. I stare into his deep-brown eyes and caress his lids. My fingers sink into his bright chestnut coat. He is so soft. I absorb the sensations into every cell of my body.

"Thank you," I say. "You saved me. You are the love of my life."

I lie across JJ, feeling the immensity of his equine body. This horse with whom I have had so many wonderful adventures. This horse whose canter could bring me to a different dimension. "Thank you for my long goodbye," I whisper.

I hear the telltale screeches piercing the air, awakening me to this world. Two red-tailed hawks circle above me.

My spirit horse is forever the light in my life. He showed me the way to my purpose: I use my horse wisdom to empower myself and others. He gave me the gift of worthiness—that was mine all along.

FROM DARKNESS INTO LIGHT

The hawks called today
Beckoning my earth angel

Will he guide me from the spirit world, dropping hawk feathers at my feet?
Will he grace me on the wings of butterflies?
Will he watch from the eyes of an owl?
Will he be the light in my life and the air that I breathe?

This luminous being lives forever in my soul and in my heart
The bright chestnut horse who brought me from darkness into light

February 1, 2021

EPILOGUE

Un-Engineering My Life

The salty ocean air fills my lungs. I take in the majestic beauty of the Bodega headlands. I am spending this weekend in Sonoma County to work with Ariana. My drive from Pacifica has brought back memories of my time with JJ. I passed by the farm where my horses lived so many wonderful years and Ariana's old ranch in Valley Ford. I think back to my journey into natural horsemanship and equine-guided education. My bright chestnut thoroughbred pushed, pulled, and navigated me on this amazing life journey I have had thus far. Gratitude fills my heart as tears stream down my face.

After JJ passed, so many people sent me kind messages and cards—sharing how JJ had transformed their lives either through our equine-guided coaching or in reading his story in *Horse of Fire*. I received weavings from his mane, tail, and forelock. After my final farewell, women had gathered around his body to say their own goodbyes, asking if they, too, could take some of his mane, tail, or forelock. Torrents of tears flooded the field that day. I truly saw the impact of this magnificent being with whom I had been so blessed to spend much of my life.

I gave away much of my equine equipment. I sold my custom Western saddle, but I could not part with his bridle—it hangs in my home alongside the halters that once belonged to JJ and Juan.

I thought I would let horses fade from my life. I started obedience training with Goose with the long-term goal of having her be a therapy dog. I envisioned that she could come to campus with me and be a part of my leadership work. She and I are now on this journey together, and we are constantly reinforced with the call of ever-present hawks. I am convinced that JJ brought Goose into my life to ensure that I would stay the course.

In March, still raw with the emotions of my loss, I received an email from Sky Horse Ranch. Ariana was planning a Healing with Horses workshop in mid-May. My heart fluttered, and my inner guide nickered, "Yes!" I quickly enrolled, knowing this was the weekend I needed to process my feelings and to better define what was next for Fire Horse.

The weekend provides everything I need. I soak up the amazing wisdom of Ariana, my modern-day medicine woman, and the healing energy of her horses. My spirit is refueled amongst the tall trees holding space on her coastal ranch. I absorb the cry of hawks and the butterflies that flicker near me.

My weekend culminates much like my true journey to healing began: in her round pen, aside an equine companion, pondering deep questions about my life. I feel the sand under my boots. I feel the soft eyes of Ariana's equine guide, Sky. I hear her questions: *Where am I going? And who is going with me?*

Something stirs. I hear the hawks screech above and sense a butterfly in my presence. It is time for a change. I know now in my heart that horses will remain in my life. What that looks like, I do not yet know. I just need to remain curious and listen to my still, soft inner voice and my spirit horse.

A thought bubbles up. I don't know if I want to stay in academia or what that looks like either. I no longer want to work like a machine. I want to focus on the parts of my life that feed my energy. *What is that?*

"Perhaps I want to expand my Engineering Your Life course out into the world," I say, with a bit of trepidation.

Ariana laughs lightly, "But your journey to your authentic self has been about realizing that you were not a problem that needed to be solved. In fact, you have been un-engineering your life."

I laugh, a deep belly laugh. The donkey in the adjacent pasture gives a bray, and Sky aligns with my new inner energy. My declaration flows from my heart.

"I am un-engineering my life." The statement resonates with my life purpose. There is no trepidation—no sense of unworthiness attached. Yes, I am joyfully and wholeheartedly un-engineering my life, and I will use my horse wisdom to continually empower myself and those who wish to follow, wherever that may be.

My beacon of inner light will never dim again. Fire Horse and JJ are forged with an unbreakable bond that knows no boundaries between this life and the spirit world beyond.

ACKNOWLEDGMENTS

I am indebted to my family. I am ever grateful to my mom and dad. They have offered me ongoing love, support, and encouragement throughout my life. I am grateful to my sister Karen and the precious time she had with us. She planted seeds for me that later blossomed so that I could be the person I was meant to be. My sister Beth has inspired me in so many ways—in education, pedagogy, and in life. Beth has stood by me at some of the lowest points in my life, and she has always encouraged me toward personal growth. I am grateful to have her as my sister.

Aunt Jackie was a force in my life—my fairy godmother, friend, ally, and accomplice all rolled into one. She instilled a sense of playfulness and joy that I still carry with me in my heart. I am grateful to my cousins Laura and Dan. They have been like siblings to me—we have shared love, loss, and wonderful memories.

My husband, Ric, has offered me love, encouragement, and inspiration through my ongoing life journey. I am grateful to share my life with him. I am so fortunate to have Savanna in my life—she is an old soul and a beacon of light. I hope her life journey will not be as tumultuous as mine!

The University of Rhode Island afforded me an incredible education and phenomenal mentorship. I am especially appreciative to Professors Tom Rockett, Otto Gregory, and Rich Brown in Chemical Engineering. These mentors believed in me before I could believe in myself. They inspired a deep love of engineering materials that remains to this day.

Brown University provided me with an environment that instilled a sense of academic excellence and a thirst for lifelong learning. I had extraordinary teachers, colleagues, and peers and the great fortune of having Professor Subra Suresh as my PhD advisor. I could not have asked for a better mentor or academic father. I am also grateful to my lab-mates Yuki Sugimura and Pranesh Aswath, who have been lifelong friends.

UC Berkeley provided me with the privilege of teaching exceptional students. Teaching puts me in an energetic flow—I have always enjoyed the energy in my classrooms. The Berkeley students never disappoint—they are thirsty for knowledge that will enable them to serve society. I am especially grateful to the students who enrolled in my personal leadership courses. We have shared sacred spaces and soul circles, and we will continue to blossom together on our journeys.

The students in the Medical Polymer Group are my academic children. I am especially grateful to Farzana Ansari, Sofia Arevalo, Sara Atwood, Lisa Bailey, David Baker, Noah Bonnheim, Latisha Bradford, Matt Carney, Ayyana Chakravartula, Dezba Coughlin, Deborah Crane, Cynthia Cruz, Giuliana Davis, Donna Ebenstein, Audrey Ford, Jevan Furmanski, Ally Gleason, Marni Goldman, Jove Graham, Hannah Gramling, Christine Gregg, Namrata Gundiah, Shika Gupta, Mera Horne, Kerry Hughes, Sheryl Kane, Cathie Klapperich, Anne Labine, Cheng Li, Andre Lundkvist, Louis Malito, Richard Meyer, Scott Niedzwiecki, Eli Patten, Rekha Ranganathan, Marco Regis, David Rondinone, Anurag Roy, Kathleen Simis, Bethany Smith, Lisa Torres, Becca Usoff, Jingli Wang, Tianzong Xu, and numerous undergraduates who have worked in our lab.

My research students have been the rivets in my armor—they have held me together through incredibly challenging times in my life. The success of my academic career is owed in great part to these phenomenal people.

I am grateful to the chairmen of Mechanical Engineering who have supported me throughout my career: David Bogy, Karl Hedrick, Al Pisano, Dave Dornfeld, Roberto Horowitz, and Chris Dames. The College of Engineering has had stellar deans throughout my career at Berkeley: David Hodges, Paul Gray, Rich Newton, Shankar Sastry, and Tsu-Jae King Liu. I am especially grateful to Dean Newton, who delegated me as his Associate Dean for Outreach Education and Lifelong Learning. I am also deeply grateful to Dean Tsu-Jae King Liu who entrusted me as her Associate Dean for Students and who supported me in the development of personal leadership courses for our students.

At Berkeley, I have been afforded many wonderful colleagues. Alice Agogino served as a pivotal role model for me, especially at a time when there were so few women faculty in engineering. Tony Keaveny has been a longtime friend and collaborator in the pedagogical realm of engineering education. Hami Kazerooni and Dorian Liepmann have been good friends throughout my career. Grace O'Connell has been a wonderful friend—it has been an honor to be her mentor. Rob Ritchie has been an inspiration and phenomenal collaborator.

Marvin Lopez and Tiffany Reardon have served as my co-facilitators for Engineering Your Life. I am grateful for their passion, wisdom, and commitment to our students. Dr. Keith Gatto helped me launch Introspective Leadership and served as my copilot—I am grateful for his wisdom in executive education and positive psychology.

I am also grateful to the extraordinary staff I have had the opportunity to work with in Mechanical Engineering, Engineering Student Services, and the College of Engineering. I especially thank Yawo Akpawu, Fatima Alleyne, Isabel Blanco, Debra Chin, Donna Craig, Vicky Garcia, Sharon

Mueller, Kedrick Perry, Stephanie Prince, Shareena Samson, Melissa Varian, and Ricky Vides.

Throughout my academic career, I have been fortunate to work with extraordinary people. There are too many to list, but a few have had a great impact in my life. Dr. Doreen Ball was my first female role model, and she instilled a love of metallurgy and forensic engineering. Dr. Clare Rimnac inspired me throughout my academic life—she helped me navigate a research field that intersects both engineering and medicine. Dr. Anuj Bellare has been a steadfast friend and collaborator—I remain ever grateful that Marni Goldman pulled us together. Dr. Mike Ries has been a great clinical collaborator and friend—he has been an anchor in my total joint replacement research. Professor Henning Kausch influenced my love of polymer physics and believed in me throughout my career.

Horses have been a godsend for me. It goes without saying that the most transformational horse in my life was JJ. This bright chestnut thoroughbred navigated me out of darkness and into light. Through him, I was introduced to natural horsemanship, equine-guided education, and personal leadership. I am indebted to Blaze, Juan, and Tristan—they were pivotal in my life trajectory. I am also grateful to the many horses I have ridden in Portugal, England, Mexico, Africa, and across the United States.

I am indebted to numerous people in the equine world who helped shape me as a horsewoman and the person I am today. Carol Franco provided me with the basics of riding and entrusted me with her horses at Hawkswood Farm, especially Bad Boy Nick.

Charles Wilhelm introduced me to the concept that the horse is always right. Dennis Reis transformed my life through natural horsemanship—his love of bringing out the best in our horses remains in my heart. Buck Brannaman offered a life philosophy through working with horses that continues to resonate with me.

Ariana Strozzi Mazzucchi is my modern-day medicine woman. She guided me through equine leadership, animal medicine, and the wisdom of nature. She helped me find my inner light.

Many incredible horsewomen have supported me through thick and thin. Shirley Park has been a true friend, mentor, and matriarchal leader in my life. Eleanor Criswell has offered an all-knowing wisdom that I continue to cherish. The Wetzel women have been anchors in my life: Merry Morrison, Winnie Crittendon, Peg Duggan, Peggy Koepke, and Robyn Boucher are enduring friends.

I am indebted to Diane Johnson and Lisa Gray at Moss Beach Ranch— these amazing women helped me care for JJ and Juan, and they enabled me to keep some semblance of life balance between my academic and equine worlds. I am grateful to everyone who offered their love and support to me when my horses moved on to their spirit realms.

Recovery is a long and arduous journey. I am grateful to the many people who helped me in this odyssey. I am especially grateful to Julia Ross for her help with my adrenal system and Ariana Strozzi Mazzucchi, who helped me find a creative path to recovery. Robert Rudelic was instrumental in helping me release long-held emotions from my body, and he continues to aid in keeping me in top form so I can maintain an active life with horses.

As part of my healing journey, I embarked on a path of self-reflection. I immersed myself in the inspirational teachings of Brené Brown, Wayne Dyer, Louise Hay, Gordon Hinckley, Michael Singer, Eckhart Tolle, and Oprah Winfrey.

As part of my introspective journey, I immersed myself in various leadership courses. Through Bill George's True North Leadership course at 1440 Multiversity, I deconstructed my life crucibles and learned that my greatest strengths were honed in adversity. Ariana's equine-guided leadership courses enabled me to harness my inner creativity and intuition.

Through Embodied Leadership at the Strozzi Leadership Institute, I utilized a martial arts foundation to explore my emotions and the power of body language in leadership. In Mark Rittenberg's High Impact Leadership, I learned the power of sharing story through a theater arts platform.

It takes a village to bring a memoir to light. I am grateful to all who have been a part of this journey. My academic daughters, Farzana Ansari and Ayyana Chakravartula, were the first in the academic world to read my story. It was through their encouragement that I sought to share my story in a way that could broadly impact others.

Albert Flynn DeSilver served as a creative writing coach and helped me with the art of memoir. He introduced me to the use of "free writing." The little girl within was awakened in this process, and creative prose found its way to my pages. Jonathan Balcombe and Diane Stockwell at The Editorial Department helped me with my first round of functional edits.

Donna Mazzitelli at Merry Dissonance Press helped me open my heart and enabled me to breathe life into my narrative. She is not only an extraordinary editor, but she is also a literary healer. She helped me find my inner voice—I am eternally grateful for her wisdom and insight.

My memoir is dedicated to JJ—the luminous horse who gave me light. He awakened a strong sense of spirit within me, and he is woven into my soul.

ABOUT THE AUTHOR

Lisa Pruitt received her PhD from Brown University and joined the faculty of Mechanical Engineering at UC Berkeley in 1993. She has authored more than three hundred publications in her research field of failure analysis, biomaterials, and medical devices. The recipient of numerous awards and honors, her research has been recognized with a Congressional citation, a National Science Foundation CAREER award, an Office of Naval Research Young Investigator Award, and she was elected to the American Institute of Medical and Biological Engineering.

Professor Pruitt has also been honored for her commitment to excellence in mentoring, teaching, and outreach. She has received the

American Association of Advancement of Sciences Mentoring Award; the Presidential Award for Excellence in Science, Mathematics and Engineering Mentoring; the UC Berkeley Distinguished Teaching Award, as well as the A. Richard Newton Educator Award. Professor Pruitt has taught undergraduate and graduate courses in Mechanical Behavior of Engineering Materials, Failure Analysis, Polymer Engineering, Medical Device Design, Personal Leadership, and Equine-Guided Leadership.

Pruitt has authored three books, including *Mechanics of Biomaterials: Fundamentals for Implant Design* (textbook, Cambridge University Press, 2011); *Horse of Fire: The Story of an Extraordinary and Knowing Horse as told by JJ Luck* (novel, Authorhouse, 2008; Amazon, 2019); as well as *Savanna and the Magic Boots* (children's book, Authorhouse, 2011).

To learn more about Lisa A. Pruitt and her work, visit LisaAPruitt.com.

INVITE LISA TO YOUR BOOK CLUB!

As a special gift to readers of *Soul of a Professor,* Lisa would love to visit your book club either via video conferencing or in person.

Please contact Lisa directly to schedule her appearance at your next book club meeting.

To contact Lisa, go to LisaAPruitt.com.

ABOUT THE PRESS

Merry Dissonance Press is a hybrid indie publisher/book producer of works of transformation, inspiration, exploration, and illumination. MDP takes a holistic approach to bring books into the world that make a little noise and create dissonance within the whole so ALL can be resolved to produce beautiful harmonies.

Merry Dissonance Press works with its authors every step of the way to craft the finest books and help promote them. Dedicated to publishing award-winning books, we strive to support talented writers and assist them to discover, claim, and refine their distinct voices. Merry Dissonance Press is the place where collaboration and facilitation of our shared human experiences join together to make a difference in our world.

For more information, visit merrydissonancepress.com.

Made in United States
North Haven, CT
27 January 2023

31669652R00217